JOYCE, DERRIDA, THE TRAUMA OF

C000075694

In *Joyce, Derrida, Lacan and the Trauma of History*, Christine van Boheemen-Saaf examines the relationship between Joyce's post-modern textuality and the traumatic history of colonialism in Ireland. Joyce's influence on Lacanian psychoanalysis and Der-rida's philosophy, Van Boheemen suggests, ought to be viewed from a postcolonial perspective. She situates Joyce's writing as a practice of indirect "witnessing" to a history that remains unspeak-able. The loss of a natural relationship to language in Joyce calls for a new ethical dimension in the process of reading. The practice of reading becomes an act of empathy to what the text cannot express in words. In this way, she argues, Joyce's work functions as a material location for the inner voice of Irish cultural memory. This book engages with a wide range of contemporary critical theory and brings Joyce's work into dialogue with thinkers such as Žizek, Adorno, Lyotard, as well as feminism and postcolonial theory.

Christine van Boheemen-Saaf is Professor of Literature in English at the University of Amsterdam. She is the author of *The Novel as Family Romance* (1987), *Joyce, Modernity and its Mediation* (1989), and numerous essays on Joyce, Lacan, and literary theory.

JOYCE, DERRIDA, LACAN, AND THE TRAUMA OF HISTORY

Reading, narrative and postcolonialism

CHRISTINE VAN BOHEEMEN-SAAF

CAMBRIDGE
UNIVERSITY PRESS

CAMBRIDGE UNIVERSITY PRESS
Cambridge, New York, Melbourne, Madrid, Cape Town, Singapore, São Paulo

Cambridge University Press
The Edinburgh Building, Cambridge CB2 2RU, UK

Published in the United States of America by Cambridge University Press, New York

www.cambridge.org
Information on this title: www.cambridge.org/9780521660365

First published 1999
This digitally printed first paperback version 2006

A catalogue record for this publication is available from the British Library

Library of Congress Cataloguing in Publication data

Boheemen-Saaf, Christine van.
Joyce, Derrida, Lacan, and the trauma of history/Christine van Boheemen.
p. cm.
Includes bibliographical references and index.
ISBN 0 521 66036 X
1. Joyce, James, 1882–1941 – Knowledge – History. 2. Psychoanalysis and literature – Ireland –
History – 20th century. 3. Psychological fiction, English – Irish authors – History and
criticism. 4. Literature and history – Ireland – History – 20th century. 5. Lacan, Jacques, 1901
– Contributions in criticism. 6. Joyce, James, 1882–1941 – Knowledge – Psychology.
7. Derrida, Jacques – Contributions in criticism. 8. Postmodernism (Literature) – Ireland.
9. Psychic trauma in literature. 10. Decolonization in literature. 11. Colonies in
literature. I. Title.
PR6019.09Z525976   1999
823'.912–dc21   98-32270 CIP

ISBN-13 978-0-521-66036-5 hardback
ISBN-10 0-521-66036-X hardback

ISBN-13 978-0-521-03531-6 paperback
ISBN-10 0-521-03531-7 paperback

Contents

v

Acknowledgments

This book is deeply indebted to two intellectual communities: first of all the International James Joyce Foundation. The plenary address Vincent Cheng, Margot Norris, and Kimberly Devlin invited me to give at the "California Joyce" Conference at Irvine in 1993 grew into this book. I am grateful for their kindness and confidence. I thank the James Joyce Research Group at Leeds, where I profited from discussion with Richard Brown, David Pierce, Alistair Stead, and Pieter Bekker. At the 1995 Miami Joyce Conference Jean-Michel Rabaté pressed me to articulate my position on Joyce and Lacan; without his publications on Joyce, this book would not have been possible. Terence Doody and Colleen Lamos made it possible for me to use Rice Library. Kimberly Devlin and Marilyn Reizbaum's volume *Ulysses: Engendered Perspectives* made me start a project that evolved into chapter 4 of this book. I thank the University of South Carolina Press for permission to reprint. At the Zurich James Joyce Stiftung's August Conference on "Joyce and the Negative," Fritz Senn took the trouble to comment on part of this text. Throughout the process of composition, he served as point of reference on sources and archival material unavailable in the Netherlands. Sheldon Brivic kindly granted me permission to adapt his schedule for the structure of *A Portrait of the Artist*. Enda Duffy generously donated a copy of *The Subaltern Ulysses* which was not then available in Dutch libraries. I am indebted to John Rickard for trading books with me. In short, I am deeply appreciative of the help, friendship, inspiration, and encouragement of Joyce scholars.

Secondly, I wish to thank the Amsterdam School of Cultural Analysis which provided an intellectually challenging environment of interdisciplinary research, and made it possible to profit from lectures by Cathy Caruth, Samuel Weber, Martin Jay, and others. Most of all, I wish to thank Ernst Van Alphen, who first mentioned Cathy Caruth's work to me. His views on trauma and contemporary culture made me rethink

Joyce's relation to representation and language. In 1996, my colleagues in the English Department granted me a welcome six-month reprieve of teaching duties, without which this book could not have been written. Finally, I thank Mieke Bal for her comments on my manuscript.

Most closely to home, my gratitude goes to Maarten Souwer, to whom I dedicate this book, for the faith, hope, and charity with which he supported me during its writing.

Abbreviations

CW	Joyce, James. *The Critical Writings of James Joyce*, ed. Ellsworth Mason and Richard Ellmann. New York: Viking Press, 1959.
D	Joyce, James. *Dubliners*, ed. Robert Scholes in consultation with Richard Ellmann. New York: Viking Press, 1967.
FW	Joyce, James. *Finnegans Wake*. New York: Viking Press, 1939; London: Faber and Faber, 1939. These two editions have identical pagination.
GJ	Joyce, James. *Giacomo Joyce*, ed. Richard Ellmann. New York: Viking Press, 1968.
Letters I, II, III	Joyce, James. *Letters of James Joyce*. Vol. I, ed. Stuart Gilbert. New York: Viking Press, 1957; reissued with corrections 1966. Vols. 2 and 3, ed. Richard Ellmann. New York: Viking Press, 1964.
P	Joyce James. *"A Portrait of the Artist as a Young Man": Text, Criticism, and Notes*, ed. Chester G. Anderson. New York: Viking Press, 1958.
PSW	Joyce, James. *Poems and Shorter Writings*, ed. Richard Ellmann, A. Walton Litz and John Whittier-Ferguson. London: Faber and Faber, 1991.
SE	*Sigmund Freud, The Standard Edition of the Complete Psychological Works of Sigmund Freud*, ed. James Strachey. London: Hogarth, 1964–74.
SH	Joyce, James. *Stephen Hero*, ed. John J. Slocum and Herbert Cahoon. New York: Viking Press, 1975.
SL	Joyce, James. *Selected Letters of James Joyce*, ed. Richard Ellmann. New York: Viking Press, 1975.

U   Joyce, James. *Ulysses*, ed. Hans Walter Gabler, et al.
                New York and London: Garland Publishing, 1984,
                1986. In paperback by Garland, Random House,
                and Bodley Head, and by Penguin, 1986–92.

CHAPTER I

The stolen birthright: the mimesis of original loss

> Literature bears testimony not just to duplicate or to record events, but to make history available to the imaginative act whose historical unavailability has prompted, and made possible, a holocaust.
>
> Shoshana Felman and Dori Laub, *Testimony*

This book argues the cultural-historical importance of James Joyce's Irish modernity. His projection of a traumatized discursivity encapsulating the life-in-death of Irish experience, his syncretic manner of representation, his paradoxical approach to Irish nationalism, his complex attitude to language and cultural memory anticipate insights which we are only beginning to grasp at the end of the century. Joyce, an Irish Catholic born in 1882, grappled with the realities of colonial experience and the hegemony of the English language; and this struggle entailed an engagement with the evaporation of the presence of the material, and the devaluation or dissolution of art and truth – problems besetting contemporary culture. Not surprisingly, Joyce's writing has had an informative impact on contemporary theory: Joyce's presence in the texts of Derrida, Lacan, and Slavoj Žižek is pronounced; and the simplest way of describing this book is as a study in the informative presence of what Freud called the "death instinct," and what I see as the peculiarly traumatizing and uncanny effect of Irish historical experience in the rivalry for truth of three disciplines: deconstructive philosophy, Lacanian psychoanalysis, and Joycean Irish modernist literature. My claim will be that, where the "death instinct" undermines any title to full truth, Joyce's encrypting of the experience of destitution in the material location of his text opens up a new, intersubjective realm of communication which may help to make it possible to work out the heritage of the past and transform the ghostly uncanniness of the "death instinct" into full discourse.

My argument, which does not require the reader's specialist knowledge of either Joyce or poststructuralist theory, has several implications. It unsettles the conventional distinction between theory and literature in showing that literature may be a form of *theoria* (this seems especially important in postcolonial studies struggling with western theories); it historicizes poststructuralist theory as itself a product of a certain resistance against the trauma of history; and finally, it argues for a new understanding of reading which emphasizes the reader's responsibility to listen beyond the conventional systems of sign and structure, and claims the ethical obligation to hear the pain which may not have been expressed in so many words.

This new perspective is made possible by the theoretical groundwork of Jean-François Lyotard, who conceptualizes the atrocity of the Holocaust as a discursive deadlock in which language and narrative representation are no longer able to express the horror or import of the experience. The concept of discursive trauma, elaborated in this chapter, is central to my argument. It entails a revision of our notion of subjectivity. Instead of the split subject of psychoanalysis with an unconscious preceding discourse and history, Lyotard's perspective allows us to understand Joyce's dramatic materialization, or literalization, of the possibility of failure of symbolization itself as a "death-in-life of discourse," or an unconscious *within* history and discourse which adds a psychic dimension to textuality. It should be noted that this study does not present an analysis of Joyce's psyche, but of the texture of his discourse.

Such a revision has radical consequences. When we re-conceptualize the notion of the subject-in-language to include the constitutive instability which comes from placing an unconscious inside the subject rather than outside or before it, we must also redefine the discourses of subjectivity such as literature or history. What is "literature" or "history" after the break-up of being and the displacement of colonialism which forces the subjected self to breach "the great divide" and relocate itself in space, time, or language? Separated from an original mooring, a postcolonial subject can only mourn the gap that divides himself or herself from the possibility of interiority and self-presence that might have been had history been different. In the case of an Irish writer, growing up with English as his first language, the aspiring artist is forced to allude allegorically, and in the *sermo patris* of the oppressor's language, to what can never be voiced with immediacy: the loss of a natural relationship to language, the lack of interiority of discourse and coherent selfhood. In his texts, Joyce gave material presence to that nothingness which Adorno and Lyotard (in different ways) would later locate in World War II. Joyce's texts enshrine the inexpressed and inexpressible experience of discursive death-in-life, long before the poems of Celan. By means of a detailed mapping of the informative presence of discursive trauma in *A Portrait of the Artist as a Young Man*, I hope to outline the concept sufficiently to lend it conceptual force in postcolonial studies, and to illustrate its radical effect on our understanding of "literature," "representation," "text," or "reader."

This introduction, which lays out the parameters of the concept of discursive trauma, is followed, in chapter 2, by a reading of Joyce's *A Portrait of the Artist* which shows the presence of discursive trauma in seemingly traditional novelistic representation and draws out its effects on our understanding of representation. Since trauma sets up a progressive dialectic of repetition-with-a-difference, subsequent readings of later works will demonstrate how Joyce, with ever-increasing self-consciousness, strove to gain mastery over the informative presence of discursive trauma in his texts. I chose "Cyclops" and "Penelope" because these episodes are central to the postcolonial and feminist debates about Joyce; and my reading of "Penelope" argues that Joyce's attitude to gender cannot be divorced from his Irish heritage. It is best seen as a defensive, and paradoxically Irish, strategy of dealing with the trauma of Irishness. Thus this book also offers a contribution to the discussion of gender in Joyce's works. After these readings, I shall turn towards Lacan and Derrida, to suggest that their controversy about Poe's "The Purloined Letter" is re-enacted in their perspective on Joyce, and that they remain locked in opposition because they fail to accept the possibility of the death of discourse that Joyce lived. My discussion concludes with an attempt to articulate the different notions of "materiality" at work in Joyce, Derrida, and Lacan because Joyce's materialization of the spectre of nothingness of colonial experience in *Finnegans Wake* is different from Derrida's "writing" or Lacan's "materiality of the letter." Their notions shore up the full acceptance of the reductiveness of colonial experience which stereotypes its subjects as pure body. This book does not present a survey of the French reception of Joyce, which is available elsewhere.[1]

My Joycean reader will find that he or she will have to engage more theory than is customary in Joyce criticism, whereas the theorist will be

---

[1] See Geert Lernout's *The French Joyce* (University of Michigan Press, 1990), for those factual details which this study does not supply.

exposed to detailed readings of a literary text. This is both unavoidable
and deliberate. That the importance of Joyce in the twentieth century is
not limited to the realm of the aesthetic can only be demonstrated by
going outside it. If theory maintains its discursive superiority by means
of a repression of the affective address of the literary text and its
intersubjective appeal, and in doing so kills its ethical impact, this can
only be countered by reading. Thus each group of readers will be
exposed to unfamiliar material.

The epigraph from Ovid's *Metamorphoses* which Joyce gave his autobiographical *A Portrait of the Artist as a Young Man*, is commonly read as a
reference to the myth of Daedalus and the escape from the labyrinth.
If we understand the words "*Et ignotas animum dimittit in artes*" [And he
applied his mind to obscure arts] as bearing on the author's artistic
intention rather than on that of the protagonist, and also note that
Joyce stopped short of the words "*naturamque novat*" [and he renewed
nature], a different message emerges. The epigraph may be a sign to
the reader that what follows presents a transformatively novel notion
of textual practice deriving from the unknown, occult, or the unconscious [*ignotas artes*]. Perhaps we should see Joyce not only as a wor-
d*smith* like the great artificer Daedalus, but also compare him to another artist figure in Ovid's collection of stories, the raped and muted
Philomel who managed to communicate by indirect means – color
and texture – a story which could not be told in words. Philomel's
strategic shift seems resonant in relation to James Joyce. Deprived of a
sense of linguistic interiority because history had ousted the use of the
"mother tongue," he had to resort to "obscure arts." Although Gaelic
was all but extinct at the time Joyce was born, and although Joyce was
raised as a native speaker of English, his life and his works nevertheless
trace the symbolic event of the entry into language as a disruptive and
violently fracturing moment splitting body from discourse and initiat-
ing an endlessly repeated attempt at arriving at a signification of itself.
In other words, Joyce's work demonstrates an attitude to language
which highlights the presence of a void or a gap opening up within
representation and memory. Stephen Dedalus, Joyce's autobiographical *alter ego*, speaking on the subject of his alienated relationship to the
English language in contrast to that of his English master, notes his
own ambivalent sense of its simultaneous "familiarity" and "foreignness." "His language, *so familiar and so foreign*, will always be for me an
acquired speech. I have not made or accepted its words. My *voice* holds
them at bay. My *soul* frets in the shadow of his language."[2] Joyce

worked in that split, and in that affective gap, writing in an English which, in its defamiliarization and slips of the tongue (*lapsus linguae*) evokes the continuous spectral presence of what, for want of a better image, we may denote as the felt presence of the lapsing of the mother tongue.[3] Moreover, he especially turned his attention to the physical or material aspects of language, because he located his resistant Irish "soul" in his body, his "voice."

In a sequence of works, beginning with the portraits of the melancholic "paralysis" or "hemiplegia of the soul" of Irish-urban existence in *Dubliners*, Joyce increasingly opened the void gaping between the "foreign" and the "familiar" to end up giving the materialization of that void a local habitation and a name in *Finnegans Wake*, published on the eve of World War II, which inscribes the darkness and dislocation of discursive death as a blot upon the screen of history. I use the word blot, because *Finnegans Wake* is both intensely funny and utterly unreadable in conventional narrative terms. But what seems important is not just that Joyce published an unreadable work. The point I want to make rests on the fact that this unreadable text, notwithstanding its unreadability, or perhaps precisely owing to its hermetic nature, became part of the cultural history of western Europe as a recognized masterpiece. The event of its publication also got Joyce's photograph on the front cover of *Time* magazine. Thus the material existence of this enshrined instance of discursive death confirmed the transformation of James Joyce the louse-eaten, starved, and possibly syphilitic Irish exile into "Joyce the genius," the internationally famous modernist author residing in Paris, permanently inscribed in the book of culture. Joyce at once demonstrates the always already modern condition of Irishness and turns it into the emblem of global culture.

Joyce achieved this by inventing a curiously hybrid and covertly double strategy of storytelling in the oppressor's language, which unweaves its very texture as it narrates. At first sight, Joyce's earlier works seems to present a recognizable world. On closer inspection, Joyce's method of weaving his texts – looping, unlooping, noding, disnoding –

[2] *A Portrait of the Artist as a Young Man: Text, Criticism, and Notes*, ed. Chester G. Anderson (New York and London: Penguin Books, 1977), p. 189. Hereafter *P* and cited by page number.

[3] I wish to emphasize that "the lapsing of the mother tongue" features as an image, a metaphor or *Vorstellungsrepräsentanz* (see chapter 1) to fill in the gap in history left by the traumatic nature of its occurrence. To support my suggestion, I wish to point to Thomas Kinsella's words in "The Irish Writer," "I simply recognize that I stand on one side of a great rift, and can feel the discontinuity in myself. . . . The death of a language . . . is a calamity. And its effects are at work everywhere in the present." *The Field Day Anthology of Irish Writing*, vol. 3, ed. Seamus Deane (Derry: Field Day Publications, 1991), p. 626.

focuses the reader's attention on an absence which defies representation and which highlights the inability to tell in one's "own" words. Writing in the English language, Joyce refused to identify with the structure of predication of language, and points us to the presence of an absence, a lacuna at the heart of his linguistic subjectivity. Instead of a story about the young Stephen Dedalus, we end up "reading" (experiencing) a texture which, like Philomel's web, indirectly betrays the muted violence of its occasion.

Philomel's story resonates in relation to Joyce in yet another way. Tereus's violation of the sanctity of his familiar bond in raping his sister-in-law initiates a series of events which blur the distinction between inside and outside, familiar and foreign, generation and consumption, ending in Procne's murder of her child, and the father's forced feasting on the flesh of his own son. This incestuous violence reminds me of Stephen Dedalus's fear of Ireland as the "old sow" eating her own children. An initial transgression sets up a pattern which keeps generating new violence – until the protagonists are delivered from the cycle of repetition through a metamorphosis. In Ovid they turn into birds. Not so in Joyce's works. Stephen's desire to fly away, his definition of his muse as a "birdgirl," the preoccupation with metempsychosis in *Ulysses*, the continual shapeshifting in *Finnegans Wake* may express the wish to end the chain of repetition and undo the history "which is to blame" as one of Joyce's characters puts it; but Joyce's universe does not allow of the magical transformation which Ovid granted his sufferers. Caught in the web of history, Joyce's characters as well as their author keep repeating the symptomatic expression of their condition to tell us, by indirect means, not about their deliverance but about the repressed historical condition which occasioned their imprisonment.

In this book, my intention is not only to demonstrate the peculiar nature of what I call Joyce's "mimesis of loss." I especially want to argue the effect on the reader of its unusual textuality. As a form of what Dori Laub and Daniel Podell call the "art of trauma,"[4] Joyce's *œuvre* does not communicate meaning directly, but may generate meaning in receptive minds; in non-receptive minds it may set up a defensive impulse to contain the threat of the text and subject it to coherent interpretation. No other writer, other than Shakespeare, perhaps, has produced such markedly obsessive as well as contradictory responses in his audience. There are Joyce-adepts who virtually live *in* Joyce's work, trying to

---

[4] "Art and Trauma," *The International Journal of Psychoanalysis* 76 (1995), 992.

master it by finding the definitive answer to some seeming riddle; and Joyce scholarship has a history of exclusivist opposition reminiscent of Irish history itself. Indeed, Joyce has had a splitting effect on his readership. His idiosyncratic strategy of representation, put down in "double dye"[5] just as Philomel wove her cloth in purple and white, has had a curiously divisive influence on its readers. Since its true "meaning," the inexpressibility and pain of the trauma of its occasion, can at best only present an address which invites the reader "to become engaged in a dialogue of his own with the trauma,"[6] readers aiming at uttering the whole truth about Joyce's texts tend to pick up one of the two threads of its hybrid texture. Consequently, Joyce criticism is characterized by a number of ongoing debates in which his readers take radically oppositional, mutually exclusive stances: Joyce is feminist or anti-feminist; humanist or ironist, modernist or nationalist, political or apolitical, etc.

In retrospect, Joyce criticism enacts the effect of what, in the seventies and eighties, reductively following Barbara Johnson and Shoshana Felman, was labelled "the castration of truth as the truth of writing." Here the term "castration" indicated the reader's sense of lack and diminishment at never arriving at full mastery or a definitive interpretation. The important point to note, however, is that in their writings this effect was presented as a universal and transhistorical aspect of literary language. My claim here is that the instance of Joyce disrupts that ahistoric universalism. Certain forms of deconstructive criticism (I am not speaking of Johnson or Felman) may be acts of textual fetishism complicit with the symptom Joyce. If, rather than elevating it into truth itself, we accept "castration" especially in its wider cultural application made possible by Freud,[7] a new but paradoxical historical perspective

---

5 *Finnegans Wake* (London: Faber, 1971), p. 185.32. Hereafter *FW* and cited by page and line number.   6 Laub and Podell, "Art and Trauma," 993.

7 The phantasy of castration is one of the primal mythic scenarios with which the small child puzzles out anatomical difference, and which has a different configuration in boys (generating anxiety about the possibility of loss) or girls (bringing the perception of a wrong suffered). To me, the importance of the concept resides in its wider application. In line with Freud in "Fetishism," *The Standard Edition of the Complete Psychological Works of Sigmund Freud*, ed. James Strachey (London: Hogarth Press, 1964–74), vol. 21, pp. 149–59, I take castration as a principle of cultural rather than just an individual psychosexual dynamic: "In later life a grown man may perhaps experience a similar panic when the cry goes up that Throne and Altar are in danger, and similar illogical consequences will ensue' (p. 153). Thus castration anxiety is a concept which may refer more generally to any threat to that which is central to our self-image; nor is castration anxiety permanently transcended in youth. See not only Jean Laplanche, *The Language of Psychoanalysis*, trans. Donald Nicholson-Smith (London: Hogarth Press, 1983), pp. 56–60, but also Jean Laplanche, *Problématiques II: Castration, Symbolisations* (Paris: Presses Universitaires de France, 1980).

opens up. Joyce's perverse, fetishistic textuality dramatically enacts the presence of a condition that in its extremity questions a facile generalizing use of "the castration of truth as the truth of writing." Some forms of writing, the symptomatic "art of trauma" of a Joyce or a Celan, re-enact an occurrence of an act of violence which affects symbolization itself, and add to history a new dimension, a spot of numbness or failure of articulation, which becomes an unconscious *within* discourse, adding a psychic dimension to discourse. The muted suffering of colonial oppression may be understood as an actual historical event which inscribed the experience of death-in-life into history and subjectivity, encrypting an ontological void.

In other words, in Joyce, and through Joyce who materializes that death-in-life, we notice the advent of a new dimension to discourse. Lacan looked upon it as the confluence of the "real" (denoting the unpresentable, death, sexuality, in contrast to the everyday use of the term which understands "real" as referring to the existent) with the symbolic of language. It was the example of Joyce which forced Lacan to this conclusion. He conceded that the historical example of Joyce's textuality upset his conceptualization of the relation between the imaginary, the symbolic, and the real. Until the late seventies, Lacan's "real" was located safely outside the symbolic and the imaginary – non-representable although the aim of representation, ahistorical while framing history: the transcendent still point of a turning world. Lacan's study of Joyce in the seventies confronted him with an instance of the binding of the real onto the symbolic and into history, as well as a dramatization of the usually repressed consciousness of the material determination of human subjectivity. It was this confrontation with the symptom Joyce (Joyce as the telling symptom of what supports human subjectivity) that led Lacan to revise his earlier schema, and admit that the symbolic, imaginary, and real, tied together in a Borromean knot – a fourth agent – may also be kept from psychotic fraying through a peculiar form of symptomaticity. Thus a distinction is to be made between "Lacan" and the "late Lacan" of the mid-seventies onwards, who mentions his intense preoccupation with Joyce, for instance in his "Preface" to *The Four Fundamental Concepts of Psycho-Analysis* (1976). The point seems especially relevant, because Slavoj Žižek's work on popular culture, e.g. Hitchcock's movies, resorts to Lacan's concepts of the "real" and the "symptom," without sufficiently indicating that his use of these concepts derives from the late Lacan working on Joyce. If the intrusion of the "real" describes a peculiarly modern form of horror, I suggest that it is from Joyce's work that the model of that modernity implicitly derives. His texts provided a material location in which the hitherto unincarnated experience of death-in-life found a living habitation and a name.

Central in all this is that Joyce's encryption of an ontological void (or discursive death-in-life) opened up an extra-communicative but non-articulable dimension *within* discourse, making it possible to honour the "presence" of the non-articulated "story" that cannot be told in so many words – the "story" of the oppressed, the muted, the ignored. Moreover, Joyce's historical example re-aligns the place of poststructuralist theory in current postcolonial studies. Hence this book hopes to refine Homi K. Bhabha's claim that postcolonial writing "occupies that space of double inscription, hallowed – no, hollowed" by Jacques Derrida.[8] I propose that the theoretical insights of Derrida and Lacan which have proven so useful in postcolonial studies, are best understood through the struggle for subjectivity of the Irish writer James Joyce. His linguistic materialism "hollowed" the supplementary location which nestles the truth of their concepts – from "dissemination" to the "two deaths." Derrida's writing is littered with his debt to Joyce ("nothing but a reading of *Finnegans Wake*"[9]), while the later Lacan who speaks of woman as symptom and Joyce as "symptôme"/"sinthome" and grapples with the place and definition of the death-drive, is also the Lacan currently prominent in cultural studies and postcolonial criticism. My intention is not to demonstrate the applicability of Derrida or Lacan to Joyce. I argue that their abstract concepts have a concretely embodied textual precursor in Joyce's complex textuality. It was Joyce's text which made their ideas possible, so to speak, by providing textual-material collateral. In other words, if, as Bhabha claims, Derrida occupies the space "hollowed" by Heidegger's revision of western metaphysics, his precursor Joyce already occupied the conceptual space hollowed by the historical condition of colonial rule. Thus the affinity between Derrida and Joyce solicits a query with regard to the historical provenance of philosophy's revision of metaphysics and the

---

[8] Homi K. Bhabha, *The Location of Culture* (London and New York: Routledge, 1994), p. 108. Bhabha quotes from *Dissemination*: "whenever any writing both marks and goes back over its mark with an undecidable stroke . . . [this] double mark escapes the pertinence or authority of truth: it does not overturn it but rather inscribes it within its play as one of its functions or parts. This displacement does not take place, has not taken place once as an *event*. It does not occupy a simple place. It does not take place *in* writing. This dislocation (is what) writes/is written." (Jacques Derrida, *Dissemination*, trans. Barbara Johnson [University of Chicago Press, 1981], p. 193).

[9] *La Dissémination* (Paris: Seuil, 1972), p. 99, my translation. Derrida also used a passage from *A Portrait of the Artist* as epigraph.

postulate of an *arche*-dimensionality. Is the history of philosophy not also influenced by the lived experience of the embodied and suffering historical subject whose alienation hollows the experiential need, and conceptual possibility, of thinking from the place of this originary presence of absence? It has often been remarked that the revision of western thought coincided historically with the rise of women; perhaps we should also note that it coincided with the end of colonial expansion.

The emphasis on such a foundational role and such historical precedence of a literary text to theoretical concepts is not just intended to make these theories less controversial tools in postcolonial studies. In undoing theory's aloof transcendence as a pure metalanguage, and tracing its debt to the lived struggle of the postcolonial situation, I also turn theory into a form of literature.[10] I find that important, because I want to reclaim the importance of literature as a socially necessary source of knowledge, especially in its *affective demand* to witness literature's occasion.

What do I mean by the "affective demand to witness"? Here Adorno's point is crucial: "We will not have come to terms with the past until the causes of what happened then are no longer active. Only because these causes live on does the spell of the past remain to this very day unbroken."[11] Just as Tereus's violence keeps generating new acts of transgression, the wounds of the past will remain active and spoil the present, unless we heal them through mourning. We must become conscious, accept the past, and find the words to voice and feel the desolation it occasions. Coming to terms with the causes of a past which keeps haunting us, as it still does in Northern Ireland, Albania, or Rwanda, depends upon an imaginative act of witnessing sympathy as well as the reorientation of subjectivity. While reading literature cannot take the place of the work of mourning imposed by history, reading the "art of trauma" may engage the reader in a dialogue with that trauma which might open him or her up to begin to acknowledge its hitherto repressed presence. Thus literature may help the reader to bracket

---

[10] See also Bill Ashcroft, Gareth Griffiths and Helen Tiffin, *The Empire Writes Back: Theory and Practice in Post-Colonial Literatures* (New York and London: Routledge, 1989), p. 173, where they argue that "political orientations and experimental formations . . . deliberately designed to counteract . . . European assimilation . . . have themselves provided the cultural base and formative colonial experience on which European theorists have drawn in their apparent radicalisation of linguistic philosophy."

[11] "What Does Coming to Terms with the Past Mean?" (1959) in *Bitburg in Moral and Political Perspective*, ed. Geoffrey Hartman (Bloomington: Indiana University Press, 1986), p. 29.

formative identifications, and generate a willingness to listen to the other. The work of mourning may, perhaps, follow. I am hesitant here, afraid of overstating my claim. Nevertheless, I emphasize the historical importance of Joyce's invention of a new way of writing which encrypts trauma into the text and traps the reader in an intense involvement. Although Joyce's work has haunted modernity, it seems its impact is still largely repressed – hence not heard and not worked through. My suggestion is that it will remain misread, enlisted in the service of transcendent truths or narcissistic play, unless we learn to receive and confront it in its sensuously embodied form as the "art of trauma." Joyce's discursiveness, however funny, brilliant, and intellectualized his texts, ought not just solicit our complicity in his laughter, but also our tears and our witnessing testimony. Thus this book contains (and, I hope, demonstrates) an ethical appeal to read differently and read whole.

At issue, then, is a new notion of mimesis. This is neither the reifying *imitatio* of the specular copy critized by Derrida in "The Double Session," nor is it the endlessly disseminating and performative self-inscription advocated by poststructuralism. Joyce's writing with "double dye" performs two activities at once, practising a cultural politics not couched in the traditional parameters of representation.[12] It answers Bhabha's question: "How does one encounter the past as an anteriority that continually introduces an otherness or alterity within the present? How does one then narrate the present as a form of contemporaneity that is always belated?"[13] It inscribes the hollowness of the experience of the loss of linguistic interiority into the heart of the specular copy. It also projects a writerly subjectivity propelled by the historically traumatic nature of its inscription to self-dialectical repetition *as the only means of working this heritage out*. I call this a "mimesis of loss." This self-dialectic, an ongoing process of self-conscious self-revision which keeps re-enacting the basic traumatic tension at ever more sophisticated levels, will eventually lead to the blatantly self-conscious but symptomatic writing of *Finnegans Wake*. Although the implied author never escapes the compulsion to repeat, albeit in incrementally complex and self-conscious

[12] See also David Lloyd, *Anomalous States: Irish Writing and the Post-Colonial Moment* (Durham: Duke University Press, 1993), who addresses the inadequacy of traditional "forms of representational politics and aesthetics" for the understanding of Irish nationalism, and the need to "conceive of a cultural politics" "outside the terms of representation" (p. 89); and Enda Duffy, *The Subaltern "Ulysses"* (Minneapolis and London, University of Minnesota Press, 1994), who argues that *Ulysses* "marks . . . a new episteme in what the Irish poet Seamus Heaney has described as 'the government of the tongue'" (p. 4).

[13] "DissemiNation: Time, Narrative, and the Margins of the Modern Nation," in *Nation and Narration*, ed. Homi K. Bhabha (London and New York: Routledge, 1990), p. 308.

ways, I argue that his text testifies, beyond its knowing, to the un-speakable moment of destitution and repression.

Irish culture is deeply divided, even in its contemporary reactions to its colonial history. For centuries, culture in Ireland was, in fact, dis-placed English culture. Ireland was neither able to develop authentic modern forms of life nor to maintain the cultural and linguistic con-tinuity of its Gaelic heritage. That traditional deadlock has not yet been fully overcome. Robert Welch, in a recent discussion, points out that, on the one hand, such a "traumatic reading" of Irish history is "catas-trophic," and "for that reason, satisfying."[14] It implies the admission that "something went wrong," and lays the blame with the "English presence in Ireland." The only remedy this vision sees is to discount all of its culture of the last centuries up to the last twenty years or so when Ireland began to join the mainstream of Anglo-American world culture:

> The logic here leads to setting up the Irish language as the only sure icon of Irishness: everything else is pussyfooting and special pleading. We see writers like Alan Titley, Michael Hartnett and Nuala ní Dhomhnaill either explicitly or implicitly making this analysis and taking appropriate action. They write in Irish because no other language will do; no other language will convey, for them, those interior states of being that all writers who are real writers want to talk about. They experience the trauma of the fracturing of Irish culture and attempt the healing process in their own work and language. (2–3)

Seen as a "cataclysmic blow to the psyche of the Irish people in that it ripped out and tore asunder all the secret interiors," the loss of the Irish language has given rise to a new form of writing in Irish which is marked by the intensity with which it addresses the entire question of language and representation itself. There is also the contrary reaction, however. Thus the "linguistic or cultural behaviourists" want to get on with modern life and enjoy capitalism. Forgetting the past, they just wish to build a successful new future – which is best done through writing in English.

The opposition sketched here, schematic as it is, would, at first, anachronistically, seem to place Joyce in the latter category of the writer who adopted the English language and made himself into a metropolitan, high-living, and world-famous success – sealed by the 1939 appearance of the cover of *Time* magazine. Indeed, this is the Joyce of the New Critics, of modernist scholars, even of such an ironic

[14] Robert Welch, *Changing States: Transformations in Modern Irish Writing* (London and New York: Routledge, 1993), p. 2.

Joyce scholar as Hugh Kenner, all of whom place Joyce as an exemplary internationally oriented modernist genius. Even in such a historically sophisticated discussion of the development of Irish literature as Joep Leerssen's *Remembrance and Imagination*, Joyce's *Ulysses* is presented as the achieved attempt to overcome Irish isolation, "normalizing and calibrating the position of Dublin in space and time."[15] It is not the Joyce I shall present. Though Joyce's drive to be modern and metropolitan is an incontrovertible fact, that appearance of modernity seems to me to have been a strategy to ensure the transmission of his work. Underneath that modernity, that work, I propose, participates in the sense of the traumatic nature of Irish experience of those who now write in Irish; but in a tragic mode, without its revivalist "dreamy dreams."[16] The obsessiveness with which it addresses the entire question of representation and language, elevating it to a meta-level, points to its Irish provenance.[17] Moreover, although in a different manner and with different intention, Joyce, too, inscribes Irishness into his work. Analyzed closely, his texts prove traumatically repetitive, "telling the old story afresh, like a needle stuck in the groove, in an uncanny, obsessive recycling process of the past," to use Leerssen's characterization of Irish discourse.[18] The paradox is that Joyce, who was raised and educated in English and aspired to modernity, wrote *in* English, but with the continuous awareness of the sense of loss of the mother tongue, a loss which he enshrined in his texts. As I said, his experience of the English language, although that was his native tongue, was traversed by the split of its simultaneous "familiarity" and "foreignness." Joyce, who referred to his native country as "Irrland's split little pea" (*FW* 171.06), managed to inscribe this alienation and sense of loss into the English novel itself, to query our understanding of mimesis, and to make his Irishness a

---

[15] *Remembrance and Imagination: Patterns in the Historical and Literary Representation of Ireland in the Nineteenth Century* (Cork University Press, 1996), p. 230.

[16] Joyce's words in the poem "The Holy Office" (1904), which defends his own poetics and points out the cathartic function his realism has for his countrymen involved in romantic idealization: "That they may dream their dreamy dreams/ I carry off their filthy streams." *James Joyce: Poems and Shorter Writings*, ed. Richard Ellmann, A. Walton Litz, and John Whittier-Ferguson (London: Faber and Faber, 1991), p. 98. Hereafter *PSW*.

[17] Note, for instance, his meeting with the young aspiring Irish writer Arthur Power. When the latter told Joyce that he aspired to write like "the French satirists," Joyce cautioned: "You will never do it . . . you are an Irishman and you must write in your own tradition. Borrowed styles are no good. You must write what is in your blood and not what is in your brain." Joyce countered Power's expressed wish to be international like the Russians with: "They were national first . . . and it was the intensity of their nationalism which made them international in the end, as in the case of Turgenev." Richard Ellmann, *James Joyce*, new and rev. edn. (Oxford University Press, 1982), p. 505.   [18] *Remembrance and Imagination*, p. 156.

model for modernity. He did so at a moment in history when the English language, although the language of the oppressor, was certainly the language in which his "catastrophic" testimony would be most likely to be heard worldwide.

Here my epigraph with its reference to the Holocaust comes in. It needs commentary, because it might seem that, like a Benetton advertisement, I appropriate the misfortune of others to enhance my particular point. First of all, as I conclude in my final chapter, I see *Finnegans Wake* as a pedagogic attempt to inscribe racial darkness into western culture on the eve of World War II. Secondly, Joyce's writing seems an "event,"[19] a coming-into-historical-being, which permanently affected representation, just as "Auschwitz" permanently altered our understanding of the concept of history.

One might argue an analogy – however abstractly structural – between the Irish experience and that of the repression of the documentation verifying the historicity of the extermination camps, which is most clearly brought home by Lyotard's discussion in *The Differend*. Lyotard is fascinated by "Auschwitz" as a deadlock of signification. Not only did the Germans exterminate the Jews, they also destroyed a large quantity of the records, the documents necessary for the validation of that fact. Lyotard proposes the following analogy. Suppose that during an earthquake all seismic instruments necessary to measure it were also destroyed. Should we then have to conclude that history has no means of establishing its occurrence? Though it cannot be quantitatively measured, it would still impress upon the survivors the overwhelming presence of the emotional force of the event. The experience would be recorded as a "feeling" "aroused by the negative presentation of the indeterminate. *Mutatis mutandis*, the silence that the crime of Auschwitz imposes upon the historian is a sign for the common person. Signs . . . are not referents to which are attached significations validatable under the cognitive regimen, they indicate that something which should be able to be put into phrases cannot be phrased in the accepted idioms."[20] We can, I suggest, transpose this situation to Irish history. Though the autochthonous language, and with it the directly transmissible cultural memory of destitution, starvation, and slavery has been suppressed, that situation lives on in two ways: there is the sign of the absence of the

---

[19] See Jean-François Lyotard, *The Postmodern Condition: A Report on Knowledge*, trans. Geoff Bennington and Brian Massumi (Minneapolis: University of Minnesota Press, 1984), p. 81.

[20] Jean-François Lyotard, *The Differend: Phrases in Dispute* (1983; Minneapolis: University of Minnesota Press, 1988), pp. 56–57.

language, and the non-figurable feeling, which travels through history divorced from a referent. In other words, the lapsing of the language – note how demonstratively Joyce resorts to the slip of the tongue – is a sign that something which ought to be or to have been expressed cannot (yet) be uttered discursively. Neither the revival of the Irish language – with its illusion that interiority has been regained by restoring the ancient speech, repressing the painful lapse in its own history – nor the turn to cosmopolitanism copes with, or addresses, the historical sign of the loss of the language and what that means: a muted history of suffering which works its effects on everyday life in the generation of nomadic affect disproportionate to the present occasion. Affect, no longer attached to story, no longer embodied as knowledge, hence no longer controllable, travels randomly like a will-o'-the-wisp.[21] As I said, neither of the two contemporary choices formulated by Welch (to write in cosmopolitan English and become rich, or to write in the Gaelic language with a reclaimed interiority) attempts to articulate and address the *feeling* attending the historical suppression of cultural memory. Unless that experience is confronted and mourned, however, it will keep haunting the present. Even if there is no "story" to pass on, each succeeding present will be inhabited by its ghost until the crime is eventually worked through.

I suggest that Joyce's *'œuvre* is a "ghost story": the location of the presence of that something not-expressed or inexpressible, that sense of loss transcending articulation, incarnated in his texts as the informative effect of a transcendent presence of absence, a matrix of negativity, a *chora* of loss, the black hole of muted history. Not only does it work its effect on Joyce's textuality, Joyce also attempts to allegorize it, to make its presence felt, and give it a local habitation and a name – to make it controllable through figuration.

Important in Lyotard's discussion is not only the question of finding language for what cannot be named. Especially relevant is Lyotard's manner of referring to it. In Lyotard's text the placename "Auschwitz" functions as the signifier for something prior to speech and declaration which has just been declared unnamable. He uses the geographical-historical name "Auschwitz" to fill in the void that gapes in history. But in choosing to take this signifier from the discourse of history to denote an unavowable loss prior to its discourse and declaration, he practises a secondary positivization of that unavowable moment. Lyotard discur-

---

[21] On the place of affect in the "resistence" of transferential repetition, see Mikkel Borch-Jacobsen, *The Emotional Tie: Psychoanalysis, Mimesis, and Affect* (Stanford University Press, 1992), p. 143.

sively re-materializes as placename the discursive death which inaugurates the condition of which the inception can never be given in its
positivity but only pointed to as the unnamable moment of advent. This
name thus functions as a substitute figuration for what cannot be
named. As I shall argue in chapter 2, Joyce's realistic presentation of
Dublin is to be understood like Lyotard's "Auschwitz" as a secondary
positivization, a material substitute in the shape of the representation of
a place and its people, offered to take the place of the story which
happened there but which cannot be articulated directly.

In tandem with the forwardly propelling self-dialectic imposed by
discursive trauma, the location, shape, and nature of Joyce's representation of the non-figurable shifts and self-consciously redoubles throughout his career. The ambition to articulate a meaning which is "still
unuttered",[22] begins when the young writer, ensconced in the sense of
moral superiority of youth, intends to show his fellowmen their "hemiplegia of the will" in *Dubliners*. He hopes to create the "uncreated
conscience of his race," the lacking "Irish soul."[23] Here Joyce under-
stands representation as a neutral instrument, an objective mirror,
independent of his writerly subjectivity, and he locates the trauma of
Irishness outside the artistic self. As my discussion of *A Portrait of the Artist*
will show, Joyce soon shifts the *locus* of the nonfigurable. If in *Dubliners*
paralysis affected the object of representation, now it is related to the
traumatically violent entry into subjectivity and naming of the artist-
figure himself. This painful inscription has both a splitting and repetitive
effect upon the text, setting up a repetitive internal dialectic, a continuous process of self-mirroring and self-correction which will continue
throughout subsequent works, and which subverts the distinction between autobiography and fiction. Thus *Ulysses* splits the self and stages
the asymptotic double quest of two protagonists (young–old; gentile–
Jew; artist–citizen), and unravels the unity of the text into two gendered
layers between which gapes the cold emptiness of "interstellar spaces."[24]

---

[22] *Stephen Hero*, ed. John J. Slocum and Herbert Cahoon (New York: Viking Press, 1963), p. 73. Hereafter *SH* and cited by page number.

[23] Note that Joyce uses these words also to express his own intention in letters to the publisher Grant Richards and to his wife Nora. An early and important discussion of postcolonial Joyce was Seamus Deane, "Joyce and Nationalism," in Colin McCabe, ed. *James Joyce: New Perspectives* (Sussex: Harvester, 1982), pp. 168–84, which is closest to my own approach since it addresses Joyce's attempt to revise the medium of representation itself. Deane writes: Joyce's "[a]rt is itself in service to the Soul of Ireland. This soul is still uncreated. It is the function of true art to create it – a function all the more necessary since all other forms of Irish activity had failed by producing a debased version of that spiritual reality" (p. 172).

[24] Quotations from *Ulysses*, ed. Hans Walter Gabler (New York and London: Garland Publishing, 1984), are indicated by episode and line number e.g. *U* 17.1246.

The darkness of unmeaning which *Ulysses* opens up is in turn staged in *Finnegans Wake* as the allegory of its own condition of impossibility. Joyce's career concludes with the blatantly demonstrative, heroic assumption of the dark stain of meaninglessness and racial denigration as the cross of *Finnegans Wake*. It blurs reality and dream and inhabits the inexpressible which is transmitted to the reader as ambivalent "feeling" (at once laughter and despair). Always arguing that "his shape" and his "destiny"[25] were those of Ireland herself, his career is the demonstration of the increasingly self-conscious, dialectical confrontation with the irrecoverability of the language of self-presence which has been lost, and the attempt to figure and articulate as presence what history only transmits as "feeling." Thus my reading of postcolonial Joyce is new, and perhaps to some disconcerting, because I locate his struggle with difference not as a theme in his work, nor as an attempt to redress injustice *in* representation, but at the more fundamental level of the transmission and figuration of an untold and untellable trauma which some might wish to forget *through* representation.

The analogy with Lyotard's discussion in *The Differend* is instructive in several ways. Firstly, he argues that "Auschwitz" is a moment when history must change its self-conception. Since most of the records are absent, it will have to learn to pay attention to the non-figurable, the "feeling," if it wants to do justice to what happened during World War II. Lyotard faces the possible counterclaim that history is not made of feelings, and that only facts establish truth, and points out that such historians do a "wrong" to the "sign that is this silence." Indeed, he claims that Auschwitz is so important in western history, because it inaugurates the event of something which can only be "sign" and not "fact" since "the testimonies which bore the traces of *here's* and *now's*" have been obliterated. It marks the end of historical knowledge as we have traditionally understood it. Now it is up to the historian, or the reader, to *understand* the situation in its "suffering of this abeyance [*cette souffrance*]." To do so, the historian must break with the monopoly over history granted to the cognitive regimen of phrases, and he or she must venture forth by lending his or her ear to "what is not presentable under the rules of knowledge."[26] Transposing Lyotard's argument to the "sign"of the absence of the Irish language in Joyce, we learn that the literary historian will have to lend his or her ear to "what is not presentable under the rules of knowledge."

Just as historians will have to learn to read differently after Auschwitz,

---

25 Frank Budgen, *James Joyce and the Making of "Ulysses"* (1934; repr. Bloomington: Indiana University Press, 1960), p.152.　　26 Lyotard, *The Differend*, p. 57.

I think the example of the "event" of Joyce is an injunction to learn to read literature in a new way. In order to bring out the truth or reality of what is present as absence or as lack, we must pay attention not so much to *what* is said, but to its *how* and *to what effect*. Moreover if, just as in psychoanalytic sessions, the meaning of signifiers is produced intersubjectively by the transferential context, part of the meaning of Joyce may reside in his *Wirkung* on the reader.[27] In short, we must relearn to hear, and literally see, what informs the text behind or between the words or beyond its words. Ideally, we shall become engaged in a dialogue of our own with the core of absence and trauma of Joyce's text. Although it is *Finnegans Wake* which forces the reader into a witnessing attitude because it frustrates all attempts at making sense of it, all of Joyce's major works demand this style of reading. In order to be true to the inexpressible in Joyce, we shall have to use our intuition and empathy in addition to our cognitive skills and our learning.

Thus another point argued by Lyotard proves of consequence. He suggests that henceforth the addressee, in our case we as readers, is implicated in the framework of communication. "That, in a phrase universe, the referent be situated as a sign has as a corollary that in this same universe the addressee is situated like someone who is affected, and that the sense is situated like an unresolved problem, an enigma perhaps, a mystery, or a paradox." Here it is certainly worthwhile to turn to Lyotard's text itself to note how he hesitates in using the word "feeling." In whatever form or how we understand the aftermath of Irish experience as a "feeling," the absence of the language "is the sign that something remains to be phrased which is not, something which is not determined."[28] Absence of language signals meaning left unarticulated which demands articulation: "The indetermination of meaning left in abeyance . . . , the extermination of what would allow them to be determined, the shadow of negation hollowing out reality to the point of making it dissipate, in a word, the wrong done to the victims that condemns them to silence – it is this, and not a state of mind, which calls upon unknown phrases to link onto the name of Auschwitz." In short, we, the readers of Joyce, are asked to respond to the tacit demand in the

---

[27] Shoshana Felman, "Turning the Screw of Interpretation," in Shoshana Felman, ed. *Literature and Psychoanalysis: The Question of Reading Otherwise* (Baltimore and London: Johns Hopkins University Press, 1982): "Reading here becomes not the cognitive observation of the text's pluralistic meaning, but its 'acting out.' Indeed, it is not so much the critic who comprehends the text as the text that comprehends the critic. Comprehending its own criticism, the text, through its reading, orchestrates the critical disagreement as the performance and the 'speech act' of its own disharmony" (pp. 114–15).   [28] Lyotard, *The Differend*, p. 57.

text, and articulate the meaning which is left "in abeyance."

Although my perspective is more Lyotardian or Foucauldian than psychoanalytic, I use the term "trauma," following Shoshana Felman and Cathy Caruth, to denote a presence which exceeds narrrative discourse as traditionally understood. Though the term may, perhaps, carry a negative connotation of pathology, in trauma studies, as the theoretical field is now called, the concept of trauma is used to denote a structure of subjectivity split by the inaccessibility of part of its experience which cannot be remembered. Caruth speaks of the "fundamental enigma concerning the psyche's relation to reality."[29] In trauma, experience may be stored in the body without mediation of consciousness, and return as flashback, or keep insisting through a compulsion to repeat. The concept is important, because it forces us to rethink the relationship between consciousness, memory, and language.[30] It also links subjectivity to Lacan's "real." In Lacan, "the real" refers to that which cannot be directly inscribed or experienced, such as death or sexual difference, but which keeps insisting, and manifesting its presence through repetition. As Slavoj Žižek points out: "it is something that persists only as failed, missed, in a shadow, and dissolves itself as soon as we try to grasp it in its positive nature." Žižek also suggests that "this is precisely what defines the notion of traumatic event: a point of failure of symbolization, but at the same time never given in its positivity – it can be constructed only backwards, from its structural effects."[31]

Trauma is thus a paradoxical structure, working by means of indirectness: it manifests itself through and as its consequences, its aftermath and effects, but is itself not directly accessible to consciousness or memory. It shows within the text of subjectivity what seems to remain outside it and what must be presupposed if all other elements are to retain their consistency. Freud called this situation "*Nachträglichkeit*," the retroactive production of meaning. Thus trauma breaks up the forward movement of time, to inscribe metalepsis as a structuring principle. Finally, trauma is always the effect of a history, even if that history is not accessible to memory – a shocking event or situation which overwhelmed consciousness to inscribe itself as a death-in-life.

[29] Cathy Caruth, *Unclaimed Experience: Trauma, Narrative, and History* (Baltimore: Johns Hopkins University Press, 1996), p. 91.

[30] Note Ruth Leys' definition of trauma as "the mimetic affection or identificatory dissociation of the 'subject' that occurs outside of, or prior to, the representational–spectatorial economy of repressed representations of the 'subject–object' distinction on which recollection depends." "Traumatic Cures," *Critical Inquiry* 20 (1994), 644.

[31] *The Sublime Object of Ideology* (London and New York: Verso, 1992), p. 169.

The importance of trauma in this study rests on the notion that trauma is always "the story of a wound that cries out, that addresses us in its attempt to tell us of a reality or truth that is not otherwise available. This truth, in its delayed appearance and its belated address, cannot be linked only to what is known, but also to what remains unknown in our very actions and our language."[32] Speaking "beyond its knowing" of the impossibility of having its own history, the text of Joyce may work to "tell" us something about the incomprehensibility of Irish history which resists symbolization, even today. If we accept the peculiar temporal logic of trauma, which makes itself only evident in "another place, and in another time" owing to the latency inherent in its structure, we may also come to read Joyce's works as the record and location of such a return of the unexpressed of Irish history as symptom. Moreover, Joyce's texts may be understood as its incarnated vessel of preservation, if not transmission.

As a structure which manifests itself in its *Nachträglichkeit*, we can only know trauma through its effects. Thus, in the chapters that follow, I seek confirmation for my suggestion of the traumatic textuality of Joyce in both the extraordinary intensity of the response it has received, as well as in its curiously split nature. Joyce is named as an important influence or strong precursor by major writers from Borges to Rushdie.[33] He stimulated imitative productivity in several modern languages. Thus T. S. Eliot's paradoxical conclusion that *Ulysses* is a "book to which we are all indebted, and from which none of us can escape,"[34] proved prophetic. Today, a search for Joyce's *Ulysses* produces over ten-thousand hits on AltaVista; there are *Finnegans Wake* reading groups on several continents; almost more criticism is written about Joyce than about Shakespeare; and even recently a major Irish writer, referring to himself as a "survivor of Joyce," figured Joyce as the "stone Nobodaddy at my shoulder," the "great looming Easter Island effigy of the Father."[35] Joyce is at once contagious and non-masterable.[36] On the

[32] Caruth, *Unclaimed Experience*, p.4.
[33] See, for instance, Ivo Vidan, "The Continuity of Joyce: Traces, Analogues in Later Foreign Writers," in *International Perspectives on James Joyce*, ed. Gottlieb Gaiser (New York: Whiston, 1986), and Morton P. Levitt, *Modernist Survivors: The Contemporary Novel in England, the United States, France and Latin America* (Columbus: Ohio State University Press, 1987).
[34] "*Ulysses*, Order and Myth," *Dial* 75 (November 1923), 480-3, repr. in *James Joyce: The Critical Heritage, Volume 1: 1907–1927*, ed. Robert H. Deming (London and Henley: Routledge and Kegan Paul, 1970), p. 268.
[35] John Banville, "Survivors of Joyce," in Augustine Martin, ed. *The Artist and the Labyrinth* (London: Ryan, 1990), pp. 73–74.
[36] See Roland McHugh's *The Finnegans Wake Experience* (Dublin: Irish Academic Press, 1981), for a personal account of an intense preoccupation with Joyce which changed a life.

contrary, he masters us, upsetting rigid demarcations between literary periods such as modernism and postmodernism – marking the advent of the impossibility of such a distinction[37] – and frustrating our attempts at a definitive reading or interpretation. My reader may think that I am arguing Joyce's importance. That is not so. I am arguing the paradoxical peculiarity of Joyce's effect. Derrida's testimony points to that Joyce-effect: "Here the event is of such plot and scope that henceforth you have only one way out: *being in memory of him*. You're not only overcome by him, whether you know it or not, but obliged by him, and constrained to measure yourself against this overcoming."[38] This sense of Joyce as an *event* altering history once and for all, present already in Eliot's reaction, was, perhaps, most usefully voiced by C. G. Jung, who spoke of the author of *Ulysses* as "the unwitting mouthpiece of the psychic secrets of his time," "often as unconscious as a sleepwalker": "He supposes that it is he who speaks, but the spirit of the age is his prompter, and whatever this spirit says is proved true by its effects." Jung conclusively labelled *Ulysses* a "cosmic Ash Wednesday" comparable in the effect of its advent to "August 1, 1914," the beginning of the World War.[39]

In the chapters which follow I do not only emphasize this notion of a discursive trauma which confirmingly constitutes its identity through its impact, I also focus on its divisionary effect on criticism as the tell-tale sign of its presence: "[W]hen I think of Joyce I am split in two," John Banville confesses; and like Poe's story "The Purloined Letter," which generated an ongoing dispute about its meaning, Joyce's texts have a tendency to engender contradictory interpretations and endless debates. Thus they enact and effectuate what Shoshana Felman, in a reading of "The Turn of the Screw," first noted as the performative effect of the presence of the "real" in the text (in her example, sexuality): "In [its] dramatizing, through a clash of meanings, the very functioning of meaning as division and as conflict, sexuality is not, however, the 'text's meaning': it is rather that through which meaning in the text *does not come off*, that which in the text, and through which the text, *fails to mean*, that which can engender but a *conflict of interpretations*, a critical debate and

---

[37] See Lyotard, *The Postmodern Condition*, p. 81: "The artist and the writer, then, are working without rules in order to formulate the rules of what *will have been done.*"

[38] "Two Words for Joyce," in *Post-Structuralist Joyce: Essays From the French*, ed. Derek Attridge and Daniel Ferrer (Cambridge University Press, 1984), p. 147.

[39] "Ulysses: A Monologue" (1932), in *Hidden Patterns: Studies in Psychoanalytic Literary Criticism*, ed. Leonard and Eleanor Manheim (New York: MacMillan, 1966), pp. 206 and 211. My reason for giving such prominence to Jung, whose theories I do not endorse, is the professional psychoanalytic interest he took in Joyce and his schizophrenic daughter.

discord."[40] From the beginning of Joyce studies, there has been a split in the field marked by, on the one hand, the work of Richard Ellmann, Joyce's biographer (and also a critic of Yeats and Wilde), and, on the other hand, Hugh Kenner, gifted reader of Pound as well as of Joyce. The "Ellmannites," historical, and myth-oriented in their understanding, read Joyce as a humanist genius whose work advocates perennial values; the "Kennerites" tend to see Joyce as an ironist, a genius with words and literary conventions whose playfulness delights and outwits us. Whereas the "Ellmannites" tend to see Joyce as Irish, the "Kennerites" read Joyce as a cosmopolitan who presents the Dublin of 1904 as a modern technological city.[41] Important to me here is not the history of Joyce criticism, but the curious polarity of the positions which seems pre-programmed by Joyce's text itself. In fact, the effect of polarization is anticipatingly inscribed in *Finnegans Wake* in the figure of the two rivalling twin brothers, the dependable and commercial Shaun the Post who believes in facts and delivers the letter, and the slippery artist Shem the Textman who obsessively scribbles fictions and, improvidently, wallows in filth. While the insistent recurrence of this polarity, replayed in many variations in Joyce's prose fiction, might be naturalized as a stylization of his relationship with his brother Stanislaus (who claimed he was his "brother's keeper"), or even of Joyce's split-personality, I propose that we understand it as the trace, or the textual itinerary of a discursive trauma pointing to an unspeakable historical cause.[42] Just as the purloined letter in Poe's story (a document significant owing to its material presence rather than its content) inspires rivalry for its possession, Joyce's texts generate rivalry and polarity among those who attempt to subject them to a totalizing vision. The difference in approach to Joyce taken by Derrida and Lacan, therefore, may be just one more illustration of the splitting effect of Joyce's letter, and needs no resolution. If Derrida is the "Kennerite," Lacan is the "Ellmannite." Both have truth on their side, albeit not the whole truth. Each transferentially inscribes himself into a partial, differently gendered layer of

[40] "Turning the Screw of Interpretation," p. 112.
[41] The presentation of the "Critical and Synoptic Edition" of *Ulysses* in 1984 held a tense moment. In older editions, Stephen Dedalus's cry to his mother to tell him the "word known to all men," had been left unanswered by a blank. Now, that word suddenly appeared as "love," to the delight of the "Ellmannites." Since the 1984 edition did not prove "definitive," however, the last word has not been spoken on this issue.
[42] Ricardo J. Quinones, *The Changes of Cain: Violence and the Lost Brother in Cain and Abel Literature* (Princeton University Press, 1991), discusses the archetype in Joyce, and points out that it denotes the presence of a break in being.

Joyce's textuality.[43] Their reactions to Joyce will be examined in chapter 5 after the analysis of gender in *Ulysses*.

As I said, the concept of trauma brings with it a new notion of representation. The trauma victim, instead of reflecting on the trauma in a narrative account, lives out and repeats the event which always escapes conscious articulation. Only through repetition and replay may the event which caused the trauma eventually crystallize into experience and narrative – if it ever does. Joyce depicts his artist-figure Stephen Dedalus as involved in such a circular and retrospective quest for access to the self through compulsive repetition. But over and above this representation of Stephen Dedalus as propelled by the forward drive of repetition (rather than desire), Joyce's textuality is itself a form of acting out, a performative speech act of the trauma of Irishness rather than the constative speech act which portrays it. Like drama, which has the magical power to make present rather than to just narrate, Joyce's fiction always partakes of its object. Eroding the distinction between origin and copy, citation and non-citation, it sets up a correspondence between rhetoric and psychic process. It forges an existential or in-dexical relation between words and the colonial body. The expression of the discourse of the text becomes the infinitely repeated attempt at the constitutive self-expression of its author's purloined writerly subjectivity – his personality, "first a cry or a cadence or a mood and then a fluid and lambent narrative, finally refines itself out of existence, impersonalizes itself . . ."(*P* 214). Meanwhile, the literary work becomes what Wallace Stevens spoke of as "the cry of its occasion,/ Part of the res itself and not about it."[44] Seamus Deane put it thus: Joyce's writing, which was itself a political act, rather than *about* politics, "achieves its aspiration by coming into existence. It serves only what it is. Between the idea of service and the idea of the thing served, the distance has disappeared. In pursuing this conception of the artist and art, Joyce was presenting himself, via Stephen Dedalus, with a specifically Irish problem which

---

[43] Transference is a "projection, in that the subject expresses or exteriorizes through speech the identifying *imago*, until then 'imprinted in his person.'" What the analyst, in this case Joyce's text does, is return the image to the patient. See Mikkel Borch-Jacobsen, *The Emotional Tie: Psychoanalysis, Mimesis, and Affect*, trans. Douglas Brick (Stanford University Press, 1992), p. 81. On Lacan and Derrida's implicit rivalry about Joyce, see Christine van Boheemen-Saaf, "Purloined Joyce," in *Re:Joyce, Text, Culture, Politics*, ed. John Brannigan, Geoff Ward, and Julian Wolfreys (London: Macmillan, 1998), pp. 246–58.

[44] "An Ordinary Evening in New Haven," in *The Palm at the End of the Mind: Selected Poems and a Play*, ed. Holly Stevens (New York: Vintage, 1972), p. 338. In this context it is interesting to note Joyce's superstitious fear that words might come true and kill.

had wider implications."[45] One of those wider implications is that this conception of writing, which is of a piece with the understanding of trauma as the psychic extension of the effects of the overwhelming threat of bodily harm, necessitates our revision of the ontological status of literature. Instead of a metalanguage situated above or about life, literature becomes coextensive with life, writing with living. The literary text becomes the effective index of the presence of that which cannot be articulated directly.

As performatives, however, Joyce's narratives still maintain a dual charge: they may be read as referential texts descriptive of their single object: Dublin life at the beginning of this century. They may also be understood in the sense I outlined above. But if we reflect on the nature of trauma as by definition an unclaimed and perhaps unclaimable experience, it becomes clear that the representational side of Joyce's works is *ersatz*, counterfeit, "Shem." They substitute for what cannot be told because it cannot be remembered. Joyce's texts do not nostalgically express a recalled reality, however factual his Dublin may seem; they attempt to "forge" an "uncreated conscience."[46] They take the place of that which cannot be accommodated within representation because history has not yet allowed its coming-into-being. Joyce's Dublin still life (*nature morte*) inscribes the colonial death-in-life which deprived Irish culture of its autonomy, self-presence, or "conscience." As such it is, just as the absence of the Irish language itself, not an iconic, but an indexical sign. We might understand Joyce's works, even the most realistic *Dubliners*, as the mimicking performatives of a signifying mode of representation, at once deceptively obedient to his master's voice, but opening up a gap between conventional reality and a hidden emotional reality in the same gesture.[47]

Paradoxically, then, Joyce answers Adorno's call in "The Position of the Narrator in the Contemporary Novel," that the novel, if it *"wants to remain true to its realistic heritage and tell how things really are, . . . must abandon a realism that only aids the facade in its work of camouflage by reproducing*

---

[45] "Joyce and Nationalism," p. 175.

[46] Again, Joyce also spoke about his own intention in these words. In *Finnegans Wake*, Shem, issuing "piously forged palimpsests" (182.2–3), studies "with stolen fruit how cutely to copy all their various styles of signature so as one day to utter an epical forged cheque on the public for his own private profit" (181.14–17).

[47] See Homi K. Bhabha, "Representation and the Colonial Text: Some Forms of Mimeticism," in Frank Gloversmith, ed., *The Theory of Reading* (Brighton: Harvester, 1984), pp. 93–122. The structural congruence with the situation of women under patriarchy, as demonstratively and parodically performed by Luce Irigaray, will be clear.

it.''[48] Joyce erodes realism from within. But the subtlety of his procedure is such, that, like the work of termites, it may go undetected by those non-alert to it. Joyce's subversive rendering of "how things really are" splits his readership. We may read him as the modernist genius, or as the inventor of a postcolonial, subversive mode. In fact, like the transferential mirror of the analyst in the psychoanalytic session, the text reflects perhaps most of all where we ourselves stand.

In *Occidentalism*, Xiaomei Chen suggests that criticism is "best served not by separating dichotomies such as Orient/Occident, Self/Other, traditionalism/modernism, and male/female, but by engaging these binary oppositions in a constant and continuing dialogue without ever claiming one version of 'truth' at the expense of celebrating the diversities of all 'truths.'"[49] The peculiarity of Joyce's poetics is that, while it manifests the unsublatable tension of constitutive dissociation, it is at once a syncretic attempt to counter splitting. The text labors to keep body and soul together, so to speak, and operates at a level of hybridity and ambiguity in which form and formlessness, creation and destruction reverse into each other. The material object of the book creates a location in which the partial is always subsumed in and betrayed by the material integrity of the artifact.

Thus the text as symptomatic body, as substitute material location, provides a utopian place where the breach in existence, the fractures in being, whether of race, gender, or class, are placed in non-collapsing juxtaposition. The materiality of inscription, the physical location of the book, provides the *locus* for an "otherworld"[50] in which mimesis is given back its ancient ritual function of dramatizing the lived indistinction of the trance, and in which rhythm sutures the *différance* of temporality. It is a place in which one can "keep No and Yes unsplit."[51] In Joyce's texts dream and memory, disavowal and recognition, the conceptual and pre-conceptual fuse. But, it must be remembered, this linguistic-materialist utopia is not an escape from cognition or from a real world, like the transformation into birds of Ovid's protagonists. It is rather an attempt to provide an embodied location in which inarticulate experience not accommodated and articulated by history may nevertheless be preserved as unclaimed memory for future generations. In fact, Joyce per-

---

[48] Theodor W. Adorno, *Notes to Literature*, vol. 1, ed. Rolf Tiedemann (New York: Columbia University Press, 1991), p. 32.
[49] *Occidentalism* (Oxford University Press, 1995), p. 155.
[50] I take the term from Irish mythology which fuses the material and the spiritual.
[51] John Felstiner, *Paul Celan: Poet, Survivor, Jew* (New Haven: Yale University Press, 1995), p. 100.

forms a literalization of the original, Platonic notion of mimesis: as in a mirror, in his work reality appears *where it is not*. The history of mimesis begins with Plato's objection to its use of reported speech as potentially untruthful. Only first-person speech can be considered authentic and true. The mirror of mimesis is deceptive because it displaces, and lets language appear in a place where it did not originate.[52] Joyce perversely applies Plato's dictum about the *location* of truth to the letter. The fetishized "warm" "human" (*P* 179) pages of Joyce's embodied texts offer themselves as the material locus of the truth of the unconscious of the historical process.[53]

Joyce's fetishized linguistic materialism requires a new way of analyzing narrative. Just a sense of Joyce as Daedalian "wordsmith" is not sufficient, especially as the architecture of his texts is unprecedented and demands that we expand our register to accommodate the materiality of Joyce's inscription, which exploits the shape of dots, doodles, the size of letters, in short, the physical dimension of textuality. Joyce practices a kind of hieroglyphic narrative, a lithography (writing in stone), presenting a graven image, "epic cryptograms,"[54] in which the manner of its material inscription itself conveys meaning. He adds a new dimension to the semiotics of narrative. As we know, Joyce was obsessively particular about graphic design. He insisted that direct speech not be indicated by quotation marks but by a dash. He attached expressive importance to page numbers, chapter headings, typeface, size of initial capital letters, presence or absence of punctuation, the blue color of the cover of *Ulysses*. He experimented with the representational conventions of different genres: playing visually with musical scores, the layout of poetry and drama. Ultimately, *Finnegans Wake*, would contain graphs, parodic footnotes, diagrams and marginal commentary, in addition to characters whose names are configurations of letters to be retrieved from the text by the reader. As I shall argue in chapter 3, "The language of the outlaw," this is not an early form of postmodernism's parodic awareness of the limits of representation, but an attempt to tear through the screen of representation itself, and make the text concretely present. In order to compre-

---

[52] Aristotle's definition of mimesis as the representation of an action, which has become dominant in literary history, shifts away from Plato's emphasis on truth as located in direct speech, to redefine truth in relation to the accuracy of imitation.

[53] See also Emily Apter, *Feminizing the Fetish: Narrative Obsession in Turn-of-the-Century France* (Ithaca: Cornell University Press, 1991), who constructs "female fetishism" as a praxis of "materialized social construction" (p. 98) which I see as similar to Joyce's "subaltern fetishism."

[54] Adorno's description of Joyce's style. *Notes to Literature*, p. 35.

hend Joyce, we must take this emphasis on the materiality of the letter literally.

Thus this study emphasizes a level of textual existence and a manner of reading which includes awareness of immanence, even of ourselves as readers. Such affirmation is, by definition, inaudible to classical philosophical discourse. Derrida's revisionary readings of older texts are presented as a correction of the lack of attention to "writing" in classical philosophy. That Derrida's own texts show visual and textual features reminiscent of those of Joyce needs no further argument.[55] The question is how or whether Derrida's "writing" (or Lacan's "materiality of the signifier") is comparable to Joyce's linguistic materialism.

Here it suffices to note that Joyce's works provide a textbook illustration of Derrida's and Lacan's major concepts. The following chapters offer a reading of Joyce in which *"différance"* proves to be the textual pattern of *A Portrait of the Artist*, "dissemination" the mode of "Cyclops," and "supplementarity" the structural pattern of the text of *Ulysses*. Lacan's theory of the split subject, which breaks up the rational autonomy of the humanist self and points to its determination by an other – language or the symbolic system – may be most poignantly appropriate as a description of the split sense of self-awareness of subaltern consciousness. Dublin's scotoma illustrates Lacan's theory of "castration." The "gaze" is easily understood as the sense of surveillance, not only of paranoia but of an oppressive regime in which subjectivity has become an imaginary function of signs and meanings always determined from elsewhere. Joyce's excessive writerliness was Lacan's example of the persistence of *"jouissance."* As we shall see in the final chapter, Joyce's liminality, the effect of the death-in-life of the condition of trauma, illustrates Lacan's theory of the "two deaths," whereas Lacan's "real" enters Joyce's texts as an informative presence to litter its pages with repetition and the informative *lacuna* of death. Thus it is in Joyce's texts that we can "read the real."

In choosing to speak of Joyce's textual subject-position as "traumatic," I also imply that there is a curative force at work in the condition itself. Traumatic memory, unclaimed experience, keeps insisting until it is worked through. Thus Freud's "death-drive" is also a signal of the necessity and possibility of cure, the necessity of mourning and psychological "work" to undo the negativity which history has inscribed. Instead of being unchangeably determined by our past, we can, if we

---

[55] See: Christine van Boheemen, "Deconstruction after Joyce," in Bonnie Kime Scott, ed., *New Alliances in Joyce Studies* (Newark: University of Delaware Press, 1988), pp. 29–37.

learn to listen to the symptom and accept the pain implied in what it tells us, undo the heritage of history. "Something exists," Robert Welch argues, "whereby people can get outside their history, their given, fated narratives."[56]

Joyce's strategy of writing makes explicit an ethical dimension which must remain inarticulate in theory. As I shall argue in chapter 5, "Materiality in Derrida, Lacan, and Joyce's embodied text," my analysis of Joyce's discourse leads to the suggestion that we must turn our ear to the affect of the text if we hope to escape the negative determinism of history. It is a psychoanalytical tenet that without attending affect, there is no psychological change. If it was the text of Joyce which inspired Lacan's revision of his theoretical schema, it may also be the confrontation with the encrypted trauma in Joyce's works which will help the reader "change his or her mind," and acquire a future-oriented perspective which opens new vistas beyond the tyranny of the Same and the One.

Joyce's example also teaches that we do not need to choose between either Derrida or Lacan in their attribution of truth to literature – psychoanalysis locating "truth" in the textual example, philosophy in the act of writing. I think their conjunction proves most enriching. If Lacan's "real" is that "which prevents one from saying the *whole* truth about it,"[57] there is more truth in combining Derrida and Lacan than in privileging one perspective to the other. In other words, I am advocating a syncretic approach which shuttles between the two without the drive to adjudicate. I am not writing as a philosopher or theorist, but as a student of Joyce. And it is Joyce's syncretic text which provides a demonstration of the pedagogic necessity of keeping self-projected contraries in dialectical tension. Shem, the dirty alchemist whose masturbatory "act of writing" transforms bodily waste into indelible ink, is thus ventriloquized or narrated through his opposite, the pompously common-sensical materialist Shaun – a bourgeois Don Juan obsessed with money and success whose pretence to learning and truth kills the spirit of the letter. Shaun, in turn, is perceived through the discourse of Shem as the source of bad, pedestrian prose, and exploitatively self-interested sociability. The text oscillates from one interpenetrating perspective to the other without settling on a definitive image. Thus the literary text is the material location of the intersubjective experience of transference, in which patient and analyst undergo the unsettling effect of mirroring: the

[56] Welch, *Changing States*, p. 289. See also Kaja Silverman, *The Threshold of the Visible World* (New York: Routledge, 1996).
[57] Lacan, *Television: A Challenge to the Psychoanalytic Establishment*, trans. Denis Holier, Rosalind Kraus, Annette Michelson, and Jeffrey Mehlman (1974; New York and London: Norton, 1990), p. 31.

self-image is projected in the mirror of the other where it seems to belong as long as one's own projective activity is not recognized and understood. If traditionally the novel *depicted* the process of psychological change of its protagonists, as in Jane Austen's *Pride and Prejudice* or Dickens' *Great Expectations*, Joyce's works dramatize that reading is an activity which may emotionally affect the reader, and involve him or her in a processual dynamic which restructures subjectivity itself, not just our cognitive *understanding*.

Joyce's syncretism (some traditional scholars would speak of his "ambivalence") provides the material location to stage a mode of intersubjective being and perception which can, otherwise, only be experienced directly, or, perhaps, through the effect of drama. The both – and as well as the neither – nor of transference undercuts logic. Moreover, reading Joyce teaches one to understand the fixation of perception on one single and singular point of view, as, at once, a reduction and falsification. Joyce's reader grows to see the self as always already in relation to an other and to an unconscious. In this pedagogy, Joyce is close to his compatriot Yeats, who even envisioned the whole historical process as the movement back and forth in a system of interpenetrating cones. Thus Joyce holds up the analytical mirror to the western reader. He also confronts western literary theory with its inability to cope with the radical exteriority of *Finnegans Wake*. The more closely it engages Joyce's difference, the more closely White Mythology confirms its own underlying Oedipal bias and ontological imperialism, even if only in the negative.[58] Thus conventional readings of Joyce's practices of gender, sexuality, nationalism, or realism inevitably must come to the conclusion of his indeterminacy, ambivalence, elusiveness, perversion, perverseness, errancy, parody, or negativity, because they lack the conceptual tools to cope with such hybridism.

In chapter 4, "The primitive scene of representation," I shall discuss Joyce's handling of gender, because it is deeply interwoven with conceptualizations of the nation and the race. As Padraic Pearse's use of the figure of the mother – in mother Church, motherland, and mother tongue – as a sustaining metaphor of the nation demonstrates, the foundational myths of Irish identity are infused with the feminine; and so, historically, is the notion of the ("feminine") Celts as a race different from the ("masculine") English.[59] In such a situation, the supposed

---

[58] See Robert Young, *White Mythology: Writing History and the West* (New York and London: Routledge, 1990), p. 14.
[59] See Elizabeth Cullingford, " 'Thinking of Her . . . as . . . Ireland': Yeats, Pearse and Heaney," *Textual Practice* 4 (1989), 3–21.

"femininity" of his fiction, or, conversely, Joyce's misogyny, must be understood in connection with Joyce's own double implication in the discourse of gender. Not only is he a male, but as an Irishman he also shares in the participation mystique with the mother, which, feminizing him, also provides the security of maternal origins. I suggest that, although Joyce did not share the return to the foundational myths of the national revival, his relation to the maternal *imago* bears an Irish cathexis. Perhaps it is this double inscription of gender which also made possible the textual strategy of splitting which, as we shall see, supports his texts. From such a perspective, it becomes possible to understand Joyce's portrayal of the sexual liberation of Molly Bloom as not only the reflection of the drive to reveal the secrets of female sexuality of the turn of the century, but, allegorically, as phantasized vehicle for the liberation of the mother tongue. At the same time, we shall be in a position to note the fetishism which supports Joyce's textual metamorphosis, and the opening up of an abyss of meaninglessness and reductive materialism.

Blurring the boundaries between art and litter, realism and allegory, high and low, ink and excrement, metadiscourse and cry, Joyce's art is both mirror and symptom, both icon and index, about our world as well as a product in and of it. In the chapters which follow, I shall especially try to bring out the second element in these binarisms, because Joyce has traditionally been framed in their opposite. I am not trying to turn a Shaun-like Joyce into a Shem-like one, however. The unique distinction of Joyce, and his terrible beauty, is that he increasingly opted for the second term, relinquishing the first and sacrificing meaning, referentiality, the acclaim of fellow writers and friends, driven to express in and through words the violence history had suppressed, and the death-in-life of colonial experience.

CHAPTER 2

Representation in a postcolonial symbolic

It is a symbol of Irish art.
The cracked lookingglass of a servant

Ulysses

A "purloined letter" is not defined by its contents, but by its material presence and its *effect* on those who receive or hold it. Thus the letter is not valued for its message. It is seen as a "performative."[1] In this chapter, I will focus on the unsettling effect of *A Portrait of the Artist* to argue that Joyce's traumatic and resistant textuality produces a trembling and redoubling. The text is both presentational and representational. It syncretically inscribes two different ways of relating to the world at once, so that the performativity of *différance* is woven into the constativity of a stable "portrait." This produces vacillating contours, and positions the author as anxiously engaged in an ongoing process of negotiation of the boundary between self and persona, inside and outside, language and matter, psyche and history. The reader, who cannot read in two contradictory manners at once, is caught wanting in perceptiveness and comes to share the anxiety of the text.

Stephen Dedalus's qualification of Irish art as "the cracked looking-glass of a servant," is richly suggestive. A cracked mirror is a flawed object to be discarded or handed down to a servant: Irish art makes do with the outmoded models of representation of the master culture. Moreover, when we look into a cracked mirror, we see a redoubling and splitting reflection. We never see ourselves whole. In his fable of the mirror stage, Lacan points out that the vision of the unified self in the reflective surface allows the subject the illusion of wholeness. This phantasy of wholeness, overriding a fragmented body-image, provides a

---

[1] Laurent Milesi, "The *Poetics* of 'The Purloined Letter' in *Finnegans Wake* (narrative foresight and critical afterthought)," in *A Collideorscape of Joyce*, ed. Ruth Frehner and Ursula Zeller (Dublin: Lilliput Press, 1998), pp. 306–23, provides an exhaustive study of the applicability of the term to Joyce's textuality.

relation between inside and outside that "projects the formation of the individual into history."[2] Lacan's fable situates the ego's wholeness as at once imagined, exterior, and visually determined. In contradistinction to the effect of the mirror in the mirror stage, a cracked mirror gives us a split and schizoid image of the self. Thus the contradictory condition of Irish subjectivity – part of the United Kingdom but perceived as racially and culturally different by the English; English-speaking while aware of the loss of the mother tongue – is allegorized in a "cracked lookingglass" which can never achieve wholeness.

But it is not only allegorized. Joyce, the author of Stephen Dedalus, takes up this image; and deliberately structuring his texts in a similar fashion, he reflects the cracked surface back to his reader. Thus he visits his own condition of oscillating subjectivity on us. The reader looking in Joyce's mirror for a unified image of the world is deprived of the satisfaction of wholeness that reading conventionally provides. He or she is placed in the position of the Irish servant, lacking a unified identity since one is always already identified in relation to a disconcerting "other." Reading Joyce thus works to unsettle the fixity of the illusion of coherent selfhood that is assumed in the mirror stage, and which is conventionally attributed to the effect of *Bildung* of the literary text.

In 1915, on the eve of the publication of Joyce's *Portrait* and of de Saussure's lectures which have become identified with the beginning of poststructuralism, Edmond Laforest, a prominent member of the Haitian literary movement La Ronde with a fine instinct for symbolic gesture, positioned himself on the highest point of a prominent bridge. There he tied a volume of the heavy *Larousse* dictionary around his neck, and jumped to his death.[3] What Laforest's mutely fatal act expresses is the painful dilemma of a writer of a minority culture inheriting the language of the oppressor. Unable to find or forge a language free from the hegemonic sway of the dominant discourse (or the dominance of discourse), he preferred to radically enact his pain and rage, turning them against himself rather than adopting his master's voice. Laforest did not speak or publish his suffering. His body expressed it without words. His action and gestures communicated more forcefully than language can that language – that abstract and immaterial medium – has the power to cause pain, to cripple and maim the body, to block the desire to live.

[2] Jacques Lacan, *Ecrits: A Selection*, trans. Alan Sheridan (1966; New York: Norton, 1977), p. 4.
[3] Henry Louis Gates in *"Race," Writing, and Difference* (University of Chicago Press, 1986), points to Laforest's sense of "overwhelming indenture" (p. 13).

In contrast to Laforest, Joyce does assume the condition of imprisonment in the linguistic web, but he reflects it back on the reader. Tying the dictionary around our necks, he visits his own state of painfully "cracked" subaltern subjectivity on all of us. A deadly serious performance artist *avant la lettre*, Laforest's gesture points to a painful reality which may have remained suppressed in Joyce criticism. Taking Joyce as a "Revolutionary of the Word" – Eugene Jolas's term which may be taken as shorthand notation for the French avant-garde attitude to language which underlies poststructuralism – we may have been deaf to the affect motivating Joyce's text.[4] Criticism tends to ignore the pain inscribed in his writing – the pain of linguistic dispossession, of the radical severance at the point of origin which belonged to growing up Irish around 1882. This avoidance of affect and pain would itself seem a characteristic feature of contemporary culture; but it also implies a form of lingering complicity with Eugene Jolas's intentions. His "new artist of the word," recognizing the "autonomy of language," would "hammer [out] a verbal vision that destroys time and space."[5] The revolution of the word would abolish contingency. Taking a different stance, I argue that Joyce's double inscription of the literary text as a cracked mirror enforces our empathetic witnessing of the "servant's" brokenness.

But Joyce's praxis remains paradoxical and double. *A Portrait* is also, and in the same movement, a gesture of defiant resistance against splitting into either a purely readerly or writerly mode. It ambivalently combines and holds in anxious suspension contradictory concepts. I begin my demonstration with a discussion of an attempt to fit Joyce in the unified framework of descriptive poetics, which uncannily shows up the disturbing peculiarity of Joyce's writing: Resisting a unified, transcendent, or metalingual perspective on life, it inscribes forgery and mimicry as a textual mode.

---

[4] Note Attridge and Ferrer's *Post-Structuralist Joyce*. Patrick McGee's *Paperspace* aims at a "broader historical framework" (p. 11). Note Eagleton's critique of "the libertarian pessimism of poststructuralism" in *Ideology: An Introduction* (London: Verso, 1991), p. 38: "It is libertarian because something of the old model of expression/repression lingers on in the dream of an entirely freefloating signifier, an infinite textual productivity, an existence blessedly free from the shackles of truth, meaning and sociability. Pessimistic, because whatever blocks such creativity . . . is acknowledged to be built into it, in a skeptical recognition of the imbrication of authority and desire."

[5] "The Revolution of Language and James Joyce," in Samuel Beckett et al., *Our Exagmination round his Factification for Incamination of Work in Progress* (1929; repr. New York: New Directions, 1972), p. 79.

THE (IN)DIVISIBILITY OF THE LETTER

Our problems in reading Joyce begin as soon as we pose the obvious question: What in Joyce's style of writing qualifies his texts as "purloined letters"? Asking this, we inevitably step on the tail of the condition highlighted in this chapter: The impossibility of defining, de-limiting, or circumscribing it. "Definition" derives from Latin "*finis*," meaning "end." Joyce's works blur a determinate end. As Johnson and Derrida taught us to note in their discussion of Poe, the act of reading involves a decision. Traditional reading strategies such as New Criticism isolate the text from its context. They mark the text as a circumscribed object; they fix the text like a butterfly sprawling on a pin, killing its performative effect. This objectivation of the literary work makes it safe for scholarship. Barbara Johnson, following Derrida, placed Poe's story back into the context of the surrounding tales.[6] Thus the frame of the individual work, which safeguards its representational function in policing the difference between citation and non-citation, is opened up. Returned to the library in which it literally begins and ends (in the form of a quotation from Crébillon), that extension of the frame generates an "openness" within the work itself – repressed at all cost by traditional readings. In fact, poststructuralism is characterized by its re-absorption of the citationality, or non-firstness, of the first word into the projective act of the constitution of linguistic subjectivity itself. The story, lacking a moment of irreducible origin outside textuality, produces its powerful effect through what Derrida might call the "double invagination" of the frame of reference into and back over the purloined letter's interior.[7] Thus framed by its own content, the story performs the thesis it communicates.

The peculiarity of Joyce is that he pre-inscribes the sublation of the poststructuralist strategy of reading as a feature of his work. He deliberately blurs the margins. His work is characterized by the trembling of its contours; it is at once openended and circular. *Finnegans Wake* "really has no beginning or end," Joyce wrote, explaining: "(Trade secret, registered at Stationers Hall). It ends in the middle of a sentence and begins in the middle of the same sentence."[8] Thus the last words of the text: "A way a lone a last a loved a long the" (628.15–16) run on to join the

---

[6] "The Frame of Reference," in Shoshana Felman, ed. *Literature and the Question of Psychoanalysis*, pp. 457–505.
[7] See "Living On: *Border Lines*," in *Deconstruction and Criticism*, ed. H. Bloom et.al. (New York: Continuum, 1979), p. 98 for a definition of "double invagination."
[8] *Selected Letters of James Joyce*, ed. Richard Ellmann (New York: Viking, 1975), p. 314.

opening words: "riverrun, past Eve and Adam's . . ." (3.1). This hermetic construction which ties the end of the text into its beginning and unmoors the text from an anchor-point in a referential world, characterizes, in different manner and degree, all of Joyce's authorized narrative works. Thus *Dubliners* ends with "The Dead," and begins with a story about death. (The title of the first story "The Sisters," might equally fit "The Dead."[9]) *A Portrait* begins as the memorized citation of a fairy tale in which the subject inscribes himself and ends as a diary. *Ulysses* connects the "s" of Molly's conclusive "Yes" with the initial letter of "Stately . . ." Thus all Joyce's prose published during his lifetime participates in the technique of the serpent biting its own tale, or "Doublends Jined" (*FW* 20.15).

The paradoxical redoubling and preclusion of closure of Joyce's works is so insidiously all-pervasive that criticism has had to adapt itself to this "lubricitous conjugation of the last with the first" (*FW* 121.31). It has demonstrated that the later work recycles versions of the earlier work, disrupting the boundary of the individual work. Since *Finnegans Wake* also includes citations of newspapers that Joyce read, and even quotes from the critical reception of *Ulysses*, the distinction between life and text, metalanguage and object language is blurred. How do we find a frame to determine "the text"? This question prevails in its most literal meaning. The debate over "the scandal" of the "definitive version" of *Ulysses* has made clear that it is difficult to determine the "text" of the work, owing to Joyce's habit of adding and revising up to the last moment, and even beyond that. The work was never complete and finished. Add to that Joyce's failing eyesight, and the scholar is left with no possibility of ascertaining whether misspellings are just that or approved by Joyce. Consequently, some now study the text in the context of the *avant-texte*, the drafts, notebooks, proofs etc., not as a stable, material object, but as an ideal construction or a process of creative production.

The subversiveness of Joyce is highlighted in his habit, after "The Dead," of ending the text with a personal postscript: "Dublin, 1904/ Trieste, 1914" in *A Portrait of the Artist;* "Trieste-Zurich-Paris/ 1914–1921" in *Ulysses;* "Paris, 1922–1939" in *Finnegans Wake.* Work and life, text and self, reality and fiction, the objective and subjective are deliberately fused. This fusion is incremented by Joyce's habit of making his own life the subject of his art, so that it grows difficult to distinguish between the

---

[9] See John Paul Riquelme, *Teller and Tale in Joyce's Fiction: Oscillating Perspectives* (Baltimore: Johns Hopkins University Press, 1983), p. 97.

experience of Stephen or Shem and that of his author. Joyce also projects his sense of himself into personae like Bloom, and, transgressing genderlines, even a Molly, Milly, or Anna Livia. As Arthur Power relates, Joyce answered the query: "[I]s literature to be fact or is it to be an art?" with: "It should be life . . ."[10] The Scylla and Charybdis of the opposition between factual history and imagination is dodged in placing literature, no longer a metalanguage, on the same ontological level as existence itself. The dates postscripting Joyce's texts trace an unbroken, seemingly linear itinerary of writing as living – as if writing were the substance of life. They fuse self and text, self as text. In short, it becomes impossible to know what composes the inside or the outside of a work; the death or absence of presence of an "outside" is inscribed in the inside of the text.[11] More important even: Joyce forces us to extend our attention to the material object, the text as book.

A structure with indeterminate boundaries, a Moebius strip construc-ted to subvert the distinction between inside or outside, text and world, Joyce's texts may stage the "purloined letter" as defined by poststruc-turalism, but, as I hope to demonstrate in this chapter, his suggestion is not the Derridian tenet that there is "nothing outside the text." On the contrary, I claim that Joyce's "design" was to point to the presence of that which language cannot accommodate. Just as Stephen Dedalus tried to fly by the nets of nationality, language, and religion thrown by Irish culture to stunt his emotional and intellectual growth to indepen-dence and freedom, Joyce turned himself into the Houdini of literary elusiveness by weaving his webs without an end or beginning from which one may to start to unravel them.[12] Instead, his webs trap the reader into witnessing the unspoken moment of their occasion. Rather than free-play, his syncreticism and impenetrability are a resistance against the self-righteous "colonizing" power of hegemonic readings (structuralist, poststructuralist, or hermeneutic) over the literary text. But his doubleness also frustrates attempts to arrive at objective scholar-ly conclusions.

---

[10] Arthur Power, *Conversations with James Joyce*, ed. Clive Hart (London: Millington, 1974), p. 34.

[11] See also Derrida's discussion of the "parergon" in *The Truth in Painting* (University of Chicago Press, 1987): a supplementary, foreign, or extrinsic object, an aside or a remainder, which is neither simply within nor simply outside [a text]. As frame, a parergon rests next to and in addition to a work. Its effect is to question the notion of the essence or purity of presence of/in the work itself: it points to a lack or absence at the heart of the work. It generates an effect which "comes as an extra, *alterior* to the proper field . . . but whose transcendent exteriority comes to play, abut onto, brush against, rub, press against the limit itself and intervene in the inside only to the extent that the inside is lacking. It is lacking *in* something and it is lacking *from* itself" (p. 56).

[12] John Banville, in "Survivors of Joyce": "Joyce was never silent, but he was certainly cunning . . . He was the supreme escape-artist, a Houdini of the word . . ." (p. 80).

Already noted in the previous chapter was the radical doubleness of the Joyce-effect. *A Portrait* and *Ulysses* may be read as realist novels, or as writerly performances.[13] Derrida's claim was the letter's divisibility: *Ulysses* shows a "subatomistic micrology . . . (the 'divisibility of the letter')."[14] However, Joyce's writings, I propose, are *at once* infinitely divisible *and* radically indivisible, depending on how we read them. They accommodate contradictory perceptions.

If "Shakespeare is the happy huntingground of all minds that have lost their balance" (*U* 10.1061–62), Joyce is the objective correlative to almost all attempts to define the modern or the postmodern. From T. S. Eliot to Umberto Eco, from Adorno to Lyotard, Joyce's *Ulysses* or *Finnegans Wake* provides the illustration. Ever since Ihab Hassan's "*Finnegans Wake* and the Postmodern Imagination,"[15] Joyce's works also provide material for the descriptive definition of modernist and postmodernist styles. As may be expected, Joyce trips up scholarly endeavor.

Brian McHale's *Postmodernist Fiction*, published the year before Linda Hutcheon's *A Poetics of Postmodernism*,[16] may serve as illustrative example. Steering away from Hutcheon's emphasis on gender, as well as from questions of ethnicity, nationality, or race, McHale aims to describe the distinguishing characteristics of the universal postmodernist literary text without differentiating between phases, locations, or nationalities.

McHale's claim is that postmodernist literature distinguishes itself from modernist literature in relinquishing the latter's epistemological perspective – its thematic and formal emphasis on questions of knowledge: How do we or can we know? What is knowledge? Instead, postmodernism holds to an "ontological" perspective: The possibility of the simultaneous existence of a plurality of worlds, of more than one reality, as if all realities were virtual. McHale illustrates this claim in a series of readings of postmodernist works, pointing to typical postmodern textual strategies such as excluded middles, forking paths, infinite regress, postmodernist constructions of the world as zone, the collision of worlds, fantasy worlds, carnival. This is a clear and useful work, a necessary complement to Hutcheon.

13 Note that *Dubliners* and *Finnegans Wake*, the first and last of Joyce's major works, inversely double their emphasis on one mode, whereas *Dubliners* seems predominantly readerly, the *Wake* appears primarily writerly.
14 "Ulysses Gramophone: Hear say yes in Joyce," in *James Joyce: The Augmented Ninth*, ed. Bernard Benstock (New York: Syracuse University, 1988), p. 50.
15 *Paracriticisms: Seven Speculations of the Times* (Urbana: University of Illinois Press, 1975), pp. 77–97.
16 *Postmodernist Fiction* (New York and London: Methuen, 1987); *A Poetics of Postmodernism: History, Theory, Fiction* (New York and London: Routledge, 1988).

While McHale locates the transition from modernist to postmodernist poetics in Beckett's trilogy of the early fifties, he frequently refers back to Joyce: "*Molloy* juxtaposes two different, contrasting minds . . . This is a minimal structure of modernist perspectivism – its *locus classicus* is the 'Nausicaa' chapter of Joyce's *Ulysses* (1922) – and Beckett has further reduced and stylized it, converting a minimal structure to a minimal*ist* one."[17] What McHale locates in the fifties and in Beckett could just as well be located in *Finnegans Wake* and the thirties. This subverts the self-containment of postmodernism as a circumscribed period in literary history. Instead of noting this, McHale ends his text with a chapter entitled "Coda: The Sense of Joyce's Endings," which is headed by the following quotation from Beckett's *For to End Yet Again/ Pour finir encore* (1976): "Thus then the skull last place of all makes to glimmer again in lieu of going out."[18] To the reader's surprise, McHale begins a discussion of Joyce which argues that the endings of Joyce's works show similarities; each focuses on husband and wife and:

the possibility (or actuality) of unfaithfulness on the part of one or both of the partners. Each involves a merging or confusion of personal identities – of Gabriel Conroy with Michael Furey and the hosts of the dead, of Leopold Bloom with Molly's first lover Mulvey (in Molly's memory), of Anna Livia Plurabelle with Finn MacCool, the sea. And each ends by circling back, one way or another, to its beginning. Such similarities tell us something about Joyce's sense of an ending – about, that is, a recurrent pattern which is specific to Joyce. The *differences*, however, tell us something about modernist and postmodernist fiction in general, and what distinguishes one from the other. (233).

His claim is that all Joyce's endings are filtered through the medium of consciousness; but in *Finnegans Wake*, in contradistinction to the earlier works, that consciousness is not individual but collective: "Molly Bloom's soliloquy notoriously represents the 'stream of consciousness,' but Anna Livia is the thing itself: the personification of the River Liffey, she literalizes the metaphor 'stream of consciousness'" (234). Moreover, just as her speech unifies all discourse into flow, it also erases the projected world of the fiction. "[T]here is no stable world *behind* this consciousness, but only a flux of discourse in which fragments of different, incompatible realities flicker into existence and out of existence again, overwhelmed by the competing reality of language" (234). Thus *Ulysses* is a modernist fiction and *Finnegans Wake* a postmodernist one.

---

[17] *Postmodernist Fiction*, p. 12.   [18] *Ibid.*, p. 233.

It might be that McHale here forgets the caution he practices earlier on when he points out that the difference between the two period styles is one of a relative predominance of certain features – a question of more or less – rather than an absolute distinction. The problem with Joyce's *œuvre*, as we saw, is that it is a homogeneous continuum: it (re)writes the "seim anew" (*FW* 215.13). It resists splitting. In Joyce, consciousness is collective and is embedded in language from the opening words of *Portrait*: "Once upon a time . . ."

Another point in McHale's argument is that Molly "represents" her "stream of consciousness" whereas Anna Livia *is* her monologue. Since Molly's monologue will receive extensive coverage later, let me just suggest that this distinction does not hold either. As Joyce told Frank Budgen, Molly and her monologue were composed from an abstract principle of femininity (flow, the lemniscate, the four feminine holes), which he translated linguistically into unpunctuated liquidity and silent flow. Molly may *seem* real, but like Anna Livia, she is the elaboration of a concept, she *is* language. In fact, as Kimberly Devlin argues, there are many points of similarity between the two monologues; and Devlin calls ALP Molly's "dream avatar,"[19] while Clive Hart even sees ALP's monologue in the light of Eveline in *Dubliners*.[20] Again, the unified texture of Joyce's works, which Devlin demonstrates so convincingly, defies definition. The later texts cite and rework the earlier ones, so that it becomes impossible to draw lines of absolute difference between them. We are confronted with one continuously recirculating flow.

C. G. Jung, writing about *Ulysses* in 1932, proves unexpectedly authoritative: "[t]he pitiless stream, [which 'begins in the void and ends in the void'], rolls on without a break, and its velocity or viscosity increases in the last forty pages till it sweeps away even the punctuation marks."[21] Moreover, it betrays "the secret of a new cosmic consciousness." "All the Daedaluses [*sic*], Blooms, Harrys, Lynches, Mulligans, and the rest of them talk and go about as in a collective dream that begins nowhere and ends nowhere, that takes place only because 'Noman' – an unseen Odysseus – dreams it . . . The ego of the creator of these figures is not to be found."[22] Thus the consciousness in and of *Ulysses* seems no less "depersonalized," "detached," or dreamlike than

---

[19] *Wandering and Return in "Finnegans Wake": An Integrative Approach to Joyce's Fictions* (Princeton University Press, 1991), p. 169.
[20] *Structure and Motif in "Finnegans Wake"* (London: Faber and Faber, 1962), pp. 53–55.
[21] "*Ulysses*: A Monologue." *Europäische Revue* 8 (1932), repr. in Leonard Mannheim and Eleanor Mannheim (eds.), *Hidden Patterns: Studies in Psychoanalytic Literary Criticism* (New York: Macmillan, 1996), p. 193. [22] *Ibid.*, pp. 208, 209.

that in and of *Finnegans Wake*, and it is foreshadowed in *A Portrait*.

While McHale's argument about the radical difference between the *Wake* and *Ulysses* shows up Joyce's resistance to clear-cut definition, I am intrigued by McHale's decision to give Joyce a separate and final section in his text. He excised Joyce from his main argument, while giving him pride of place at the end in a reading of Joyce's endings, "simulacra of death" in McHale's words.[23] Not only is the suggestion that *Ulysses* ends in death wildly far-fetched, while inapplicable to *A Portrait*, McHale shifts from a descriptive mode into interpretation. In short, Joyce seems to trip McHale up in several ways. The fact that Joyce is not "dead," that his *Finnegans Wake*, even if published more than a decade earlier than even the earliest "postmodernist" text, remains vitally alive to anachronistically subvert the categories of literary-historical periodization, brings McHale to write a separate piece about Joyce in which he claims that Joyce's works end as "simulacra of death." Is it McHale's realization that Joyce's works are not "dead and buried" that surfaces here as a break in the self-identity of this study?[24]

Indeed, postmodernism's "ontological" perspective may itself be a defense against death: in an infinite plurality of worlds death cannot be final. My sense that McHale's Coda is uncanny grows acute when we read McHale's text along Joyce's lines, including the "parergon" in the work. McHale's page of dedication reads: "*In memory of/* Robert J. McHale 1927–85/ Steve Sloan 1952–85/ Arthur A. Cohen 1928–86." This phantom-like apparition of the names of McHale's personal dead on the material screen of the book suggests a symptomatic logic at work. "[W]hat is excluded from reality reappears as a signifying trace (as an element of the symbolic order: a name, a teabrand [in this case a dedication]) on the very screen through which we observe reality," Žižek observes.[25] It is as if McHale had placed the contamination of death before and after his text, to safeguard the scholarly text and its transcendence from the infective threat of blurring and indistinction present in Joyce.

What this encounter between descriptive poetics and Joyce teaches is twofold: First of all, Joyce's text seems constructed to project a dual, simultaneous image of both divisibility and indivisibility. The text is

[23] McHale, *Postmodernist Fiction*, p. 233.
[24] See Barbara Johnson who speaks of the truth of the purloined letter as its "materialization of my death," or, citing Derrida, "the truth of being as non-being." "The Frame of Reference," p. 464.
[25] *Everything You Always Wanted to Know about Lacan (But Were Afraid to Ask Hitchcock)* (London and New York: Verso, 1992), p. 238.

both re-presentational and presentational, "allographic" and "autographic," both a sequence of individual works and one continuous *œuvre*. It allows itself to be read in different ways. Jung's memorable metaphor for this (in)divisibility of Joyce's work is that of the tapeworm: "Objective and subjective, outer and inner, are so constantly intermingled that in the end, despite the clearness of the individual images, one wonders whether one is dealing with a physical or transcendental tapeworm." The tapeworm (which survives after severance into fragments) is a "whole living cosmos in itself and is fabulously procreative . . ."; but "[i]n every segment of the book, however small, Joyce himself is the sole content of the segment."[26] This self-defensively armoured (in)divisibility, which made the psychoanalyst's enjoyment of *Ulysses* impossible, applies equally to the earlier and later works: All of Joyce's infinitely divisible and citational prose fiction paradoxically refuses division and objectification: It is "one continuous present tense integument" (*FW* 186.1). We might apply Jean-Michel Rabaté's epithet for *Finnegans Wake*, a "Series-machine," to the whole *œuvre*.[27]

Secondly, the nature of this subversive tapeworm, which inscribes death on the screen of a text which tries to mirror it objectively, would seem to be what Lacan might call the "real" insistence of the death-drive, the insistent force of the repetition of the same. Jung still spoke of the "intangible," "secret purpose" of the work, expressing "something whose nature we cannot grasp";[28] Lacan, writing later, is more explicit in his elaboration of Freud's articulation of the "compulsion to repeat" in relation to the "death instincts" in "Beyond the Pleasure Principle" (in which Freud takes the "traumatic neurosis" of World War I as example), which was published in 1920 and conceived simultaneously with the essay "The Uncanny." That this insistence of the "real" is itself not to be regarded with "single vision" as just a reifying force leading to stasis, but that its repetitive drive may also be understood as aimed at eventually resolving the traumatic condition of its neurotic inception, will be the argument of the rest of this chapter.

My entry into this discussion is facilitated by another attempt to capture Joyce in a unified perspective: *Modernist Conjectures*.[29] Its object is to define modernism, its method Yury Lotman's semiotics of culture, its

26 "*Ulysses*: A Monologue," pp. 195–96.
27 See "Lapsus ex machina," in *Post-Structuralist Joyce*, pp. 79–103.
28 "*Ulysses*: A Monologue," pp. 207.
29 Douwe Fokkema and Elrud Ibsch, *Modernist Conjectures: A Mainstream in European Literature 1910–1940* (London: Hurst, 1987).

praxis to draw a distinction between modernism and postmodernism, its conclusion that modernist textuality is marked by the dominance of three semantic fields: consciousness, detachment, and observation. Postmodernist writing, on the other hand, privileges assimilation, multiplication, and permutation, sensory perception, movement, and mechanization. To the authors, *Finnegans Wake* marks the entry of the postmodern, whereas *A Portrait*, like *Ulysses*, is representative of modernism.

It is not my intention to disprove the accuracy or relevance of this description, but to show that there is a crack in the looking-glass which subverts attempts to fix Joyce in neat categorizations. Let us take *A Portrait* as our example. The semantic features of "consciousness, detachment, and observation" at first sight perfectly describe Stephen's attitude: "I will try to express myself in some mode of life or art as freely as I can and as wholly as I can, using for my defence the only arms I allow myself to use – silence, exile, and cunning" (*P* 247). Stephen's ideal art leads to objectivity and "static" contemplation. To that aim he devises an authorial persona indifferently paring its fingernails behind the screen of representation. Moreover, Joyce himself chooses exile – physical detachment – as the precondition for artistic creativity; and the plot of *A Portrait* seems to work to the *telos* of Stephen's assumption of this very authorial stance as its one great goal.

My query, therefore, does not concern the *correctness* of this reading. I am interested in how much it must exclude to draft a unified image. This is important, because the theory of distinct literary periods, which, in turn, has given us the "heroic artist" Stephen Dedalus and "the genius" Joyce, is grounded in this act of descriptive perception. The seemingly tailored fit between this description and Joyce's text is itself the product of an attitude to the text which is pre-emptively predicated upon assumptions of "detachment" and "observation" – its *parti-pris*. In fact, historically speaking, the theory of Joyce as the representative modernist writer may itself be the product of a "modernist aesthetic" which is projected back upon the text. "How you see (or read) is what you get." This implies a *petitio principii* in our reading.

What we are alerted to is the informative presence of two ideological assumptions about textuality operative in conventional scholarly reading. First: In order for *A Portrait* to be the apotheosis of Stephen's access to detachment, we must understand it as a linear progress of development towards *Künstler*hood. Thus we actualize the text as the record of an informative temporal teleology, which we might call "history." Secondly, colluding with the epic illusion, we assume that the end of the text frames the representation and lends it stability and self-identity – thus making metalanguage possible. This manner of reading seems heavily involved in an aim-driven identity politics, supported by the assumption of the informative concreteness of the frame. Just as the infant seeing its unified image in the mirror founds its illusionary sense of integrity on that visual projection, the reader of a unified story relies on the fixity of its conclusion to conceptualize self-identity and history.

What immediately strikes anyone familiar with Joyce is that *A Portrait* is not just the reflective expression of transcendent detachment. It is full of "purple" passages charged with the emotional desire for fusion and surrender:

> an inaudible voice seemed to caress the soul, telling her names and glories, bidding her arise as for aspousal and come away, bidding her look forth, a spouse, from Amana and from the mountains of the leopards; and the soul seemed to answer with the same inaudible voice, surrendering herself: *Inter ubera mea commorabitur.*
>
> This idea of surrender had a perilous attraction for his mind . . . He seemed to feel a flood slowly advancing to his naked feet and to be waiting for the first faint timid wavelet to touch his fevered skin. (*P* 152)

This passage shows that the text is not just constituted dialectically in the sense suggested by Kristeva,[30] but that that implicit dialectic of the process of constitution is *staged* in the narrative text as a continual debate between the need for, and attitude of, detachment, and the attraction of fusion and merging. In fact, the voice of desire speaks no less loudly than the call to detachment in *A Portrait*. It is hard to decide which of the two voices is dominant. The text is split between two rival positions – it is a cracked mirror. Like the picture of the rabbit slipping into that of a duck used in gestalt psychology, the image of *A Portrait* can be actualized in two different ways – depending on which voice in the text we hear most loudly.

If we open the frame of the text, we generate a structural effect: The teleological impetus of the *Bildungsroman* makes way for a sequence of repetitions. In his early sketch for this novel, Joyce had spoken of its

---

[30] Kristeva sees language as the product of a moment of psychological constitution, implying a split, which is reflected in language itself as a "thetic" layer (our notion of clear and rational language), and in and underneath it a "semiotic" layer which is informed by and keeps a connection to the infantile drives. See *Semeiotike: Recherches pour une sémanalyse* (Paris: Seuil, 1969).

identity as the "curve of an emotion."[31] If we suspend the epic illusion, each of the five chapters proves to be embroidered as the same "curve of an emotion." In each Stephen meets with a similar conflict between contraries. The attraction of surrender and fusion is personified in a series of female figures: first the mother, then the girlfriend, then a prostitute, the Virgin Mary, and the Muse – the incarnation varies according to Stephen's age and maturity; they represent the same desire for *amor matris* however. On the other hand there is the paternal prohibition or command, the patriarchal law which demands detachment from the feminine and its lure in order to join a homosocial bond. Unable to solve this conflict, in each new chapter Stephen flies away, wandering aimlessly in sheer forward movement in order to escape the dilemma, until he finds himself in a situation which offers a temporary compromise resolution. We might draw a diagram of this repetitive emotional "structure" of this "portrait" which is to be read both vertically and horizontally:[32]

Chapter	1	2	3	4	5
Structure					
New setting	school	society	nighttown	church	university
Maternal image	mother	E— C—	prostitute	virgin	muse
Prohibition	Wells and Doran	Heron	Fr. Arnall	director	friends
Exile	upstairs to Rector	nighttown	confession	beach	Europe
Compromise	popularity	sex	communion	epiphany	art

Thus chapter 4, often read as the climax of the novel because it describes Stephen's epiphany on the beach, is now seen as *one in a series*. Like the other chapters, it begins with the depiction of Stephen in a new role: The very devout adolescent whose "daily life was laid out in devotional areas." Though he now seems to have his sexuality under control, the new danger of "spiritual dryness" looms, while the thought of surrender, both spiritually and physically, keeps insisting. His relation

---

[31] In "A Portrait of the Artist" of 1904, he argued that his portrait "is not an identificative paper but rather the curve of an emotion" (*PSW*, p. 211). Note David Hayman's essay, "The Fractured Portrait," in *Myriadminded Man: Jottings on Joyce*, ed. R. M. Bosinelli (Bologna: CLUEB, 1986): "a text that oscillates between temporal and spatial developments, between synchrony and diachrony" (p. 87).

[32] I gratefully take this structure from Sheldon Brivic, "Joyce in Progress: A Freudian View," *James Joyce Quarterly* 13, 3 (Spring 1976): 306–27.

to the feminine – now in his function as prefect of the sodality of the Holy Virgin – proves unstable when he is offered the possibility of becoming a priest. This invitation to become a member of this celibate homosocial group awakens his resistance to the restrictiveness of the Church, and he embarks on an aimless walk through the city, musing about language and poetry, until he sees a girl on the beach as the self-projected, birdlike, mystic incarnation of the resolution of the conflict between the maternal and the paternal: "He would create proudly out of the freedom and power of his soul, as the great artificer whose name he bore, a living thing, new and soaring and beautiful, impalpable, imperishable" (*P* 171).

By extrapolation, the ending of chapter 5, the moment of Stephen's departure in exile, is also just one in a series, even though it ends the story. Exile may be just as precarious a resolution of conflict as Holy Communion had been when he was younger. What guarantee do we have that Stephen's vocation is fixed?[33] Repetition will keep occurring. Perhaps, no, probably, once he arrives on the continent he will find himself in a new social group, encounter another mother-*imago* and a fresh paternal prohibition. Just as Stephen outgrew his devotion to the Virgin, he may become unfaithful to his Muse. He may end up a solid *pater familias* with a mistress or an interest in Madonna. The end freezes the action but does not offer a semantic resolution. Thus the finality of the ending, its framing effect, is undermined by the repetitiveness of structure, the crack in the looking-glass which repetitively subverts the stability of the image.[34] Consequently, like *Finnegans Wake*, *A Portrait* manifests itself as holographic and infinitely divisible. Just as each element in a holographic design contains the image of the whole from its own unique point of view, so each element in *A Portrait of the Artist* mirrors the dialectical theme of the total book. Perhaps the true subject of *A Portrait* is this irresolvable dialectic between contraries, as it is of *Finnegans Wake*.

Read thus, Stephen's artistic vocation can no longer be regarded as the brand and seal of the identity of the protagonist, or the grand aim of this novel. It is one stage in a structured sequence of possibly infinitely repetitive modulation which may be extrapolated outside the frame-

---

[33] See also Phillip F. Herring: In *A Portrait* we see the "uncertainty principle at work in characterization . . . [A] major reason for this in Stephen's case may be that he is blocked in the apprentice stage by an experimental forebear he cannot go beyond." *Joyce's Uncertainty Principle* (Princeton University Press, 1987), p. 205.

[34] I am radicalizing Kenner's ironic perspective in "*The Portrait in Perspective*," in *Joyce: A Collection of Critical Essays*, ed. William M. Chace (Englewood Cliffs, NJ: Prentice-Hall, 1974), pp. 33–50.

work of the text. It certainly seems impossible to keep seeing Joyce's text as only a modernist work illustrating the centrality of "detachment," "observation," and "consciousness." We must also, and at the same time, see the other half of the mirror, where the text appears as a poststructuralist serial construct. The text provides an image with a double exposure.

What the reader meets here is more than the "internal division of the trait, impurity, corruption, contamination, decomposition, perversion, deformation, even cancerization, generous proliferation or degeneration"[35] denoted by poststructuralism. The double image produced by the generative crack stages the internal division, giving a local habitation to the insistence of repetition and the death-drive. Joyce materializes it. My aim is not to present a rival interpretation to contravene the depoliticized one. The point of my reading is to argue the "Joyce-effect," and show that the opening of the frame which contains the repetition in and of the text has as effect the reader's implication. We can no longer maintain our illusion of transcendent objectivity; we must either engage the crack in the looking-glass or repress and ignore it. Suddenly confronted with a text which refuses to stay put in its formal boundaries, it implicates the reader in its process of articulation.[36] It spills over the psychological parameters of the distinct individuality of its reader, because it envelops the reader in its transferential web. The paradox of Joyce's style is that the utmost of constructedness is paired with the perspectival disappearance of a firm formal identity, the letter is "littered" (in both the sense of "being torn up as trash" and "reduced to literalness and materiality"), but is not destroyed. This littering was Lacan's fascination with Joyce.

Littering, the almost mystic conjunction of form or unity *and* contamination, is a feature not limited to Joyce. See, for instance, Walter Benjamin's *The Origin of German Tragic Drama.*[37] To illustrate what is at stake in Joyce, I turn to Jean Arp, the sculptor and painter. He describes how, in the 1930s, his work began to verge away from the extreme of

---

[35] Derrida, "The Law of Genre," *Critical Inquiry* 7 (1980), 58.

[36] In *Introduction à l'architexte* (Paris: Seuil, 1979), Gérard Genette addresses the crisis in poetics which I am staging here: How can the critical or theoretical text survive in the absence of stable representation? Genette posits a general transtextuality which merges metatextuality, intertextuality, paratextuality (parody etc.), and an architextuality which is omnipresent, above, below, around the text. Focusing on the self-irony in Genette's study, Geoff Bennington in "The Field and the Fence," *Oxford Literary Review* 4, 2 (1980) deconstructs this attempt to formalize the effect of the loss of boundary, pointing out that "any representation of the non-representational in language cannot be added to a schema which represents linguistic representations without casting the representativity of that schema into doubt" (p. 86).

[37] Trans. John Osborne (1928; London: Verso, 1977).

"impersonal, severe" shapes and forms – intended as defence against emotional turbulence – towards the acceptance of decay:

About 1930 the pictures torn by hand from paper came into being. Human work now seemed to me even less than piece-work. It seemed to me removed from life. Everything is approximate, less than approximate, for when more closely and sharply examined, the most perfect picture is a warty, threadbare approximation, a dry porridge, a dismal mooncrater landscape. What arrogance is concealed in perfection. Why struggle for precision, purity, when they can never be attained. The decay that begins immediately on completion of the work was now welcome to me . . . The dying of a picture no longer brought me to despair. I had made my pact with its passing, with its death, and now it was part of the picture for me. But death grew and ate up the picture and life. This dissolution must have been followed by the negation of all action. Form had become unform, the Finite the Infinite, the Individual the Whole.[38]

Thus the materialization of the presence of death, its incarnated pre-acceptance as the ultimate destiny, not only of the artist but also of the work of art (in defiant contradiction of the old adage that life is short and art long), creates the paradoxical unifying effect of (in)divisibility. Jean Arp's confession suggests that the motivation of Joyce's peculiar textuality may likewise not merely be a matter of formal arrangement, but the inclusion of the gaping abyss of death into the work itself: hence its transferential effect.

In fact, Joyce places us in the predicament of Stephen Dedalus. *Portrait* lets itself be read as an allegory of its own textual practice. It presents an anatomy of Stephen's impossibility of attaining the conclusive framing which would provide a defense against the encroachment of death or otherness. Since Stephen's problems with autonomy and detachment are metonymized in his writing and reading of his own name, the narrative prefigures our problem of reading in inverse order:

He turned to the flyleaf of the geography and read what he had written there: himself, his name and where he was.
Stephen Dedalus
Class of Elements
Clongowes Wood College
Sallins
County Kildare
Ireland
Europe
The World
The Universe

[38] Jean Arp, *On My Way: Poetry and Essays 1912–1947* (New York: Wittenborn, 1948), pp. 77–78.

That was in his writing . . . Then he read the flyleaf from the bottom to the top till he came to his own name. That was he: and he read down the page again. What was after the universe? Nothing. But was there anything around the universe to show where it stopped before the nothing place began? It could not be a wall; but there could be a thin thin line there all round everywhere . . . Only God could do that . . . God was God's name just as his name was Stephen. (*P* 15–16)

Stephen's problem of detachment is rendered as a problem of framing, of definition in the sense of "demarcating the end." Stephen's query bears on the relationship of self to the surrounding world. Inscribing his name in ever-widening concentric circles of enlarged selfhood, that inflation also leads to the dissolution and voiding of identity. The concept of boundary is paradoxically married to the concept of unassimilable otherness: Without semantic boundaries there is no circumscribed selfhood or fixed meaning; but the notion of delimitation also evokes the spectre of an "other" – something outside, unknown, unnamable, and without form – which threatens the idea of self-presence. No wonder that even the most fleeting suspicion of a presence, a realm of meaning beyond rational human intellection, is repressed in favor of the stability of identity and meaning.

Stephen attempts to be an exemplary practitioner of the traditional western strategy of coping with otherness. Thinking of the end of the universe, the spectre of unassimilable difference is displaced as a problem of signification. "But was there anything around the universe to show where it stopped before the nothing place began?" (*P* 16) In addition to the invention of a "nothing place," thus denying the specter of "nothingness" through its material location in a specific point of space – a typical Joycean strategy to which I shall turn later – the sentence strikes me in its shift to the activity of writing. This, in turn, raises the question of authorship. The source of the "thin line" must be an original agency. That original draftsman must have a name. That name is provided by tradition: "God." Thus Stephen's definition of the self is related to the name of an earlier "author/writer," whose name guarantees the "thin thin line" separating meaning from chaos: "God was God's name just as his name was Stephen." In other words, the linguistic signifier "God" anchors the hierarchy of difference and identity; it lends stability to Stephen's own identity and name. Only provisionally, however. Stephen immediately begins to worry about the plurality of names for "God" in different languages. Language, and even the personal name, proves an unstable grounding. Stephen will remain obsessed with the duplicity of language, as in his worry about the meaning of "belt." What Joyce allegorizes is the abortive process of identification with language of the subaltern subject. Though Stephen seems as yet not conscious of this, the English language does not provide him with a stable point of authority, a unified mirror image, an unshakable concept of origin which can ground his identity in language.

Later in *A Portrait*, we note that Stephen's theory of aesthetics attempts to ground itself by means of practicing a reversal. God is no longer the projected stable signifier of origin, but already a form of writing. Stephen's aesthetic is pitched upon the example of the originary function of the demarcating line or wall: "In order to see that basket, said Stephen, your mind first of all separates the basket from the rest of the visible universe which is not the basket. The first phase of apprehension is a bounding line drawn about the object to be apprehended" (*P* 212). Only when the object is safely circumscribed, and has become familiar, does it grow possible to think of it as having a context and background: "the esthetic image is first luminously apprehended as selfbounded and selfcontained upon the immeasurable background of space or time which is not it. You apprehend it as *one* thing. You see it as one whole. You apprehend its wholeness. That is *integritas*" (*P* 212). But such a vision of the object against a backdrop of nothingness, suspended in a void, is the product and effect of the firm, defining draftsmanship which guarantees the illusion of boundary and meaning. It is the "wall" of the materializaton as writing which shelters us from the vertigo of the abyss of divisibility, the *"abnihilisation of the etym"* (*FW* 353.22). This act of inscription is never definitive, it remains related to the threat of the meaningless in Joyce. In the earlier *Stephen Hero* we read: "And over all this chaos of history and legend, of fact and supposition, he strove to draw out a line of order, to reduce the abysses of the past to order by a diagram" (*SH* 33). These words from *Stephen Hero* express what *Finnegans Wake* performs.

In short, in both *A Portrait* and *Stephen Hero*, Stephen's *credo* of *claritas*, *consonantia*, and *integritas* is the defensive product of the subaltern subject's frantic activity of definition and delimitation expressed in the metaphor of writing or inscription; and it is from that strategy of framing inscription that the mystic-epiphanic vision of seeing "that it is that thing which it is and no other thing" (*P* 213) derives. Just as Stephen's epiphanies are produced by an inscriptive act of preliminary definition, just so our reading of *A Portrait* as the representation of Stephen's accession to artistic authority is predicated on delimitation and repression. Such a reading draws a thin line around the text, spatializing its five-part repetitive structure to an instance of organic form where the oak at the end of the road is the apotheosis prefigured in the entelechy of the earlier acorn. Thus the *Darstellung* of Stephen's definitive crystallization into an artist (whether true or failed is beside the point) rests upon the convention of reading as framing. The stability of such a reading may, perhaps, be understood as an indication of the reader's privileged positioning in the mirror of language.

A Portrait brings into the open the reader's attitude to "the sense of an ending." The ending is where we place it, and endings serve to preserve us from the awareness of the skull beneath the flesh. The pedagogy of Joyce is that we learn to see that every time we wish to fix a circum-scribed identity on his text, its seemingly self-evident coherence has already been blurred by double exposure. The text deprives itself of its self-identical "truth" in its materialization of itself as doubly written. After all, it is not by accident that Joyce chose the verb "to forge" to indicate Stephen Dedalus's artistic intention. He selected a verb which semantically redefines creation as a citational, derivative, echoing form of making present and material.

What I am claiming with regard to Joyce is different from Phillip Herring's "indeterminacy principle," which implies that Joyce as a conscious and almost malignant God behind the scene of his creation withholds from his reader the satisfaction of closure, the "Ithaca of meaning that can never quite be reached"[39] – as if Joyce, a malicious Sheherazade, planned to frustrate the reader. Whereas Herring under-stands Joyce's textuality as the effect of rational design and planned deviance, I am arguing that it points to discursive trauma. Joyce's indeterminacy or openendedness is neither the irresponsible playfulness of *Post-Structuralist Joyce* ("it always turns up again, laughing, behind your back"), nor is it the expression of Joyce's malice.[40] Instead, it is Joyce's inscription of the death-in-life of the condition of being born Irish and lacking a natural relationship to language.

THE TRANSFERENCE OF THE TEXT

Transference is a spilling over of unconscious content beyond the frame of the individual self. Transference, the "process of actualisation

[39] *Joyce's Uncertainty Principle*, p. 170.
[40] *Post-Structuralist Joyce*, p. 10. See also *L'œuvre ouverte* (Paris: Seuil, 1965), where Umberto Eco adresses the openendedness of Joyce's works, which he locates primarily in *Finnegans Wake*, however.

of unconscious wishes,"[41] transgresses the frame of the individual. It subverts the distinction between presence and absence, presence and past, real and imaginary. Transference implies a displacement in masked form of the intensity of affect attending that which remains unconscious in the relationship between patient and analyst (in Lacan's articulation) upon the other who serves as screen for the projection of that unconscious self. Transference uproots the notion of a proper location, and spills over the boundary of what we conventionally determine as "reality." It even engages others in playing out our unconscious scenarios: subverting the tie between agency and act. Transference is not a phenomenon limited to the analyst's office, it affects the objective practise of scholarship. Through it we, as scholars, are transformed from dispassionate scientists into human beings whose histories matter.

Jane Gallop writes about the effects of transference on scholarship: "In the relation of transference, the critic is no longer analyst but patient. The position of patient can be terrifying in that it represents, to the critic who in her transference believes in the analyst's mastery, a position of non-mastery."[42] Since it causes fear of possession by the past, of losing control over the self and over the object, the threat of transference also sets in motion a counterforce: the desire to subject the text, to assert control over it through a rigid application of procedures which reinstate the duality of active reader and passive text, the position of someone who knows and an object to be known. Indeed, "[t]ransference is as much denied by an assertion of the total difference of the [text] as by its total identification with one's own 'self' . . ."[43]

Freud taught, however, that the elusive but desirable objective of an exchange with an "other" is to work through transferential displacement in a manner that does not blindly replicate debilitating aspects of the past. The question is, therefore: Can we read *A Portrait* without fearing its transference effect; without resorting to the containing strategy of seeing the text as a self-interpretative supertext which "offers the very theory of its own incapacity to signify fully as its credentials for transcending both Imaginary and Symbolic alike"?[44] Can we let the text "live" without assertions of its "free play," or "indeterminacy"? In other

---

[41] J. Laplanche and J.-B. Pontalis, *The Language of Psychoanalysis*, trans. Donald Nicholson-Smith (London: Hogarth, 1983), p. 455.

[42] Jane Gallop, "Lacan and Literature: A Case for Transference," *Poetics* 13 (1989), 307.

[43] Dominick LaCapra, *History and Criticism* (Ithaca and London: Cornell University Press, 1985), p. 72.

[44] Fredric Jameson, "Imaginary and Symbolic in Lacan: Marxism, Psychoanalytic Criticism, and the Problem of the Subject," in *Literature and Psychoanalysis*, ed. Felman, p. 389.

words, can we open ourselves up as readers to allow the text to work its effect upon us?

The repetition of the same situation of conflict, the wandering escapes (*fugues* in psychiatric discourse), the symbolic resolution at the end of each chapter involving images of nurturing, suggest to me that *A Portrait* does not merely stage the dialectic of the constitution of the subject split in language, but that it enacts and constantly re-enacts that moment as a trauma, a point of fixation. It remains riveted to that moment as the moment of a crack or fissure in being, just as the needle of a gramophone record gets caught in the scratch on the disk, endlessly repeating the same bars. What Derrida names the "double affirmation" of *Ulysses'* double inscription, its "yes, yes," may also be the repetitive attempt to escape the effect of the crack. Joyce does not illustrate the Lacanian splitting of the subject as the entry into language. That Lacanian symbolic cut entails a severance into a linguistic and pre-linguistic part; it also implies an identification of the subject with the paternal agency governing language and the symbolic. While, according to Kristeva, the pre-linguistic experience of the tie with the mother may, in some cases, affect the manner in which language is used (Joyce is one of her examples in *Revolution in Poetic Language*), what we have in *Portrait* is not an example of Kristeva's "semiotic" either. In his seminar on Joyce, Lacan, increasingly convinced that literature might be instrumental in helping the reader to revise the configuration imposed upon the subject by the original cut, pointed to Joyce's work as an example of a form of writing that traces the empty place in the system of the signifier and in the knowledge that the subject occupies. In other words, the linguistic subjectivity of Joyce points to a failure of that primary symbolization at the moment of identification with language, which allows the subject to inscribe himself in the relaying predicative power of the copula to provide identity: "I am Stephen Dedalus" or "I am a British Subject." Joyce's peculiarity is that his work illustrates the presence of a hole in the other which Lacan himself would eventually acknowledge.[45] I argue that Joyce illustrates that hole owing to his dramatization of the peculiar placement in the symbolic order of the Irish colonial subject. Instead of subjectivization, Irish history left Joyce with a traumatic discursivity always locked in the attempt to come to terms with the violence and treachery of language.

The crack beyond/within the symbolic opens up in the overture of *A*

---

[45] A very useful introduction to Lacan, tracing the development of his thought across the entire career, is Gilbert D. Chaitin, *Rhetoric and Culture in Lacan* (Cambridge University Press, 1996).

Portrait which situates Stephen as a subject who is consciously engaged
with the entry into language. Indeed, this passage in Joyce has often
been read as illustrating Lacan's theory of the symbolic cut and its
conjunction of gender-division.[46] However, let us analyze it once more
and note that the scene presents a conceptual deadlock rather than the
gendering of the subject. The story begins with projecting language or
the symbolic as a fairy tale which glosses ugly Irish reality as pastoral
bliss. "Once upon a time and a very good time it was there was a
moocow coming down along the road and this moocow that was
coming down along the road met a nicens little boy named baby tuckoo
. . ." (*P* 7). Earnestly endeavoring to identify with his own pre-inscribed
role in this scenario provided by the father – of a maternal animal
(Ireland) encountering a "nice" child – the boy is from the beginning
limited to thinking of himself in the alienated masculine third person
("*He* was baby tuckoo." "*His* father told him that story" "*his* father
looked at him through a glass"; my italics). To place himself in the
verbal picture painted by the father (a representative of symbolic authority who gazes at him through a glass), the child assuming the split
between "I" and "he," and seeing himself from the father's position,
seems to identify with the father. But as we read on, we note that this
split in the self does not provide the authority and masculinity supposedly attending masculine gender. The father's language, hence the
symbolic, is here already placed as falsely glossy and unstable. This
instability increases in the song "*O, the wild rose blossoms/ On the little green
place*" which the father, it seems, offers the child as "his" song. This
rendition, however, practices a revision of the original words in Thom-
pson's "Lily Dale," which speak of "*the little green grave.*"[47] Assuming the
father's perspective means colluding with the repressive falsification of
Irish reality and ignoring its heritage of death. When Stephen accepts
the song as his: "He sang that song. That was his song," his lisping of it
as "the green wothe botheth" in turn substitutes "green" for "wild."
The wild rose turns Irish green, a phantasy creation, and Stephen
redoubles the "fairy" element of the father's tale. The symbolic as
handed down by the father (already feminized as "fairytale" and
"song"), does not provide the stability of a God-term, nor does it allow

---

[46] See Hélène Cixous, "Devant le pome," *James Joyce: Cahiers de l'Herne* (Paris: L'herne, 1985),
pp. 193–203. Most recently: Christine Froula, *Modernism's Body: Sex, Culture, and Joyce* (New York:
Columbia University Press, 1996), who, ignoring the cultural specificity of Joyce's Irish situation,
sees Joyce as a split subject articulating the effects of the patriarchal denial of the pre-linguistic
identification with the mother.

[47] *Notes for Joyce*, ed. Don Gifford (New York: Dutton, 1967), p. 86.

escape. Intertextuality, revision or rewriting, and the inability to denote and found truth are inscribed in it from the beginning. In fact, the passage itself rhetorically enacts that groundlessness. It places us in seemingly rootless mediated speech from the first word ("Once upon a time and a very good time it was . . ."); nevertheless, it drops the line "*O, the wild rose blossoms*" as if it were Stephen's, immediately contradicting that suggestion in its lisped copy. From the first, the reader is deprived of a sure footing in Joyce's symbolic, never able to ground language in a specific human agent or referential reality: entrapped in Joyce's web just as Stephen is entrapped in the discourse of his culture.

That instability in the Irish symbolic is in turn actualized as the conflicting social reality Stephen enters. With language, he also immediately encounters the dilemma of conflicting claims and different forms of appeal and modes of being pre-inscribed in his culture. Whereas the father "frames" him in a fairy tale, the mute mother plays music to make him dance. Culture provides two forms of symbolic address: Structured Language (Narrative, Song) primarily but not exclusively associated with the father (later the mother and Aunt Dante will utter the rhyming threat to Stephen's eyesight), and music, the rhythmic periodicity of sound, pitch, and melody which enlists Stephen's body, related primarily to the mother who tends it. Neither of these modes of appeal provides the sense of interiority or stability of a "mother tongue." Each is already partial and incomplete, and complementing the other. In Joyce, the felt absence of the mother tongue is allegorized in both the failure of the symbolic to fix truth, and the heightened appeal of the material effects of tone and pitch as the possible crypt of authenticity. In contrast to earlier readings then, I do not find here a classic Lacanian allocation of the symbolic and speech to the father, and the relegation of the mother to the pre-linguistic. The symbolic, "language" itself, is split into two modes of expression which rival to engage the child. Neither the claim of the father (himself notoriously unstable given Stephen's endless list of his father's identities and attributes ending in "at present a praiser of his own past"), nor that of the muted mother offers a point of identification for a seemingly stable subjectivity predicated upon a Lacanian split. Truth and the promise of a solid positioning of the subject are lacking in the father's word, while the mother's materialization of language as rhythm and sound – while more physical and perhaps more primary – can never ground the self in language. Indeed, Joyce's redoubling of language in this scene violates Kristeva's or Lacan's temporalization of the moment of entry into language as that in which the bond with the mother is superseded and broken by the symbolic. Here the mother shares the symbolic with the father, and their joint presence seems to set up a series of splitting redoublings which the text itself must try to overcome.

We here gain insight into Joyce's attempt, throughout his *œuvre*, to create an embodied textuality which re-combines the materiality of rhythm, sound, and graphic inscription with the structuring power of narrative: As if a marriage of the mother's mode of appeal to that of the father might generate the absent grounding for identification. The constitutive gap in the subaltern symbolic will give rise to endlessly renewed attempts to ground narrative in the body, in the periodicity of the drive, the flow of (menstrual) blood, in short, in the material. This will eventually lead to the reductive materialization of the signifier in *Finnegans Wake*. Thus the constitutive instability of the symbolic also entails a redoubling and recrossing of gender. The colonial father is always already feminized: as a subaltern subject he fails as the representative of the cultural authority of language. As a Celt, moreover, he is perceived as the feminine other to the Anglo-Saxon Englishman whose language already rules the waves. The Irish father's language cannot constitute truth. This situation is emblematized when Stephen's father cannot prevent the quarrel at the Christmas dinner. The passage concludes: " – Poor Parnell! he cried loudly. My dead king! He sobbed loudly and bitterly. Stephen, raising his terrorstricken face, saw that his father's eyes were full of tears" (*P* 39). In Joyce the figure of the mother, on the other hand, is not seen as muted, but as the repository of a wordless language (a language of flowers), a public secret, a hidden letter, or a "word known to all men," which she may transmit to her son. Moreover, she seems the instance of authority when she utters the command that Stephen must apologize. From *Ulysses*, the reader will gather that Stephen's mother's authority is so powerful because it is the extension of that of the Roman Catholic Church. Here the mother is allied to the law which, in Kristeva's theory, is reserved for the father.

After situating this constitutive conceptual knot which generates splitting and redoubling, the text begins to introduce ever more complex forms of splitting. The two symbolic colors (maroon for Michael Davitt and green for Parnell) of Aunt Dante's brushes introduce the treacherous divisiveness of Irish politics ("Irrland's [Errorland's] split little pea"). This split, in turn, brings into the text the breach between Protestants (Eileen's family) and Catholics (his own). The passage concludes its build-up of repetitive splitting with the threat of violence to the boy at the moment when gender meets the divisiveness of Irish culture: "the eagles will come and pull out his eyes." This threat is not motivated in the tale. What did Stephen do to deserve this? Why does the child's confrontation with the situation of gender roles in Irish culture solicit such violence? In wanting to marry Eileen, he conforms to the paternal example and answers the mother's invitation to the dance of sexuality. In styling himself "masculine," however, the child incurs inexplicable violence. It is as if the split-reality of Irish history itself made clear gender-identity impossible, creating a conceptual deadlock or double bind. At this point in the story, Joyce leaves a *lacuna* in the text which ought to make us wonder. (We shall return to this.)

Thus Stephen Dedalus – who shows the same psychological reaction in each chapter, each new situation – not only "has" a complex, he also "is" a complex; the text which inscribes this portrait constantly hovers on the brink of the dissolution of the self, and practices strategies of containment to hold contradictory claims in one focus, while never escaping the imprisonment in the contradiction in its re-enactment of that traumatic moment of its constitution as Irish subjectivity. The later chapters of *A Portrait* rehearse this primal scene of the anxiety of the text at ever more sophisticated levels, but always repeating its invariable scenario. Through this rehearsal, the underlying split between two different modes of the symbolic, verbal-intertextual (primarily gendered masculine in Joyce's text through the association with the father's storytelling) and physical-material (primarily gendered feminine through the mother's music), becomes clearer. As I said, that split should not only be seen as a representation of the conflict of Irish identity; it is also an attempt to overcome that contradiction in the symbolic.

To illustrate this claim, we must return to the moment immediately after the scene in which Stephen tries to contain dissemination by means of drawing lines: "It pained him that he did not know well what politics meant, and that he did not know where the universe ended. He felt small and weak. When would he be like the fellows in poetry and rhetoric? . . . That was very far away" (*P* 17). Beset by a sense of his own inadequacy in this world of masculine learning, Stephen pictures the eventual inclusion in a homosocial group of men-who-know as the release from insecurity and smallness. At the same time, he begins to process the endless distance separating him from that moment as a dialectic between the maternal home and school: "First came the vacation and then the next term and then vacation again and then again another term and then again the vacation. It was like a train going in and out of tunnels and that was like the noise of the boys eating in the refectory when you opened and closed the flaps of your ears. Term, vacation; tunnel, out; noise, stop. How far away it was!" (*P* 17).

Stephen's method of coping with the unbearable discrepancy between the felt pain of ignorance and a desired self-sufficiency, is to rhythmicize the dialectic of opposition by means of using the body. The opening and closing of the flaps of the ears produces the alternating beat of the *fort-da* which Freud observed in his grandson playing with a thread and bobbin, attempting to cope with the loss or protracted absence of the mother in the re-enactment of her departure. Repetition compulsion, yes! But also the constantly renewed attempt to overcome the contradiction. The reliving of the trauma of the parent's absence is also the child's attempt at learning to cope. In Freud's parable in *Beyond the Pleasure Principle*, the boy learns to symbolize the mother's absence, and thus bear it, through a repetitive gesture which gives a sense of mastery. In Lacan's reading the same scene emblematizes the moment of entry into language and marks the detachment from the mother.[48] To both the dramatizing re-enactment of separation is also an attempt to conquer its emotional effect.

What appears significant to me is that Stephen's medium for coping with the anxiety of separation and detachment is not just a bobbin in combination with language, but the *ears* in conjunction with *language patterned as ritual play, poetry almost.* Just as the bobbin can function as transitional object for the little boy because its concrete material presence, in itself without significance, substitutes for the tangibility of the mother while its small size allows him full control, so the patterning of sound and meaning through the body alleviates the self-alienation caused by separation from the mother, mediating between the verbal paternal and the material maternal (body, rhythm, pitch, and music). It cleverly turns language – the mark of detachment – into its own object as music or art. The play which fuses language and body allows the little boy to forget his loss. It also directs the focus of attention to patterned linguistic expression, and locates the center of subjectivity in the medium itself, as a form of poetry. Lacan's reading of the *fort-da* game in particular supports this suggestion, emphasizing that the repetitiveness of the game "destroys" the reality of the object and creates a substitute "reality" that is imaginary: "His action thus negates the field of forces of

[48] Lacan, *Ecrits*, pp. 101–03.

desire in order to become its own object to itself."[49] Thus Joyce renews human nature like Daedalus, and projects an escape from the labyrinthine condition of being Irish, by making poetic language the ultimate reality.

In Joyce's *Portrait*, the child's bobbin is replaced by the child's own body, while language is patterned as rhythm as in Freud's example. But in Freud's text the value of the bobbin resided in its lack of significance. What about Stephen's relationship to his own body? He treats it as if it were an object without significance, as if language and body were split. Moreover, Joyce's child is no longer a one-and-a-half-year-old boy. It is as if Stephen never can and will accede to the detachment which the play with the bobbin or body ought to have taught him long ago. He can neither relinquish the desire for the presence of the mother, nor his attempted identification with the father. Instead, he endlessly repeats the game at increasingly sophisticated levels. As the reader notices in the later chapters of *A Portrait*, Stephen's game will more and more focus on the rhythmic and poetic features of language, turning poetic language into a fetishized substitute for presence. Thus he becomes a poet, an artist, not just out of vocation, or out of desire to transcend the limitations of the environment, but also because he remains caught in the crack of the always already contradictory moment of entry into a language always "foreign" and "familiar" owing to its colonial derivation.[50]

What about the structure and meaning of *A Portrait*, then? Is the repetition *in* the text, the repetition *of* the text? How do we know that Joyce gives us a "portrait" of Stephen Dedalus (an "identificative paper" [*PSW* 211]). Can we be sure that this is not just the "acting out" of Stephen Dedalus's or even Joyce's own "curve of an emotion"? How do we distinguish between representation and performance? How can we tell "portrait" from "auto-graph" in the sense of "inscription" of the "self"?

As will be clear, it seems to me that the distinction between those two modes of presentation is undercut in Joyce's text. Instead of a circumscribed image, Joyce provides a spacing without end, a patterning of representation through rhythm and repetition which establishes at once

---

[49] *Ibid.*, p. 103.
[50] Patrick McGee, *Paperspace*: "Stephen's discourse is perhaps the discourse of a lack, but a lack that from the beginning has been a temporal fiction of the subject-in-process which effaces the boundary between subject and object, self and other, father and mother. The subject-in-proces is between" (p. 61).

a break and a connection between the temporal and the spatial, the same and the different, the text and the world – what Derrida named "*différance*' and Les Murray spoke of as "time broaden[ing] into space."[51] Resisting the reduction to either partition, Joyce's text, a form of *archi-écriture*, moves dialectically between oppositions, inscribing the spacing that articulates all signifying. It repeats, *ad infinitum*, the traumatic moment of its original constitution as the subject-in-language, because that subject is never constituted definitively. Through this pattern of repetition venturing into the future, it breaks through circumscribing frames: the end of the individual work, the boundary between text and life, realism and postmodernism, writing as physical act and as representation.

It also sets up an internal dialectic within Joyce's *œuvre* which becomes a continual self-address. Instead of the communication of a prior sense, Joyce's writings enact the discovery of modes of coping with the tension between the opposite poles. Each work presents a new and different way of repeating the same. The forward movement within writing itself becomes a rhythmic dance which will eventually lead to the pure performativity of *Finnegans Wake* which inscribes the rhythms and acoustic patterns of narrative rather than its content. The forward movement of Stephen Dedalus's wanderings through Dublin finds its analogue in Joyce's "forward flight" in the process of confrontation with the alienation within signification itself. "[R]ear[ing his] disunited kingdom on the vacuum of [his] own most intensely doubtful soul" (*FW* 188.16), Joyce repeats that initial moment which brought a sense of nothingness, and inscribes death into representation itself.

Instead of helping his reader to distinguish between the dreamer and the dream, the narrator of *A Portrait of the Artist* compounds our dilemma. Here he acts very much like Stephen's father who fudges the distinction between imagination and fact. Joyce contaminates reality with fiction, memory with imagination, origin with copy, as if in a flaunting dramatization of his own resisting textual mode. The story continues with "How far away it was!" "It was better to go to bed to sleep," after which follows a description of Stephen's feverish phantasy of being in bed, which immediately turns into the seemingly objective description of an actual event: "It would be lovely in bed after the sheets got a bit hot. First they were so cold to get into. He shivered to think how cold they were first . . . It would be lovely in a few minutes. He felt a warm glow

---

[51] *The Empire Writes Back*, p. 34.

creeping up from the cold shivering sheets, warmer and warmer till he felt warm all over, ever so warm . . ." (*P* 17). Imagination overtakes reality, the green rose the wild rose, phantasized memory becomes actuality in the attempt to cope with the coldness of the actual. The imagined activity of the protagonist is transferred to the material object. The sheets "shiver" uncannily. The dream stage of the *Wake* is prefigured in the blurring of what "happens" and what is "thought," fact and imagination, in *A Portrait*. The text, not only here, straddles waking and dreaming, dead and alive, self and other, and subverts the possibility of telling them apart.

Imagined or real, portrait or performance, the repetition in the text speaks of a deadlock, a traumatic moment of experience which cannot be superseded, but which is also not accessible to memory and verbal expression. Such a structure of involuntary repetition is what Freud defined as the effect of a wounding moment which can itself not be symbolized. "Consciousness, once faced with the possibility of its death, can do nothing but repeat the destructive event over and over again," Cathy Caruth points out.[52] Laplanche and Pontalis define psychotrauma as an "event in the subject's life defined by its intensity, by the subject's incapacity to respond adequately to it, and by the upheaval and longlasting effects that it brings about in the psychical organisation."[53] Though there is no agreed upon clinical definition of psychotrauma, trauma is marked by the inability to remember the event which gave cause to the symptoms. The condition involves a paradox hinging on the notion of this dissociation of consciousness. The victim cannot remember the original occurrence, yet notes its influence on his life. Thus "presence" and "absence" are looped together as "presence-as-absence/absence-as-presence." The same holds for "past" and "present." Even more curious is the fact that while memory of the original event has disappeared, it apparently survives in the body. Unclaimed memory is staged as involuntary mental activity by the body.[54] This upsets the distinction between the physical and the mental, body and mind, matter and spirit. It lends to the inscription in the materiality of the body that priority and agency which, in western thought, traditionally had been assigned to the spirit. It generates the paradoxical notion of a material-memory.

---

[52] *Unclaimed Experience*, p. 63.   [53] *The Language of Psychoanalysis*, p. 465.
[54] See also Cathy Caruth, ed., *Trauma: Explorations in Memory* (Baltimore: Johns Hopkins University Press, 1995); and Ruth Leys, "Traumatic Cures," who speaks of war neuroses as articulated by the patients as related to the trauma of the *fort-da* of the desertion by the mother.

Psychotrauma, then, inscribes a paradoxical death-in-life which originates when a life-threatening event overwhelms consciousness and grafts the experience of that moment as unclaimed and unconscious knowledge. In short, trauma victims suffer from a splitting or cracking of the "self" into a conscious history accessible to memory, and an unconscious knowledge which cannot be tapped because the violence of the original event precludes its conscious experience. This break or gap in the self, inscribing nothingness into the self, is caused by the fact that the subject, literally, failed to experience what happened; and what has not been experienced cannot be remembered, cannot be worked through. The event situates itself in the constitution of the subject as a faultline which generates the effect of repetition until the original event enters memory.

A characteristic feature of trauma is its metaleptic nature. Trauma leads an encapsulated existence never manifesting itself as such until symptoms, sometimes decades after the event, point to the absent cause. Apparently, language can only approach trauma asymptotically, by indirection. One cannot articulate the trauma itself, because it materializes itself only as consequence, as implicit in form or structure, the patterning of a life or text, the gaps in the design. It is this curious discursive formation of linguistic absence – the trauma itself cannot be expressed in words – attended with experiential presence, as symptom and effect, which makes trauma such an important phenomenon in this context. It combines the incommensurability of difference, the philosophical problem which Lyotard addresses in *The Differend*, with perceptible effect – even if that effect is just the repetitive insistence of the presence of absence: a structure of repetition. It suggests that "subjectivity" may entail more than just verbal-linguistic inscription. There may be a form of unconscious knowledge or experience which resists memorization and is written in or on the body without our conscious awareness.[55] Moreover, it seems that such unconscious knowledge may transmit itself from speaker to listener without articulate entry into language, as the psychological history of the families of some of the survivors of the Holocaust or Japanese prison camps shows. Children or spouses may express in their art, their dreams, their neuroses the experience their parents never put into words, sometimes in vivid detail.

---

[55] Cf. Freud's "The Ego and the Id": "In the same way that tensions arising from physical needs can remain unconscious, so also can pain – a thing intermediate between external and internal perception, which behaves like an internal perception even when its true source is in the external world." *SE* 19 (1923), p. 22.

I suggest we return to the prelude of *A Portrait* as the impossible record of the moment of trauma which establishes Stephen's at once tenuous and over-cathected linguistic subjectivity. It is the moment of inscription of the division within the trait, infinitely repeating a failed predication, instigating the faultline in the mirror of the self. Stephen's first confrontation with threatened annihilation is here:

" – O, Stephen will apologise.
Dante said:
" – O, if not, the eagles will come and pull out his eyes.

Pull out his eyes,
Apologise,
Apologise,
Pull out his eyes.

Apologise,
Pull out his eyes,
Pull out his eyes,
Apologise."
*   *   *

The threat to Stephen's physical integrity, the impending pain, subsequent to something excluded from the story, send language into a spinning turmoil. In its chiasmic pattern of crossing over and redoubling it instigates infinite repetition – only to be framed by three asterisks already present in the holograph (cartoons use stars to indicate pain). The experience is rendered as overwhelming, annihilating, hence unconcluded and inconclusive; the young child is confronted with anxiety so massive that there is no response possible. He lacks language, words of his own to ward the experience off or work it through. No gesture or act, except trying to hide underneath the table, can let him escape. But underneath the table the voice still booms; now resounding in his own consciousness, his own interiority. The child is reduced to a passive echo of his master's voice: "pull out his eyes, apologise, apologise, pull out his eyes." Intrusive, the refrain annihilates self-sentience, the self, the core and center of his being.

The Greek noun "trauma" is related to the verb "titrooskoo" – "to pierce or penetrate." If the scene implies a threat to the eye, it presents itself as a piercing of the ear, as a rolling thundering blow to the tympanum which sends it resonating (or spinning) forever. Perhaps it is

not by accident that in *Finnegans Wake* thunder marks the com-
mencement of life as "auradrama."[56] The archetype of the paternal is
there incarnated as "Earwicker" (ear whacker?) or "Persse O'Reilly" (fr.
"perceoreille" ["earwig"] is literally "ear-piercer"), an incestuously
penetrating violator of his children's orifices. Though it is the mother
(seconded by Aunt Dante) who speaks in *A Portrait*, I suggest we do not
understand this allocation to one gender as exclusive. Important is not
the attribution to a single agent, but to note that the agency of language
is felt as piercingly invasive, a "[t]hunner in the eire" (*FW* 565.17)
entailing a colonization of the self by sound (remember that Stephen
resorted to his ears to cope with his alienation in school); a colonization
which is symbolized by the eagles of the Roman Empire, the emblems of
colonial-religious imperialism. I hardly need point out that "ear" rendered as "eire" extends the application of the trauma of the linguistic
invasion of the subject to that of the nation.

A distinctive feature of extreme pain is its paradoxical effect – it can
neither be denied, nor can it be spoken. Reducing the subject to a state
anterior to language, the memory of intense pain may even remain
unconscious, as Freud pointed out in "The Ego and the Id." The only
road to access the memory of pain is through the detour of language,
finding words which, binding unconscious content, make unconscious
thought-processes into retroactive perceptions.

The sole strategy of survival for the child deprived of personal speech
(and by extension the colonial subject invaded by the hegemonic language) is therefore, paradoxically, to cling to language, to speech, even if
in his state of shattered anxiety the only words available are the ones
sounding the trauma, and to transform those words into poetry: pattern
and rhyme. Psychotrauma, whether caused by life-threatening bodily
harm, emotional or sexual abuse, entails the economy of slavery, the
bondage of body and mind to the originating moment. This scene in *A
Portrait*, a reworking of Joyce's first epiphany, suggests a moment of
wounding constitution of the self which locks it in a perpetual struggle to
escape, while binding the self to that event in an endless repetition of
undoing, of acting out and being and denying that trauma. Since the
moment of trauma is also the moment of *naming* in the text, "Stephen" –
as he is named after the martyr from this moment – will *be* the living
habitation of this event which purloins his self (note he does not say "I").

---

[56] John Bishop, *Joyce's Book of the Dark: Finnegans Wake* (Madison: University of Wisconsin Press,
1986), p. 300.

He forever "auto-graphs" its *re-enactment*. In that sense he has "a shape that cannot be changed," to use Joyce's words for his creation.[57]

As I said, the only way to access unconscious memory is through the detour of language, finding words which, binding unconscious content, make unconscious processes into perceptions. Thus the subject is "sentenced" to the repetition within language, to "work[ing] out the enigma of [his or her] position" (*SH* 209). As Felman and Laub point out in *Testimony*: "The accident" is known through its effects, "both to the extent that it *'pursues'* the witness and that the *witness is, in turn, in pursuit of it.*"[58] The unique form of subjectivity of the survivor exists in his or her being an enactment of the event. In the act of working out he or she bears witness to the existence and occurrence of trauma which might otherwise be forgotten or denied.

In the case of Stephen Dedalus that working out must take place in the discourse of the oppressor and entails an inescapable bondage to the voice and the ear. Voices constantly pursue Stephen, murmuring, clamoring, soothing, sobbing, reproaching, bewailing, whispering not only their keen commands and claims, but also urging him to wander and escape: "he would suddenly hear a command to begone . . . a voice agitating the very tympanum of his ear, a flame leaping into divine cerebral life" (*SH* 30). The web of voices, internal and external, of flesh and culture, becomes a labyrinth in which the subject "walks through himself" (*U* 9.1044–46), enacting the dubious/dividual drama of his symbolic wound which can neither be denied nor articulated, inviting and seeking the return of the unspeakable in the self.

This labyrinth of trauma originates at the moment of the trauma itself. Stephen's chiasmic repetition "*Pull out his eyes,/Apologise,/Apologise,/Pull out his eyes.//Apologise,/Pull out his eyes,/Pull out his eyes,/Apologise*" negates command by turning it into musical language, thus appropriating it to aesthetic transformation, while also repeating and propagating it. In the same act, meaning is enclosed in a transforming echo-chamber of literal meaning: the threat "Pull out his eyes" (re)turns into a vengeful command to "Pull out his eyes," that is: compete with the aggressor. Thus language gains an extra, punning dimension, echoing as supplement to its received semantic meaning. Similarly the meaning of "apologise" turns from "presenting an apology" to "becoming an apologist." According to the *Oxford Dictionary*: a "professed

---

[57] Frank Budgen, *James Joyce and the Making of "Ulysses"* (1934; Bloomington: Indiana University Press, 1973), p. 107.

[58] *Testimony: Crises of Witnessing in Literature, Psychoanalysis, and History* (New York and London: Routledge, 1992), p. 22.

literary champion" like Stephen's hero Cardinal Newman. Affirmation is also undoing. Every repetitive "yes" is also "oyes! oyes!": "listen, watch out."

Let us try and listen to the text's "encrypting" of a drama that resists articulation.[59] From the first few pages Joyce shows Stephen's education as the desensitization of the body in order to shift the locus of reality from physical selfhood to language. Stephen's education provides an extreme illustration of Foucault's suggestion that culture harnesses the body through the "association of a prohibition and a strong injunction to speak."[60] It is a process of subjection made possible by the infliction of pain: Father Dolan's pandying, the punishment from schoolmates, the pain of loss, and the destitution of the body, pain remembered or imagined in the future, or the afterlife, but always pain inflicted in the service of a repressive ideology which denies the free use of the body, as when Nash and Boland batter, Stephen who has his back in a barbed wire fence, with a long cabbage stump in order to make him admit that the promiscuous and revolutionary Byron "was no good" (*P* 80); or pain which intends to harness the individual's productivity as when Stephen is called a "lazy idle loafer" (*P* 49) and pandied.

In *The Body in Pain*, Elaine Scarry argues that pain differs from other feelings in that it cannot be rendered linguistically. At the same time "physical pain is so incontestably real that it seems to confer its quality of 'incontestable reality' on that power that has brought it into being."[61] We might read Stephen's education as the inscription of Irishness and identity through the pain attending prohibition. Thus he is forced to acknowledge himself a "heretic" to his friends, to see himself as a "schemer" through Father Dolan's eyes, to confess himself a "sinner" after the retreat.

Curious and admirable in Stephen is that he has found a defence against the violent inscription of ideology on the body, never acceding to the "incontestable reality" of the prevailing ideology. Taking the discourse of one group or idea, he turns it against another, thus using language itself as a dagger forcing escape from the definitive stamp of linguistic-ideological determination. The five chapters of *A Portrait* show Stephen playing this game at ever more sophisticated levels. Thus the

---

59 The term "encrypting" derives from the work of Nicolas Abraham and Maria Torok, *L'Écorce et le noyau*, 2nd edn. (Paris: Aubier-Montaigne, 1987), whose analyses give dramatic insight into the complex interweaving of hidden or secret information into memory and text.
60 *Ethics: Subjectivity and Truth*, ed. Paul Rabinow (Harmondsworth: Allen Lane/Penguin, 1997), p. 224.
61 *The Body in Pain: The Making and Unmaking of the World* (New York: Oxford University Press, 1985), p. 27.

language of justice and freedom serves to vanquish Father Dolan. Against the "constant voices of his father and masters" calling him to sportliness, nationalism, manliness, courtship, all equally "hollow-soun-ding" (*P* 84) to his ears, Stephen activates the "infuriated cries within him" (*P* 92), the "voice" of nature, the "vague speech" of sexuality. The insistent claim of guilt voiced by the Church is appeased by confession; while professional allegiance to its Word is avoided by turning to the battle cry of art and freedom.

Still, however skillful Stephen may be at the dialectical manipulation of language to prevent his taking a definitive shape, somewhere along the line something has gone wrong. He is alienated from his surroun-dings (he sees his fellow playmates as body parts: "legs were rubbing and kicking and stamping. Then Jack Lawton's yellow boots dodged out the ball and all the other boots and legs ran after" [*P* 10]). Again and again alienation exacerbates into a state of fugue: "Without waiting for his father's questions he ran across the road and began to walk at breakneck speed down the hill. He hardly knew where he was walking. Pride and hope and desire like crushed herbs in his heart sent up vapours of maddening incense before the eyes of his mind. He strode down the hill amid the tumult of suddenrisen vapours of wounded pride and fallen hope and baffled desire. They streamed upwards before his anguished eyes in dense and maddening fumes . . ." (*P* 86). Once the overwhelm-ing emotion recedes, Stephen calms down by means of attending to *writing, letters*: "He saw the word *Lotts* on the wall of the lane and breathed slowly the rank heavy air." For all his pride and self-conscious superiority, Stephen's self-conscious hold over himself and the body is tenuous even at moments of triumph. Thus Stephen's exclamation "Heavenly God!" at seeing the girl on the beach, rather than to approach her, propels him to "set off across the strand. His cheeks were aflame; his body was aglow; his limbs were trembling. On and on and on and on he strode, far out over the sands . . ." (*P* 172). As Hugh Kenner once argued, wandering is one of Stephen's ways of resolving conflict. What seems to play here, however, is more than just a tendency to take long walks; the precarious alignment of body and emotion in extreme circumstances suggests that linguistic subjectivity is at times dissolved by emotion so powerful that it sets the body off in flight to recover itself and escape the emotion. The most extreme example occurs during the visit to Cork when even reading fails him:

His very brain was sick and powerless. He could scarcely interpret the letters of the signboards of the shops . . . He could respond to no earthly or human

appeal, dumb and insensible to the call of summer and gladness and com-
panionship, wearied and dejected by his father's voice. He could scarcely
recognize as his his own thoughts, and repeated slowly to himself: – I am
Stephen Dedalus. I am walking beside my father whose name is Simon
Dedalus. We are in Cork, in Ireland. Cork is a city. Our room is the Victoria
Hotel. Victoria and Stephen and Simon. Simon and Stephen and Victoria.
Names. (*P* 92–93)

To end this state of depersonalization, Stephen has recourse to the most
basic poetic form of language use, the recital of names, to keep his hold
on reality. Sometimes he seems to lose that hold. Sick at school, he
hallucinates the arrival of Parnell and the presence of ghosts. After the
sermon during the retreat, he has an auditory hallucination, hearing
the voices of the devils discuss him in hellish officialese. From the
beginning, Stephen also has the curious habit of speaking to himself, or
reassuring himself of his own existence by means of language use. He
repeats odd or remembered words or phrases, reads to himself "his
name and where he was" (*P* 15), as if in a private ritual protecting the
self from evaporating. Indeed, we might read *A Portrait* as a whole, since
it begins with speech repeated to the self, and ends as a diary – words
written by the self to the self in order not to forget the self – as a speech
act of linguistic self-maintenance in the face of the threatened dissolution of subjectivity.

But however much it tries, the *text* can never access its own unconscious. It can only speak the repetitive effect of the trauma rather than
the trauma itself. The only way the letter can arrive at its destination and
lay the repetitive force of the trauma to rest, is if it engineers a situation
of transference which seduces the listener to the story to articulate what
the text *enacts*. The text is in the situation of the ancient mariner who
must grab the wedding guest to witness his tale, in the hope that the
transference of the listener will liberate him from the death-in-life of the
spell of the albatross. Significantly, Joyce wrote a poem entitled "A
Portrait of the Artist as Ancient Mariner" in which the vicissitudes
around the distribution of *Ulysses* which prevent this work from being
read are figured as the albatross around the artist's neck (*PSW* 143–44).

That Joyce had designs on his reader is an almost proverbial cliché.
That the explicit intention to keep the professors busy for centuries, his
claims on an ideal reader with an ideal insomnia, his demand that we
devote our lives to his text are perhaps not just the manifestation of
modernist egomania, but the desperate attempt *to be heard and given
witness*, is something which gains credibility when we perceive the
ghostly echo "above" or "behind" Joyce's repetitious "handiwork,"

brought out by Brian McHale. Only the emotional response, the articulation of its meaning by the reader, stops the insistence of repetition, its "bad infinity," and stabilizes the language of the text in laying its ghosts to rest. Perhaps this is the *object* of the anxiety of Joyce's *Portrait.* Joyce waits for his reader, just as Stephen metaleptically waits for the advent of the other to find himself: "He did not want to play. He wanted to meet in the real world the unsubstantial image which his soul so constantly beheld. He did not know where to seek it or how: but a premonition which led him on told him that this image would, without any overt act of his, encounter him" (*P* 65). From this point of view, poststructuralist readings which keep meaning "in flight" engage Joyce's letter at a partial level, no less than the humanist framings of Joyce as Artist-Genius. They speak from a position which itself participatingly underwrites the dissociation that effectuates repetition. Neither speaks from the moment and place where language arises.

The rhetorical nature of Joyce's intersubjective textuality is most easily explained by means of Slavoj Žižek's joke about the conscript who attempts to escape military service. The young man goes around, frantically picking up all papers he can lay his hands on, scrutinizing them and exclaiming: "That's not it!" Sent in to the highest military psychiatrist, he flips through the letters on the desk and even rummages in the wastebasket, mumbling "That's not it," until the doctor, convinced that this young man is crazy, hands him a form warranting release. The conscript exclaims happily: "That's it."[62] Žižek points out that the piece of paper is an "object" in Lacan's terminology, because it is a thing which came into being as the product of all the to-do around it. The "demented" conscript repeats the failing gesture of looking for something ("That's not it!"), but by means of that repetition, he produces what he pretends to be looking for. "The paradox is, then, that the process of searching itself *produces* the object which *causes* it."[63]

I suggest that Joyce's text works rhetorically like the action of the conscript: it involves us in searching for, and eventually creating its desired object – a witnessing reading – which is implicitly demanded by the anxiety of Joyce's tantalizing signifying texture. The mistake of the people around the conscript, including the specialist, is in thinking that they are objective observers at a distance, outside the scenario of the other. Here is an object-lesson for Joyce's readers. The truth is that we are already participants in the "crazy" scenario of Joyce's text. The

[62] "Why Lacan Is Not a 'Post-Structuralist'," *Newsletter of the Freudian Field* 1, 2 (1987), 31–40.
[63] *Ibid.*, p. 39.

difference between the situation in the joke and our situation as readers of Joyce is that the "design" of the text is not simply the effect of a consciously formulated scheme, but of the overly self-conscious inscription of the effects of the anxiety of the colonial unconscious as text.

THE SEMIOTIC STATUS OF THE TEXT

In using the word "design," covering both meanings of "intention" and "structural composition," I engage the question of the semiotic status of Joyce's texts implied in my suggestion that we see the text as having an "object" on the reader. Can we understand Joyce's *Portrait of the Artist* itself still as a mimetic representation, a "portrait," if it is not couched in metalanguage but as "object"-language? Indeed, Joyce's *Portrait*, in addition to functioning as the *Darstellung* of a world, must also be qualified as the vehicle of the (unconscious) affect of the text. The word or text does not only correlate with an image of a character which it seemingly circumscribes, but also with the productive *effect* of the crack in the mirror. It fulfills the aesthetic of the 1904 sketch, in that it is not a mimetic representation, but an "auto-graphic" signifier "set between the mind or senses of the artist himself and the mind or senses of others" (*P* 213). The image mediates between writer and reader, between psyche and psyche. Aspiring to be more than the representation of a state or object in the world, it subverts the ontological gap between language and metalanguage, presentation and representation.

In *The Four Fundamental Concepts*, Lacan, deliberately twisting Freud's use of the term, speaks of a *Vorstellungsrepräsentanz*: a signifier which comes in the place of an excluded or repressed representation which "constitutes the central point of the *Urverdrängung*."[64] The *Vorstellungsrepräsentanz* stands in for what has been primordially repressed, and cannot be represented. Thus it is to be understood as an attempt to figure as text, hence in the symbolic, that which eludes language and representation. It replaces the impossible representation of the unrepresentable. I suggest that *A Portrait* may be understood as a *Vorstellungsrepräsentanz*.

Here another of Slavoj Žižek's jokes may help us gain clarity. In a discussion of the issue of metalanguage, Žižek zooms in on the relation-

---

[64] "Repression," *SE* 14, pp. 141–59, where "*Vorstellung*" is translated as the "idea or group of ideas which is cathected with a definite quota of psychic energy (libido or interest) coming from an instinct" (p. 152). The *Vorstellungs-Repräsentanz* is the representative of the drive in the psychic apparatus. Freud is belaboring the point that the drive is not purely biological. In *The Four Fundamental Concepts*, Lacan translates *Vorstellungsrepräsentanz* as "representative of the representation" (p. 218).

ship of title to work, and demonstrates Lacan's perspective by means of a joke about "Lenin in Warsaw": "At an art exhibition in Moscow a picture is hung showing Nadezhka Krupskaya, Lenin's wife, in bed with a young member of the Komsomol. The title of the picture is 'Lenin in Warsaw.' A bewildered visitor asks a guide: 'But where is Lenin?' The guide replies quietly and with dignity: 'Lenin is in Warsaw.'"[65] Of course, at play here is the resistance against Lenin as the bearer of paternal prohibition; but the theoretical *pointe* of the joke lies elsewhere. The title of the painting does not convey what the representation makes visible. It violates the convention of titles like "sunset" or "portrait." It points out what is lacking in the *Darstellung*. Our mistake in asking where Lenin, or by extension where Joyce's "portraiture" is, is to be caught in the snare of metalanguage. "The mistake . . . is to establish the same distance between the picture and the title as between the sign and the denoted object, as if the title is speaking *about* the picture from a kind of 'objective distance,' and then to look for its positive correspondent in the picture."[66] In other words, when we ask "where is Joyce's artist depicted?" we overlook that Joyce's title does not function as denotative metalanguage, since it may be on a level with the text itself. It is the anxious "writing" itself which demonstrates the presence of an artist, not a representative image contained in that writing. Thus the title is the productive extension of the text, which is the productive extension of its author, just as the title of the painting in Žižek's example is part of the continuum of the representation on the canvas, and just as traumatic repetition is the extension of the moment of violence. "Its distance from the picture is strictly internal, making an incision into the picture itself. That is why something must fall (out) from the picture: not its title, but its object, which is replaced by a title."[67] Here we have Lacan's *Vorstellungsrepräsentanz*: the signifying element filling out the vacant place of the missing representation (i.e. of Lenin, or the "stable" Portrait of the Irish Modernist Artist). The screen of the text, the *Vorstellung*, is the space reserved for what is to be given a local habitation and a name; but the problem is that not everything can be *named* or *represented* in language or paint: death or the unclaimed experience of trauma, or an authentic subaltern subjectivity must remain outside language. Indeed, it is of the essence of the concept of trauma that it cannot be represented directly or spoken in words. It must necessarily fall out from the representation just as Lenin must be in Warsaw. In the case of Joyce, writing takes the

---

[65] "Why Lacan is not a 'Post-Structuralist'," 137.   [66] *Ibid.*, 37.   [67] *Ibid.*

place of its missing object, the originally repressed representation, the portrait of a stable and unified Irish identity.

But that impossible originally repressed representation is also the motor of what is shown to us. If Joyce's textuality did not "enact a trauma," we would not have had Joyce's narratives which are the expressive aftermath and product of the pain of the moment of inscription of that originally repressed representation. Thus the semiotic relationship between text and life, story and object of representation is not iconic in Pearce's terminology. It does not hinge on resemblance. Instead, it is indexical: the text is the consequence of the event it cannot represent, just as smoke is the index of fire.

When we see smoke, we immediately take action to quench a possible conflagration. The notion that *A Portrait* functions as index, as pointer to something not-presentable, suggests that there is more to textuality than just language, that the poststructuralist attempt to circumscribe the world as text,[68] the psyche as language, may paradoxically backfire to draw our attention precisely to what it excludes in its originary repression. This paradoxical effect is contained in the Lacanian notion of the phallus as signifier itself. As the transcendent signifier which marks loss or the possibility of loss, usually referred to as "castration," the signifier embodies the possibility of loss. Thus a "purloined letter" points to its own deprivation of content in the very act of exercising its power as signifier. It is the index of its own impossibility. I began this chapter suggesting that Joyce syncretically constructs his texts as purloined letters as well as traditional postcards. Thus I may seem to have ranked Joyce with Lacan, while the differential textuality of *A Portrait* also places him with Derrida. However, in articulating the occasion of the originally repressed representation not as the universal condition of "castration" (Derrida's point of objection to Lacan), nor as the Derridian universal of the "internal division of the trait," but as the "traumatic" record of the violence of the inscription into the symbolic of the subaltern Irish subject lacking a mother tongue, I offer a perspective which relates Joyce's writing to the specific historical situation of Irishness around 1882.

For Derrida, and to a certain extent Lacan, the moment of originary repression is symbolized by Freud's fable in *Moses and Monotheism* relating the murder of the father which institutes the order of history. This fable substitutes the remembrance of the Name, that is, language, for physical

---

[68] See Allen Thiher, *Words in Reflection: Modern Language Theory and Postmodern Fiction* (University of Chicago Press, 1984).

presence, and institutes a social order which is based on symbolic power rather than physical force. Freud's simplistic scenario is itself a necessary attempt to fill in what can never be articulated in words, because the moment precedes history. The necessity of its telling demonstrates that there is an area of experience which inescapably lacks symbolization. The telling is an effect of the lack, and points to that lack, but cannot communicate anything substantial about it.

The difference between this *Ur*-trauma and the situation of Joyce, is, as I argued, that the splitting scenario of *A Portrait* points to a redoubling of the *Ur*-trauma *within* the symbolic. The infinite chain of splitting and redoubling is the product of a pattern of linguistic subjectivity in which the son cannot identify with or within the symbolic; nor can he escape into a "mother tongue." Living out this paradox, unable to express its destitution directly, lacking the voice to name the anxiety and loss and give it presence otherwise than, perhaps, through its belaboring of intonation, rhythm, and repetition, its denotation must necessarily remain a *Vorstellungsrepräsentanz*. Thus the specificity of Joyce contrasts with the universality implied by Derrida and Lacan. Whereas Derrida and Lacan rejoyce in "speaking" the impossibility of articulating the missing representation, Joyce indirectly "speaks" the historical outrage of certain forms of human behavior which have made the articulation of memory impossible. Moreover, he presents his culture's history in the only way in which it can be grasped, in the very inaccessibility of its occurrence. Joyce lets the ghost walk, he involves us in the intersubjective scenario of looking for interpretations, constructing meanings which might be adequate to the enormity of the event of the loss of identity or selfhood at the moment of entry into language or history. He makes us the vehicle of his anxiety. As the cracked looking-glass of an Irish writer, Joyce's texts keep asking us to repair the faultline which splits and doubles and subverts representation, and to bear witness to the original repression at the root of the constitution of identity. He demands that we instate the subject which has fallen out of the representation in to its place in the picture. We must complete his "portrait."

This reading of Joyce's writing contains a theoretical imperative with regard to the meaning of the word "text." In *Metaphors We Live By*, Lakoff and Johnson point out that human thought processes are largely metaphorical.[69] A metaphor is not a rhetorical ornament, a decorative element adorning the vehicle of meaning. Metaphor creates and expres-

---

[69] George Lakoff and Mark Johnson, *Metaphors We Live By* (University of Chicago Press, 1980).

ses meaning. The metaphor of the "text" projects the radical separation of the literary work from its author, creating two distinct realities: the living human being and the dead material object. The poet is a "makere," as he was called in earlier times. What the metaphor precludes is the metonymic vision of the continuity of self-extension between the artist and the work. How do we express, what terminology do we have to express, our sense of the living presence of the author in his work? How do we accommodate the indexicality of Joyce's writing in our metaphors? Criticism resorts to metaphors like "voice" and "tone" to approximate the intuition that there is more at work in a literary text than the arrangement of dead language, the objectifying weaving (or unweaving) of the linguistic material of the text. To humanists like Erasmus, whose interest in the written word centered on the Holy Scripture, language, especially in its written form, still contained and mediated presence. It was of the utmost necessity that the text be translated correctly in order not to interfere with the reader's participation in the presence of Christ's Word and Body. Indeed, reading, like the participation in the ritual of the liturgy, was an act of "eating" the body and "drinking" the blood.

We moderns have largely lost that participation mystique which lives on in oral cultures. Certainly the drive of structuralism has been to articulate the literary text as a material object with a determinate structure which is itself the vehicle of meaning. It would seem to me that the understanding of Joyce's work as indexical not only requires our revision of the notion of "text"; we might also need to investigate whether Joyce's understanding of the phenomenon of language approximated that of an indigenous oral tradition. I shall return to that necessity in the following chapter. Here I merely wanted to explain that in using the term "embodied" textuality, I try to do justice to the indexicality of Joyce's writings.

CHAPTER 3

The language of the outlaw

In the buginning is the woid, in the muddle is the sounddance
Finnegans Wake

Although a cracked mirror, *A Portrait* is less complex than *Ulysses*. In *A Portrait*, Joyce still offers an image which seems to represent a world we know. In *Ulysses*, for all its realistic precision of detail, Joyce deliberately sets out to frustrate the reader's expectations of encountering a unified and naturalizable representation. *Ulysses* not only offers a new style in each chapter, it violates conventions which keep representation stable – especially the assumption that a single voice is tied to a specific character whose speech and memory are his own. On a metalevel, the novel vitiates the expectation that the text can be seen as the product of a coherent authorial agent. Joyce has not absconded behind his "handiwork" – to use Stephen Dedalus's words for the impersonality of his ideal artist, who, "like the God of the creation, remains . . . invisible, refined out of existence, indifferent, paring his fingernails" (*P* 215); the author of *Ulysses* precisely calls attention to himself *as absent and improvident*. Thus the textual strategy dramatizes the impossible condition of masculine/paternal/writerly authority under colonial rule as it was sketched in *A Portrait*. It transforms stricture and absence into flamboyant and self-pleasuring mastery. In this chapter, we shall trace the strategies Joyce employed to achieve that reversal.

Homi Bhabha, following Roland Barthes, offers the metaphor of "writing outside the sentence"[1] for a style which trespasses upon the strictures under which representation is placed by western ideology. It will be my suggestion that Joyce frustrates our readerly expectations, and attempts to attain a position outside western ideological preconceptions in order to dramatize the impossibility of an authentic Irish voice.

---

[1] Homi K. Bhabha, "The Postcolonial and the Postmodern: The Question of Agency," in *The Location of Culture*, pp. 171–97.

Within the hegemony, the subaltern Irish writer cannot but be seen through the eyes and preconceptions of that hegemony. Outside that order there is no place from which to speak and be heard, just as Archimedes could not find a place from which to move the Earth. Scrambling coherent sense and meaning, Joyce increasingly performs the impossibility of his own authorial situation. Ultimately, instead of the authorial "subject who knows," he presents the author as the "subject who shows,"[2] in a dramatization of the impossibility of his condition.

Roland Barthes proclaimed the "death" of the author in 1968 at the time when Derrida and Lacan were discovering Joyce as the achieved embodiment of their theories about the autonomy of "writing" and the "materiality" of the signifier. Joyce's authorial absenteeism might well lead us to conclude that Joyce is the perfect illustration of Roland Barthes' claim as well. I submit that the crucial difference with the poststructuralism of Roland Barthes, and by extension that of Derrida and Lacan, is, again, Joyce's postcolonial situation. Joyce does not illustrate "the death of the author": His writing dramatizes the presence of a void at the point of origin because the historical condition of being Irish entails the excruciating necessity of postulating that void in the face of the overwhelming encroachment of hegemonic culture.[3] Thus a style which from a purely formalist point of view may appear identical to that of poststructuralism, proves different from a historical perspective.

It is imperative that the question of authorial agency not be left as Barthes formulated it: "It is language which speaks, not the author"; or writing is the "destruction of every voice, of every point of origin."[4] The gesture of abolishing the concept of the author at the historical moment when cultural and social minorities begin to claim their rightful share of participation is a suspect move.[5] On the one hand it seems to liberate writing from the shackles of the old personalized concept of the author as the godlike subject who knows, breaking through hegemonic restrictions,

[2] I owe this term to Maud Ellmann, "The Ghosts of *Ulysses*," in *The Languages of Joyce*, ed. R. M. Bosinelli, C. Marengo Vaglio and Christine van Boheemen (Amsterdam: Benjamins, 1992), pp. 103–21.
[3] My endebtedness to Jean-Michel Rabaté's *Joyce Upon the Void: The Genesis of Doubt* (London: Macmillan, 1991) will be obvious.
[4] "The Death of the Author," in *Image/Music/Text*, trans. Stephen Heath (New York: Hill and Wang, 1977), pp. 142–48.
[5] Note Henry Louis Gates' claim that just "when we [women and/or blacks] enter the academy, suddenly there is no more subject," quoted in Sandra M. Gilbert and Susan Gubar, *No Man's Land: The Place of the Woman Writer in the Twentieth Century* (New Haven: Yale University Press, 1989), p. 372.

since the traditional figure of the author is what Barthes calls the "epitome and culmination of capitalist ideology." At the same time, however, it deprives those who have not heard of recourse to the basic concept which they might found their claim to an audience. The concept of authority is of extreme moral and ethical importance. Socially, juridically, ethically, the concept of authority cannot be divorced from concerns with accountability and responsibility. Unless we wish to accept that the enunciative agency of the literary work is stereotyped as irrelevantly "aesthetic," we must re-articulate the manner in which literature positions itself in the cultural and political field.[6] Here Bhabha's query: "can there be a social subject of the 'non-sentence'?" seems crucial. If Joyce writes "outside the sentence" the question is how such deviant authority still carries moral and political weight. My suggestion is that Joyce's dramatization of his Irish subject-position is pedagogic. It alerts us to its injustice, and teaches us to hear a hitherto hardly heard dimension of literary communication (a new "mother tongue").

As argued in chapter 1, Stephen's exclamation: "His language, *so familiar and so foreign*, will always be for me an acquired speech. I have not made or accepted its words. My *voice* holds them at bay. My *soul* frets in the shadow of his language" (*P* 189) alerts us to the splitting and redoubling within the colonial symbolic which Joyce incorporates into representation itself, adding a dimension of unfamiliarity (defamiliarization, *Verfremdung*), as well as giving it a new, hitherto unfamiliar, dimension. That new dimension derives from that which, in Stephen Dedalus's sense of self, serves to "hold" the master's "words" "at bay": his "voice" and his "soul." Both "voice" and "soul" are elusive concepts escaping formalist determination; yet they denote that which we consider most intimately and unalienably personal. In *The Psychic Life of Power: Theories in Subjection*, Judith Butler addresses the issue of the possibility of resistance and escape from hegemonic discourse, addressing Foucault's argument in *Discipline and Punish* that the "soul" is the effect and product of the body's subjection by discourse.[7] Hence it would hardly seem a propitious instrument of escape from the net of discourse. She argues that only a concept of the psyche, and the reiterative work of melancholy, can bring into being a location offering the possibility of revision. My suggestion is that Joyce – who personally refused to mourn – used his texts as a duplicate of the self. In this duplicate he performed,

[6] Denis Dutton, "Why Intentionalism Won't Go Away," in Anthony J. Cascardi, ed., *Literature and the Question of Philosophy* (Baltimore: Johns Hopkins University Press, 1987), pp. 192–210.
[7] (Stanford University Press, 1997).

in and as writing, to perform the process of mourning reiteration that creates the possibility of escape. As an extension of the self, writing is at once Joyce's material "voice" and "soul." As I hope to demonstrate below, Joyce vitiates traditional representation to make present, through his self-conscious exploitation of textuality, an abstract, more primal and almost musical dimension of communication beyond words, "outside the sentence." He adds a psychic dimension to discourse, resonating from its materiality, and perceptible in its intersubjective effect.

Lacan spoke of the *jouissance*, the ecstatic pleasure or bliss attending Joyce's incurable symptom. Instead of speaking of *jouissance*, which is strictly personal, I think we may hear in "Cyclops" the echo of a more social sentiment: the glee of successful defiance, the triumphant transcendence of hegemonic oppression, the hysterical laughter of the subaltern subject who discovers in the meaning of his name within the hegemony ("Joys") the means of escaping its prisonhouse. Joyce's sensitivity to language extended to the semantic meaning of names. Thus he noted that "Freud" was a translation of "Joyce."[8] In adding the reverberating echo of visceral laughter to written textuality, Joyce combined the effect of the unconscious (Freud's heritage) with the meaning which his own name acquired in the language of the oppressor. Joyce dramatically literalizes the subaltern condition in which the signifier that is by definition outside meaning – the name that rivets the symbolic – acquires semantic significance in the system of the hegemonic language. His play on his own name produced variants like "Shame's Voice," or "Germ's Choice."

"In the buginning is the woid" (*FW* 378.28), *Finnegans Wake* parodies the Gospel of St. John. In Joyce, origin is a void of absence, and the Word is always already voided because of its inherent unfamiliarity or *unheimlichkeit*. It is "bugged" with foreignness. That same sentence from *Finnegans Wake* about the bugging of origin not only suggests the diagnosis of the traumatic condition of the Irish entry into language. The words which follow: "in the muddle is the sounddance," point to a new possibility of discursive agency, a different form of authority *through* language (*from* the position of the void), instead of *in* form and *as* structure – a transgressive body-poetics, or fetishized extension of the self, which speaks from the position of the sovereignty of laughter. Thus Joyce retreats to the void because the effect of doing so sets language free from the corset of a political tradition, an imperial heritage, a "white

---

[8] Ellmann, *James Joyce*, p. 490.

mythology" which is seemingly ingrained and has become identified with the structure of representation in language itself.

In fact, it is only once we perceive the non-place from which Joyce is speaking that we can hear and see another, non-discursive, dimension of narrative, hitherto unnoticed because it was considered irrelevant. My reading of "Cyclops" will argue that, in addition to the seeming projection of a representational image, the text conveys an understanding of itself as rhetorically excessive of representation.[9] Joyce's technique constitutes a way of writing "beyond the sentence" which smashes the instrumental usefulness of the mirror of representation for the practice of the mimetic self-constitution of national and individual identity. Moreover, by means of its rhetorical excess, it conveys a sense of indexical presence and meaning which breaches the ontological gap between representation and presence. Thus the question which Gayatri Spivak voiced in her essay "Can the Subaltern Speak?"[10] may be re-phrased as: "How must we read, in what manner should we listen, to hear the subaltern's voice"? Joyce demands a shift in focus away from the question of the possibility of the subaltern's speech to the assumption that the text enunciates but our ears are not attuned to the subtleness of its expression, or simply not used to perceiving the utterance of pain or desperate laughter. Our reading may have been a listening without hearing. I suggest that it is our responsibility to endeavor to learn to hear the text speak. I argue for the presence of a dimension to Joyce's writing which presents such an ethical claim.

"Cyclops" replays Odysseus' escape from the man-eating giant whom he blinds and tricks with a play on his name: "No-one." "Cyclops" is not only one of Joyce's most direct parallels to Homer, it also tends to be the focus of discussions of Joyce's nationalism and postcolonial poetics. Its major protagonists are the violently nationalist citizen and the pacifist Leopold Bloom, born in Ireland of Jewish descent. The cave-like setting of the narrated scene is a pub. The narrator who relates the events in retrospect remains anonymous (referred to as "the nameless one" in the later "Circe" chapter), and is a master of an invective discourse which reduces everything it touches to the lowest and meanest level.

The problem with "Cyclops" is that this first-person narrative is interlaced with more than twenty, sometimes very long, interrupting passages which comment on, parody, expand, and echo aspects of, or

---

[9] David Lloyd, *Anomalous States*, "Adulteration and the Nation."
[10] *The Post-Colonial Studies Reader*, ed. Bill Ashcroft, Gareth Griffiths and Helen Tiffin (London and New York: Routledge, 1995), pp. 24–29.

items in, the narrator's discourse in a number of different clichéd styles familiar from the media, popular culture, or Irish myth and history. These passages appear in the text at random, spawned by an association generated by an aspect of the story, a word used by a speaker, a historical analogy to an event, or merely a rhetorical figure. Critics tend to refer to these passages as "parodies." Since the term "parody" implies a narrowly stylistic intention and Joyce's meaning is more broadly ideological, I shall speak of "interpolations." We might say that the narrative itself seems bugged. It has a virus.

Although the chapter is complex, critics tend to focus on one of three major issues: the theme of anti-Semitism contained in Bloom's confrontation with the citizen, the problem of narrative technique which subverts narrative representation, and the question of Joyce's attitude towards Irish nationalism. This has undesirable consequences. Critics interested in style or narrative technique tend, on the whole, to ignore the political and ideological implications.[11] The critic interested in Joyce's attitude to anti-Semitism, and, more recently, (post)colonialism, is often unable to handle its narrative complexity, using terms like "metanarrative" or "materiality of the signifier" inappropriately, or failing to distinguish between levels of narrative embedding, and confusing characters with narrators. The effect is a flattening of the complexity of Joyce's text which reduces its insidious cultural politics to an outspoken representational positionality: Joyce "speaks against" the citizen's anti-Semitism, and Joyce "advocates" Bloom's gentleness.[12]

But matters are not so clear-cut. As Enda Duffy points out, the narratological irregularity of the chapter meaningfully disrupts the traditional conception of subject-centered discourse, to make way for a new version of postcolonial subjectivity which breaks traditional molds.[13] Woven into the seemingly representational narrative, there is

---

[11] Karen Lawrence, *The Odyssey of Style in "Ulysses"* (Princeton University Press, 1981) gave a stylistic analysis to which all later readings are endebted; David Hayman, *"Ulysses": The Mechanics of Meaning* (Englewood Cliffs, NJ: Prentice-Hall, 1970) attempted to cope with Joyce's "impersonality"; Hugh Kenner's *Joyce's Voices* (London: Faber and Faber, 1978) addressed the problem of "focalization"; André Topia, "The Matrix and the Echo: Intertextuality in *Ulysses*," in *Post-Structuralist Joyce*, pp. 103–27 scrutinizes the intertextuality of "Cyclops." None places Joyce's stylistic choices in a historical-political context.

[12] It should be pointed out that Emer Nolan, in *James Joyce and Nationalism* (London: Routledge, 1995), argues the complexity of Joyce's relationship to the nationalist voice.

[13] *The Subaltern "Ulysses."* See also Bryan Cheyette, "'Jewgreek is Greekjew': The Disturbing Ambivalence of Joyce's Semitic Discourse in *Ulysses*," in *Joyce Studies Annual* (Austin: University of Texas Press, 1992), p. 43, who argues that the stance of Bloom should be understood as itself a wider rejection of all "dominant discourses" which Joyce "ruthlessly parodies" in this chapter. Cheyette still identifies Bloom's enunciative position as that of Joyce, however, thus he implicitly maintains faith in Joyce's loyalty to the "dominant discourse" of representation.

an excess of elocutionary force which undermines the representational status of the text. Let us follow the rhetorical development of the chapter, to get a sense of its complexity and utter strangeness. Bloom is queried about his national origin:

Bloom was talking and talking with John Wyse and he quite excited with his dunducketymudcoloured mug on him and his plumeyes rolling about.
–Persecution, says he, all the history of the world is full of it. Perpetuating national hatred among nations.
–But do you know what a nation means? says John Wyse.
–Yes, says Bloom . . . A nation is the same people living in the same place.
–By God, then, says Ned, laughing, if that's so I'm a nation for I'm living in the same place for the past five years.
So of course everyone had the laugh at Bloom and says he, trying to muck out of it:
–Or also living in different places.
–That covers my case, says Joe.
–What is your nation if I may ask? says the citizen.
–Ireland, says Bloom. I was born here. Ireland (12.1415–31)

The story immediately continues with a long extrapolation about the citizen's handkerchief, described as an ancient Irish embroidered face-cloth of legendary beauty, ending with an exhaustive list of the places and scenes of Irish nationalist self-identification depicted on the "emunctory field" (12.1447) and closing with "all these moving scenes are still there for us today rendered more beautiful still by the waters of sorrow which have passed over them and by the rich incrustations of time" (12.1461–64).

After this mock-romantic interlude, the reader is abruptly thrown back into the humdrum reality of pub interaction: "–show us over the drink, says I. Which is which? – That's mine, says Joe, as the devil said to the dead policemen. –And I belong to a race too, says Bloom, that is hated and persecuted . . ." (12.1465–68). Bloom's reference to love triggers the extrapolation: "Love loves to love love . . . And this person loves that other person because everybody loves somebody but God loves everybody" (12.1493–501).

The text seems indiscriminate in its irony. Its object is not only the sentimentality of Irish nationalism but God's authority and the universal human value of love and fellowship are also ironized. Bloom's tendency toward grandiose phantasy is mocked by the staging of a farewell ceremony as if he were a foreign dignitary, prefiguring his ascent to heaven as Elijah which concludes the chapter. His sentimentality triggers the "Love loves to love love" interpolation, and is also commented on directly by the "nameless one": "that's an almanac picture for you" (12.1476). Bloom's tendency to want to dispense popular-scientific truths at inappropriate moments is sent up by an interpolation beginning: "The distinguished scientist Herr Professor Luitpold Blumenduft tendered medical service . . ." (12.468–69). In fact, the text frazzles Bloom's identity through hyper-inflation: "Who comes through Michan's land, bedight in sable armour? O'Bloom, the son of Rory: it is he. Impervious to fear is Rory's son: he of the prudent soul" (12.215–218), making him an Irish hero with a Jewish soul. Meanwhile, it also pokes fun at Bloom's sexual ineptitude and his secret correspondence under the pseudonym Henry Flower (a translation of his name "Bloom," which is in turn translated into Portuguese): "Senhor Enrique Flor presided at the organ with his wellknown ability . . ." (12.1288–90). Thus it becomes difficult to see even pacifist Bloom as the author's direct mouthpiece.

Indeed it is difficult to determine "who is who" in this chapter. Identities seem unstable. Is the "nameless one" the "No-man" Odysseus, or is it Bloom? Is the citizen the Cyclops, or is it the nameless narrator? Is the citizen the nationalist, or is the narrator, who also uses Gaelic terms, his *alter ego*? How do we place the citizen's unlikely use of Homeric epithets: "the winebark on the winedark waterway" (12.1298)? Can we identify the characters in Homer with characters in Joyce's text, or should we see them as discursive positions perhaps no longer identified with a speaking agent but with ideological forces in the drift of the text? Should we suspend the notion of individual character? In any case, the notion of truth as ontologically rooted in fact is itself sent-up by the fabula, when Bloom, who is of Hungarian descent, is identified as the genius behind Arthur Griffith's adoption of a Hungarian model of nationalist opposition – a wildly absurd identification which is later confirmed (at least not gainsaid) by the eminent Martin Cunningham who is in a position to know. Thus unlikely rumor becomes fact: "Well, it's a fact, says John Wyse" (12.1486).

What speaks most emphatically in "Cyclops" is not the fabula or the story, but its author's delight in the sheer inventiveness of these rhetorical fireworks. The visitors to the pub sublimate their frustration with the English as speech and articulation: "Any civilization they have they stole from us. Tonguetied sons of bastards' ghosts" (12.1199–200). They clearly identify their verbal agility as a distinguishing Irish characteristic.

And Joyce makes a point of displaying a good number of different examples of it. Joyce also, and gleefully, lays on their racism to the point of parody: Bloom is called a "white-eyed kaffir" by the citizen, and the narrator, commenting on a newspaper picture of a lynching in Georgia, adds: "Gob, they ought to drown him in the sea after and electrocute and crucify him to make sure of their job" (12.1326–28). As Vincent Cheng points out, their racist speech is, apparently unwittingly, full of quotations and references to the Old Testament, so that their anti-Semitism is, in turn, deflated by their own rhetoric.[14] Rhetoric seems to subvert all subject-positions.

If it is difficult to see Bloom as Joyce's mouthpiece, it is even more difficult to view the narrator and the Citizen in that light. None of the strategies of reading based on the notion that narrative is representational work in Joyce's text. Jean-Michel Rabaté pointed out with regard to *Finnegans Wake* that "it must be understood how the voices are not reducible to psychological instances, how they are inserted into a mobilization of the potential energies of language itself, in so far as it permits the accomplishment of acts and gestures."[15] What Rabaté points out with regard to the later work, I argue with regard to "Cyclops." Just as the rhetorical excess of "Cyclops" bugs identity and truth with irony and self-contradiction, it frustrates the reader's habit of placing and reading character as subject position. The strangeness of the text spoils the possibility of our readerly identification with one of the characters. We must find a new way of relating to the text. We must identify with the rhetorical force inspiring the text; we must share and identify with its heroic and transcendent struggle for articulation.

ACTING OUT THE STEREOTYPE

Its setting in a pub may give us a clue to the strangeness of "Cyclops." The bar is the arena of licensed familiarity and enforced togetherness, and a stage for the display of verbal power. "Give us one of your prime stinkers" (12.438) is asking for a cigar in Kiernan's. This linguistic inventiveness seemingly contrasts with the ritualized behavior of the place: drinking and standing drinks. Joyce clearly brackets those parts of the text that relate to the consumption of alcohol. Uninterrupted by

---

[14] *Joyce, Race, and Empire* (Cambridge University Press, 1995)
[15] Jean-Michel Rabaté, "Lapsus ex machina," in *Post-Structuralist Joyce*, p. 87.

asides or interpolations, they slowly and meticulously describe the process of standing a drink, ordering a round. The names and sizes, the interaction with the waiter, the arrival of the drinks, how much money changes hands, and finally the process of sharing out are recorded in detail. The narrator even comments on the speed with which others drink, his own "blue mouldy" thirst, and the process of intense waiting until someone else orders. For each new round the narrative pace falls back to slow motion; and these passages punctuate the rhythm of the chapter and its rhetorical force with the heightened intensity of surrealist art. The text makes us share the addict's obsession and the group's ritual intoxication.

Intoxication is often related to politics or nationalism in Joyce. In his early favorite, "Ivy Day in the Committee Room," Joyce dramatizes the ineffectualness of Irish canvasing. Talk about the prospective visit of the English king takes the place of campaigning. The canvasers gather around the hearth of the committee room because its heat helps to uncork the bottles of stout in the absence of a corkscrew. Instead of winning votes, rhetoric serves the recital of a poem commemorating the death of Parnell. The past is occasion for empty sentimentalism, and the present is drowned in alcohol. It is as if Joyce associated the rhetoric of Irish politics with the consumption of alcohol. Irish politics is "Ireland at the Bar," to take and twist the title of a piece Joyce published in the Triestine *Piccolo della Sera* in 1907, two years after finishing "Ivy Day."

In this piece Joyce commemorates the trial of a Myles Joyce, falsely accused of participation in murder, yet convicted and executed. Since the old man did not speak English,

[t]he questioning, conducted through the interpreter, was at times comic and at times tragic. On one side was the excessively ceremonious interpreter, on the other the patriarch of a miserable tribe unused to civilized customs, who seemed stupefied by all the judicial ceremony. The magistrate said: "Ask the accused if he saw the lady that night." The question was referred to him in Irish, and the old man broke out into an involved explanation, gesticulating, appealing to the others accused and to heaven. Then he quieted down, worn out by his effort, and the interpreter turned to the magistrate and said: "He says no, 'your worship'." "Ask him if he was in that neighbourhood at that hour." The old man again began to talk, to protest, to shout, almost beside himself with the anguish of being unable to understand or to make himself understood, weeping in anger and terror. And the interpreter, again, dryly: "he says no, 'your worship'" . . . The story was told that the executioner, unable to make

the victim understand him, kicked at the miserable man's head in anger to shove it into the noose.[16]

This grim story relates to "Cyclops" in an obliquely pertinent way which becomes clear when we read its recycled version in *Finnegans Wake*. In its replay there as the trial of Festy King, the prisoner's exaggerated gesticulation and dramatic rhetorical excess is "translated" and viewed from the point of view of English prejudice as drunkenness rather than cultural difference or the effect of sheer desperation at not understanding and not being understood. The prisoner is "soaked in methylated," and intoxicated: "ambrosiaurealised" (*FW* 85.31–32).[17]

There is no doubt about Joyce's sympathy for the old "patriarch"; and he wrote the paper, in Italian, to be published in a city which would recognize the traumatic situation of cultural deprivation it addresses. Joyce's message in this piece is the misrepresentaion of the Irish as criminals by the English media. "The figure of this dumbfounded old man, a remnant of a civilization not ours, deaf and dumb before his judge, is a symbol of the Irish nation at the bar of public opinion" (*CW* 198). Just like Myles Joyce, Ireland lacks a tongue to represent itself. What the defendant's supposed drunkenness in *Finnegans Wake* suggests, however, is Joyce's *identification* with this situation of silencing. Joyce ties a symbolic knot between rhetorical excess (gesturing, emotion, volubility), the inability to represent oneself juridically or socially, and the stereotyping of the drama of the impossibility of expressing the self as drunkenness. While Joyce seems to take the English perspective in *Finnegans Wake*, depicting Myles Joyce as drunk, he does so precisely to demonstrate that Myles Joyce still cannot be given authentic voice, in order to enforce our awareness of how we, too, are locked in our preconceptions which stereotype the other. Simultanously, all of *Finnegans Wake* is the demonstration of voluble and inarticulate rhetorical excess, *enacting* the situation of Myles Joyce.

With regard to "Cyclops," we may now be in a position to postulate a tie between the rhetoric of the visitors to the bar and the general rhetorical excessiveness of the chapter as a whole. The chapter acts out and dramatizes at a more philosophical, and non-victimised level, what the emptiness of the social ritual in Kiernan's pub and in "Ivy Day" bespeak: the impossible position of the loss of a mother tongue in which

[16] *The Critical Writings of James Joyce*, ed. Ellsworth Mason and Richard Ellmann (New York: Viking Press, 1973), pp. 197–98. (Hereafter *CW*).

[17] See Jeanne A. Flood. "Joyce and the Maamtrasna Murders," *James Joyce Quarterly* 28 (1991): 879–89.

to express authentic subjectivity. Hence rhetoric and representation themselves seem to participate in the gradual process of intoxication, as if, in volubly and excessively acting out the negative self-image projected by the hegemonic mirror of the oppressor, the text can dramatize the underlying cause of the empty rhetoric of nationalism and the alcoholic ritual which takes the place of effective political action and debate.

In other words, in a novel clearly designed by its author as analog to a human body, in which each chapter is assigned its own organ, we might understand the rhetorical inflation in "Cyclops" as the mimicking intoxication of language which gradually unties itself from referentiality and truth, thus acting out the "drunkenness" of Myles Joyce as the drunkenness of the text.

If the rhetoric of "Cyclops" exceeds any stable identification, it also vitiates the analogical relationship between the individual and the collective, and the possibility of regarding the individual type exemplary of the totality of the nation. As David Lloyd argues, the dependence on "a concept of representation which requires a narrative movement between the exemplary instance and the totality that it prefigures" is, traditionally, a vital aspect of Irish identity formation. "The identification of each representative individual with the nation constitutes the people which is to claim legitimate rights to independence as an 'original,' that is, essential, entity. Consistent representation of that essence underwrites simultaneously the aesthetic originality, or autonomy, of the literary work that takes its place as an instance of the national culture."[18] In making this identificatory traffic between the individual and the nation impossible, Joyce frustrates the allegory of the nation, and cuts the ties between reference and representation. Should we conclude then, with Hugh Kenner in *Joyce's Voices*, that all the text is is words, arranged or rearranged.[19] Is it an "Irish" novel, a product of a community which has decided – since no one knows what he (or she) is talking about and all is blarney, or so Kenner suggests – that there is nothing to know *but* talk, that all is just words? Does that imply that we have no basis from which to form an opinion of the author's moral or ethical investment in his writing? Such a conclusion would fail to appreciate Joyce's puncturing of the collusion between representations of the individual and the collective in Irish aesthetics for what it is: his attempt to forge the conscience of his race, however indirectly.

---

[18] *Anomalous States*, p. 109.   [19] (London: Faber, 1978).

THE SEMIOTICS OF NARRATIVE

As the textbooks teach us, narratology, a structuralist approach to narrative based on the ancient distinction between mimesis (dramatic enactment) and diegesis (verbal summary), untwines the strand of the narrative text into two component threads, which I shall here refer to as "fabula" ("a series of logically and chronologically related events that are caused or experienced by actors") and "story" ("a fabula that is presented in a certain manner").[20] The peculiarity of "Cyclops" is that it sabotages this critical distinction, thus vitiating the hierarchizing priority of fabula over story which grounds the objectivity of representation. The interpolated passages, triggered by associations in the story independent of a tie with a speaking subject, more often than not fail to mediate or present events in the fabula. They just appear in the text, randomly fired by a connotation or a concept in the story, or an aspect of an event in the fabula. Thus the narrator's thought of the effeminate Bloom as having a soft hand under a hen triggers the following irruption: "Ga Ga Gara. Klook Klook Klook. Black Liz is our hen. She lays eggs for us. When she lays her egg she is so glad. Gara. Klook Klook Klook" (12.846–47). This crazy linguistic irruption is not part of the fabula; but how is it part of the story? Our problem is that we cannot trace the source of this linguistic utterance. Is it the narrator? But why should that violently aggressive man suddenly speak in a child's voice? Is this a child's voice, or is it the voice of an adult mimicking a child? Can we still speak here of "voice"? Is it, perhaps, an excerpt from a primer or nursery rhyme? But how did it get into this text? What is its purpose here? Do we picture a narrator who speaks in many voices, capriciously impersonating many different styles? Do we picture the utterer as a psychotic, ventriloquizing the voices in his head? Is the text utterly drunk? In short, it becomes very difficult to account for the source of the utterance if we wish to adhere to the anthropomorphic model of the narrative speech act. The tacit assumption that one individual speaker (whether character or narrator) deploys one individual voice or style which becomes his or her *signature*, and, conversely, that a stylistic signature represents the utterance of one individual speaker, does not hold. Since "Cyclops" scrambles this process of ontological anchoring of style and voice, and randomly releases voices from the bottle, we

---

[20] Mieke Bal, *Narratology: An Introduction to the Theory of Narrative* (University of Toronto Press, 1985), p. 5. It should be noted that Bal argued for the addition of a third dimension, which she calls "text."

cannot naturalize the text unless we wish to declare the narrator insane, possessed, or overtaken by a Holy Ghost and speaking in tongues. Thus the problem returns: how can we identify Joyce's meaning?

Obviously, Joyce criticism has long struggled with this question, and David Hayman's suggestion that we see the "implied author" as a split-subject, sometimes manifesting himself as an "arranger," has been widely adopted.[21] But it does not solve the problem. Indeed, it compounds the problem of accountability. We still want to know "who" arranged, and how that arrangement relates to the authorial strategy of the text. The arranger's interpolations enlist language itself into the service of racism: "Li Chi Han lovey up kissy Cha Pu Chow" (12.1495), divorcing racism from a naturalizable human agent; thus making it more difficult to fight it. Moreover, from a narratological perspective, the concept of an "arranger" is threatening because there are no markers to separate the supposed "arranger's" presence from other aspects of the text. The interpolations are not just tagged on to the story as mere appendices. There are moments when the story, and even the fabula, is carried forward and continued by means of an aside. Furthermore, the interpolations are not so easily distinguished in tone from the first-person narrator's narrative. Sometimes they seem to emerge from the mouth of one of the embedded characters (12.1438–65). Sometimes the "parodic" style of the arranger invades or snatches the function and role of the narrator:

And lo, there entered one of the clan of the O'Molloy's, a comely hero of white face yet withal somewhat ruddy, his majesty's counsel learned in the law, and with him the prince and heir of the noble line of Lambert.
–Hello, Ned.
–Hello, Alf.
–Hello, Jack.
–Hello, Joe. (12.1008–1014)

The inane simplicity of the four separate lines of "Hello, Ned," "Hello, Alf," "Hello, Jack," "Hello, Joe," following upon the inflated style of mock-romance (where the voice of the first-person narrator has been snatched by the arranger), shows that even the most innocently realistic-seeming parts of the text have been bugged by foreign invasion. The

[21] "Cyclops," in *James Joyce: Critical Essays*, ed. Clive Hart and David Hayman (Berkeley: University of California Press, 1974), p. 265: "The asides belong to a nocturnal decorum generated by a single impulse if not a single persona, a resourceful clown of many masks, a figure apparently poles apart from the self-effacing narrator. This figure may be thought of as an *arranger*, a nameless and whimsical-seeming authorial projection . . ."

hyper-simplicity of these four lines parodies the child's primer. Thus the clear distinction between the two modes of narration and interpolation, conformism to convention and the breach of expectation, mimesis and diegesis, the forward syntagmatic drive of the text and the paradigmatic thrust of the lists and catalogues, breaks down on a number of counts. In fact, Hayman's proposal of multiple perspectivity *is a defense against Joyce's meaning.* Joyce hopes to puncture the illusion of the possibility of voicing an ontological Irish presence (however fragmented or multiple) within hegemonic realist representation.

The notion of the text as *Vorstellungsrepräsentanz* explained in the previous chapter already implies a subversion of the distinction between mimesis and diegesis; and such a subversion is a political act, first of all because the identity politics of the realist mode are intimately allied to the logic of "white mythology," the radical separation of "before"/ "after," "inside"/"outside," maintained in an immutable hierarchy by means of the controlling function of the concept of a narrator, and rooted in a phonocentric concept of voice and stylistic signature.[22] In addition, as Umberto Eco points out in "Ur-Fascism," repressive regimes have a natural interest in realist discourse, the simpler the better, "to limit the instruments for complex and critical reasoning" which might criticize the official version of the natural and the real.[23] Realism and stereotype naturalize the official version of the real, the normative standard by which the different is judged deviant and defective.

But Joyce's aim is not only to frustrate a conventional mode of reading. His criticism also bears on the illusion of self-identity of the Irish, maintained by the heady alliance of narrativized romanticism, aestheticized history, and Celticist nationalism. Part of the tragedy of a colonial heritage is that one's self-identity is unconsciously predicated upon the model and example of the oppressor. In *Rebel Hearts: Journeys with the IRA's Soul,* Kevin Toolis shows us how this guerilla force has adopted the pseudo-military, petty formality of the army it is fighting.[24] It has "Officers Commanding," "POW's," "Brigades," "Active Service Units." Its funerals resemble military honours: Pistol volleys at the grave; a black beret and black gloves placed on an Irish flag draped over the coffin. Also a historical reality in connection with the IRA is the

---

[22] Lubomír Doležel, *Narrative Modes in Czech Literature* (University of Toronto Press, 1973): "the representative function of the narrator is always coupled with the *controlling* function: the narrator dominates the narrative text structure" (p. 6).

[23] *The New York Review of Books,* July 22, 1995, p. 17.   [24] (London: Picador, 1996).

constant fear and threat of betrayal in a situation where anyone might be an informer or "tout," where double-crossing is complicated by triple-crossing in a looking-glass war with an infinity of mirroring surfaces. In this light, the Citizen's desire for purity, and his objection to foreign "bugs" ("coming over here to Ireland filling the country with bugs," (12.141–42) and "strangers in our house" (12.1150–51), might be read as a defensive symptom of his unconsciously shaky sense of self-identity; and by extension we could understand Joyce's paranoid fear of betrayal, and his insistence that Irish culture endemically betrays its heroes, as similarly motivated. Nevertheless, even if history seems to have staged the lack of self-presence of the colonized self as an ontological condition, consciousness or conscience begins with the recognition of the situation as it is, not with the projection upon others of one's own handed-down identity, or the flight into nostalgic constructions of pure origin. Thus the puncturing of realist representation in "Cyclops" – like the "drunkenness" of Myles Joyce in the Festy King trial in *Finnegans Wake* – also aims at the puncturing of the illusionary defense of Irish nationalist purist self-identification. The "bugs" and "strangers" already inhabit the self; they have also invaded authorial subjectivity.

To clarify this point I should like to turn to the conclusion of the chapter, where prejudice and aggression climax in an outburst of the Citizen's violence against the supposedly stingy Jew Leopold Bloom, who fails to stand a round. While Bloom attempts to escape the Citizen's persecution in a carriage, the story modulates into a passage which is at once the rhetorical apotheosis of the stylistic peculiarities of this narrative:

And the last we saw was the bloody car rounding the corner and old sheepface on it gesticulating and the bloody mongrel after it with his lugs back for all he was bloody well worth to tear him limb from limb. Hundred to five! Jesus, he took the value of it out of him, I promise you.

When, lo, there came about them all a great brightness and they beheld the chariot wherein He stood ascend to heaven. And they beheld Him in the chariot, clothed upon in the glory of the brightness, having raiment as of the sun, fair as the moon and terrible that for awe they durst not look upon Him. And there came a voice out of heaven, calling: *Elijah! Elijah!* And He answered with a main cry: *Abba! Adonai!* And they beheld Him even Him, ben Bloom Elijah, amid clouds of angels ascend to the glory of the brightness at an angle of fortyfive degrees over Donohoe's in Little Green street like a shot off a shovel. (*U* 12.1906–18)

The passage begins in what we have learned to identify as the voice of the nameless narrator ("the bloody car," "old sheepface" Bloom). Suddenly, however, it modulates into Biblical idiom and style ("When, lo, there came about them all a great brightness"). Since the object of description is Bloom's escape, the stylistic change would seem motivated by the event. If so, it is the event "seen through" (focalized through) the eyes of a Bloom who is no longer thinking like a citizen of Dublin but like a Jew, and who "speaks" like a Biblical prophet. Thus the narrator's discourse is snatched by this Biblical voice which represents the event of the escape of the jarvey around the corner as if it were an ascension to heaven.

There are several problems here: Not only is there the shifting of stylistic register which is hard to explain. Of course, Bloom may, perhaps unconsciously, be living out Messianic or other grandiose fantasies. On the other hand, this turn to biblical idiom makes Bloom into a "stranger in the house." It compounds the racist exclusion practiced by the Citizen. More worrisome even is Joyce's subversion of the referential value and truth of the fabula. No such event as an apotheosis is taking place. The notion of Bloom's ascension is suggested by the Biblical style which traditionally relates such an event. Thus it is the stereotypical association between style and the subject matter it conveys which produces this suggestion. In short, Joyce pushes the inquiry into the relationship between discursive style and its object to the point where the traditional ontological priority reverses. It is as if discursive register and style *generated* fabula and event instead of just *mediating* it. Connotation produces discourse and reality – as in repressive regimes.

In an article dating from 1981, Jonathan Culler points out that the relation between fabula and story is not ontologically anchored. Thus narratives often subvert the hierarchical priority of the event to its narration in the act of narrative itself.[25] A notable example of such a situation is Sophocles' *Oedipus Rex* in which Oedipus' guilt of the murder of his father is gradually established by means of circumstantial evidence. We might say that the story "produces" the event. "Oedipus leaps to the conclusion, and every reader leaps with him, that he is in fact the murderer of Laius. His conclusion is based not on new evidence concerning a past deed, but on the force of meaning, the interweaving of prophecies and the demands of narrative coherence."[26] Culler's conclusion is that every narrative text predicates itself upon an interaction

---

[25] "Story and Discourse in the Analysis of Narrative," in *The Pursuit of Signs: Semiotics, Literature, Deconstruction* (London: Routledge, 1981), pp. 169–87.   [26] *Ibid.*, p. 174.

of two different forms of narrative logic: "one which insists upon the causal efficacy of origins and the other of which denies their causal efficacy." Although "in contradiction . . . they are essential to the way in which the narrative functions. One logic assumes the primacy of events; the other treats the events as the products of meanings."[27] Thus narrative hinges on the interaction of two modes of perception – a referential logic which departs from the primacy of the events, and a discursive or semiotic one which derives signification from the coherence and internal logic of narrative construction.

It is the peculiarity of the detective novel to have thematized the interaction of these two modes, as Peter Brooks has made so clear.[28] The reason that I pause to reconsider here, is because Brooks's discussion alerted us to the problematic connection between narrative structure and Freud's theory of transference. In the course of his career, Freud was increasingly inclined to sacrifice a referential logic to a discursive or semiotic one. The question of whether seduction by the parent had actually taken place or not made way for the postulate of the primal fantasy of seduction. The narrative of his own past, slowly pieced together by the patient in analysis, was curative, not owing to its factual or historical correctness, but because it was intellectually and emotionally meaningful to the patient. Here the internal structure and logic of signification, what I call the "symbolic," works to lend "truth" to a fictional or tropological event. Although Freud perhaps never chose one mode to the exclusion of the other, the notion of transference puts great pressure on a referential logic. In the situation of transference, where the patient perceives qualities and attributes of people he knew long ago as belonging to his therapist, the referential primacy of fact is sublated by *Nachträglichkeit*. The same holds for the victim of trauma who can perceive the presence of past events only in and as their displaced repetition in the present. I suggest that Joyce, in "Cyclops," deliberately leads his reader into the maze of a world in which a discursive or semiotic logic seems to have ousted realistic referentiality, because the traumatic condition of imprisonment in the hegemony of the oppressor's language entails such a preclusion of the priority of fact.

Just like Myles Joyce, whose "drunkenness," so Joyce leads us to believe, may have been suggested to an English court because that court had its own pre-established notion of reality, Joyce's reader enters an inescapably discursive world in which logic and fact are shown up as

---

[27] *Ibid.*, p. 178.
[28] *Reading for the Plot: Design and Intention in Narrative* (New York and Oxford: Clarendon Press, 1984).

resting upon conventional, already existing, ideological associations over which he or she has no control. As I have repeatedly hinted, this universe of discourse is not to be identified with Lacan's symbolic order, because Joyce shows us not just the hegemony of "Language," but the traumatic effect of the situation in which the colonial oppressor's perspective constitutes reality. Joyce introduces the reader into the groundlessness of the colonial symbolic.

Thus, should the reader wish to naturalize this apotheosis, he or she is prevented by the complexity of the text. This sentimental self-image of the persecuted Jew as prophet and avatar of Christ partakes of the hyperbolic self-inflation of Celticist romanticism too. All narratives of the self (national or personal) are hybridized and stereotyped as already clichéd, stylistically, and structurally in terms of types of event and ending. Thus the voice of prophecy is in turn snatched back by another aspect of what the reader has learned to identify as Bloom's complex discursive identity, his "sane" and measured scientific interest which propels the text into describing his imaginary ascension to heaven with the mathematical precision of a carpenter's manual: "at an angle of fortyfive degrees." This stylistic unit is in turn displaced by the words "like a shot off a shovel," which suggest a return to the voice of the vulgar narrator. Thus the concluding sentence of this chapter features three distinct voices within the compass of a minimal narrative unit.

Joyce's *praxis* is not merely the reversal of the hierarchy of fabula and story, vitiating the concrete objectivity usually contributed to "the fact" of the event. It ruins the truth-value of any narrative construction of identity, whether referential or semiotic-discursive. His hybridization especially pre-empts the possibility of the "small personal voice" needed to constitute one's sense of "self." There is no stable "self," no consistent personal voice in *Ulysses* because all elements of human experience are already deprived of identity by the reader's awareness of the clichés of a collective cultural discourse which anticipatingly contaminates the self-presence of any narrative. Of a fortuitous escape we speak in biblical terms, of a fashion show in the style of glossy magazines, of prayer in devotional terms (preferably in Latin), of a conflict in legal terms or in the jargon of the boxing match and so forth. Thus style, always already cliché, is generated by the associative linking of language and style to event and concept. Cowboys belong in Westerns, strong handsome men in dime novels, castles and Rolls Royces in television soap, pathetic females in Victorian novels, subterranean passages and walking statues in Gothic fiction, shepherds in pastoral or the Bible, heroic liberators in popular mythology or naive versions of history, stepmothers (at least the evil variant) in fairy tales, etc. Obviously, not all these examples derive from *Ulysses*; but the principle does. It is as if *Ulysses* forces us into the awareness of a collective cultural-stylistic memory – a memory that is a reservoir of stereotyped knowledge, classification, interpretation, and meaning, which robs us of the possibility of expressing an authentic self, because that self is never rooted ontologically, but caught in the process of infinite referral of the language of the tribe.

Reading *Ulysses* we have become narrative fashion victims. All meaning shows itself as culturally determined connotation instead of denotation; and Joyce seems to have led us down the gardenpath into a Peircean universe of infinite semiosis in which the original "object" of representation "can be nothing but a representation of which the first is the interpretant."[29] Just as Flaubert left us a *Dictionary of Received Ideas*, Joyce has left us in *Ulysses* an Index of the Hegemonically Meaningful Styles which colonize our consciousness.[30]

Joyce's reader is tutored to become so alert to the presence of significant style, ideological stance, associated connotations, that he or she begins to perceive reality itself in terms of differences without ontological anchoring. Thus the effect of reading "Cyclops" repeats one of the paralyzing effects of colonization: it spoils the power narrative traditionally has to constitute a self. According to David Lloyd, this effect is a good thing. Joyce's style "insists on a deliberate stylization of dependence and inauthenticity, a stylization of the hybrid status of the colonized subject as of the colonized culture, their internal adulteration and the strictly parodic modes that they produce in every sphere."[31] What Joyce makes his reader experience with painful clarity is the impossible position of the minority writer: the work, always stereotyped, is either derivative or defective. Joyce's aim in writing *Ulysses* may have been to spoil the mirror of representation once and for all by raising his reader's consciousness of the ideological constructedness of what seems natural and realistic.

Here we may have arrived at a point where we can detect a form of intentionality, an agency however muffled. "Cyclops" demonstrates that narration is not just representation, but can itself be a form of terrorist action. The action performed by "Cyclops" is an attack on the representional value of language. It anaesthetizes the living force of

---

[29] Umberto Eco, *A Theory of Semiotics* (Bloomington: Indiana University Press, 1977), p. 69.
[30] In a letter to Harriet Shaw Weaver of July 20, 1919, while writing "Cyclops," Joyce wrote that he experienced the progression of styles of the book as a kind of "scorching" "sandblast" leaving a "burnt up field." *Letters of James Joyce*, vol. 1, ed. Stuart Gilbert (London: Faber, 1957), pp. 128–29.
[31] *Anomalous States*, p. 110.

"Shakespeare," the cultural emblem and father of English representation. Perhaps the Cyclops in Joyce's chapter of that name is not the
Citizen, but the monolithic presence of the hegemonic language from
which there is no escape. It may be that the Odysseus-figure is not
Bloom, but, as Jung suggested, the wily and hidden manipulator of
textuality who offers the forgery of the narrative of the Nameless One as
a *Vorstellungsrepräsentanz* for the subaltern self-identity that cannot be
narrated, the voice that can never resonate with full self-presence or
meaning. Perhaps what must be blinded is not the Cyclops' eye – the
possibility of perception – but the authority of his English expression, his
speech. We should not forget that the discourses which Joyce introduces
into the text of "Cyclops" are the public ones of literature, the newspaper, the yellow press, the tabloid, the police gazette, the textbook,
historical romance – in short the collectivity of written media which
constitutes the self-mirroring image of culture, the language which
constitutes cultural community.

THE PRESENCE OF THE VOID

The question which asserts itself is how or where Joyce found a point of
identification which made it possible to defy the hegemony. One of the
ways in which the Irish maintained a sense of self-identity was by means
of an analogy with the Old-Testament Jews and their bondage in Egypt.
Joyce's special hero is the figure of Moses whose presence pervades
Ulysses.[32] The "Aeolus" chapter, which especially resonates with references to Moses, includes a quoted rendition of John F. Taylor's famous
speech which draws upon this parallel between the Jews and the Irish. It
is the only extended passage from *Ulysses* which Joyce, who knew
Taylor's speech by heart, left us recorded in his own voice. The stirring
response countering the Egyptian temptation to assimilate and relinquish attempts at constructing a national identity somehow also seems to
resonate with Joyce's deeper meaning:

---

[32] Ira B. Nadel, *Joyce and the Jews* (London: Macmillan, 1989), especially the section "Moses and
Messianism" of the chapter "Joyce and the Jewish Typology," pp. 85–139. Nadel documents the
symbolic function of Moses for the Irish, as well as the place he occupied in Joyce's texts and his
life. Also see Jeanne A. Flood, "Joyce and the Maamtrasna Murders," for a discussion of the
patriarch Moses. Flood argues that Joyce "claims the English language" and in "the verbal
abundance of the book, he undoes the defect of all the failed patriarchs, including the murdered
Myles Joyce." The importance of Jewishness in Joyce's construction of an alternative authorial
identity is argued by Neil R. Davison, *James Joyce, "Ulysses", and the Construction of Jewish Identity*
(Cambridge University Press, 1995).

—But, ladies and gentlemen, had the youthful Moses listened to and accepted that view of life, had he bowed his head and bowed his will and bowed his spirit before that arrogant admonition he would never have brought the chosen people out of their house of bondage, nor followed the pillar of the cloud by day. He would never have spoken with the Eternal amid lightnings on Sinai's mountaintop nor ever have come down with the light of inspiration shining in his countenance and bearing in his arms the tables of the law, graven in the language of the outlaw. (U 7.862–70)

The figure of Moses offers not only a point of nationalist and personal identification, it re-introduces the theme of representation in a different mode. The Moses of the Old Testament stands for the insistence on the divine prohibition on mimetic representation (making graven or molten images of the venerated object), in the face of the unregenerate persistence of the Israelites in their adoration of iconic idols. Moses' law graven in the "language of the outlaw" embodies the prescription of a non-specular, non-mimetic conceptualization of origin, engraved in abstract symbols. Even the presence of the voice is replaced by inscription. The Mosaic author has absconded from the theatre of this world to leave us only the irremovably codified symbolic script, presented as indexical. This prohibition on representation, and the disappearance of the voice, is itself figured in a secondary prohibition on pronouncing the Divine Name which may be written and observed, but not spoken.

The Mosaic language of the law is a symbolic language, premarked by the void of the direct voice, as is Joyce's own *Vorstellungsrepräsentanz* in "Cyclops" which, while it begins with the first-person-narrative "I," effaces the dash which indicates direct speech in Joyce's texts (*U* 12.1). Thus Joyce's peculiar textuality already re-enacts the linguistic subject-position of Moses' God himself: present as the absence of the voice, the written substitution of its presence.[33] With one difference however: if there is uncertainty about the provenance of Moses' tables – "are they transcendental or historical, authentic or forged?" – we have absolute

---

[33] The metaphor of trauma finds a transpersonal analog here: The individual who cannot remember the event is forced to re-enact and re-count its absence as a presence until the unassimilable experience is symbolized, perhaps, eventually, thus emphasizing the void at the point of origin. Just so the Jewish people, dedicated to the Unnamable and Non-Representable God, live out the absence of His physical presence in its devotion to His law, in the hope that eventually a Messiah will bring redemption. Both narratives place the point of origin outside history, as an unassimilable real kernel which cannot be represented – a void. Since the Irish nation, too, lacks a historical origin, we have a situation of structural overlap between the narratives of self-identity of *A Portrait of the Artist*, of Irish nationalism, and Judaism – each story in its own way is predicated upon a void, each enacts the real otherness of that origin as a quest for a (national) destiny, a (personal) vocation, a (historical) fulfillment of prophecy, which, considering the presence of the void at the point of origin, seems like a retroactive back-projection on the empty position of origin.

certainty about the source of Joyce's text. Joyce occupies the empty subject-position of the God of his creation. Furthermore, the analogy has Homeric associations. In constructing his rewritten version of the epic, Joyce takes the impossible subject position of that unnameable and non-embodied object – a "no-body," a "non-entity," an "*ou-tis*" ("not-someone"), in the literal sense of a non-embodied presence. But whereas Moses brings the tables of the law in the Name-of-the-Father, Joyce, who does not write in the name of anyone or anything else, usurps that function for himself.[34] The place of the Name-of-the-Father is the place of the phallus, which, transcendent as it is, gives significance and rooted meaning to origin and paternity; and Lacanians believe that Joyce "foreclosed" it, whereas I argue that his writing allowed him the phantasy of usurpation.[35] In usurping that transcendent-authorial place and that function, Joyce transforms the impossibility of the colonized personal voice into a Heideggerian query as to the possibility and rise of the voice itself, and hollows the "ground of voice" as the place from which he will speak. Indeed, Joyce seemingly performs the impossible feat of the son turning himself into the Father. If, as David Lloyd claims, the "principal organizing metaphor of Irish nationalism is that of a proper paternity, of restoring the lineage of the fathers in order to repossess the motherland,"[36] Joyce, realizing that there is no point of origin, no memory or history to restore, prefers to constitutively inhabit that origin himself, pre-emptying and paralyzing the oppressive paternity of the English language, its false and self-imposed title to Name-of-the-Father. Inhabiting the void, occupying the transcendental point from which the tables of the law are issued, Joyce will be the Moses of the conscience of his race, taking it upon himself to cover over the absence of a father (historically or theologically) whose presence would legitimize his word, by forging a paternal signature. As Derrida argues, Joyce's "he war" (*FW* 258.12) is a form of signing himself "God," the signifier without signified.[37]

In *Moses and Monotheism*, after arguing that the name of "Moses" denotes Egyptian origin, Freud postulates that the "savage Semites took

---

[34] Valentine Cunningham, "Renoving That Bible: The Absolute Text of (Post) Modernism," in *The Theory of Reading*, ed. Frank Gloversmith (Brighton: Harvester, 1984), points out that the concept of *écriture* "has merely transposed the empirical characteristics of an author to a transcendental anonymity" (p. 1).

[35] Foreclosure or repudiation [*Verwerfung*] is different from repression [*Verdrängung*]. The first is a total expelling of the idea from the unconscious, whereas repression safely stores it there. In contradistinction to repression, associated with neurosis, foreclosure is a more risky refusal of symbolization associated with psychosis. Lacan understood Joyce as an example of a "psychosis without symptoms."   [36] *Anomalous States*, p. 105.   [37] *Post-Structuralist Joyce*, p. 157.

fate into their own hands and rid themselves of their tyrant."[38] Thus the parricidal *Ur*-murder postulated by Freud twenty-five years earlier in *Totem and Taboo*, signaling the moment of the constitution of a fraternal symbolic culture (language and writing) to replace brute physical force, is repeated as the foundational moment of Jewish history and destiny (and of Christianity as well). In fact, Freud argues, Jewish culture is based on the disavowal of the memory of the trauma of the murder, which in turn leads to the neurotic symptom of monotheism.[39] In assuming a place outside the symbolic structure of narrative, one which takes the empty place of the murdered father which should properly be taken by his totem, his Name, Joyce seems to want to go back on the entrance into history as Freud sketched it. It is as if he is disavowing the irrevocable breach, the irremediable divide between pre-history and history, trauma and narrative, in order to construct a totalizing vision:

What race, or what language (if we except the few whom a playful will seems to have preserved in ice, like the people of Iceland) can boast of being pure today? And no race has less right to utter such a boast than the race now living in Ireland. Nationality (if it really is not a convenient fiction like so many others to which the scalpels of present-day scientists have give the coup de grâce) must find its reason for being rooted in something that surpasses and transcends and informs changing things like blood and the human word. The mystic theologian who assumed the pseudonym of Dionysius, the pseudo-Areopagite, says somewhere, "God has disposed the limits of nations according to his angels," and this probably is not a purely mystical concept. Do we not see that in Ireland the Danes, the Firbolgs, the Milesians from Spain, the Norman invaders, and the Anglo-Saxon settlers have united to form a new entity, one might say under the influence of a local deity? (*CW* 165–66)

It seems to me that Joyce constructs his meta-identity in order to form a "not purely mystical," written, historical "new entity" which retroactively confirms the Ur-intended apotheosis of a Celtic soul, with Joyce as its "local deity." Instead of just adulterating narrative to make the tool unfit for the narrativization of Irish identity, Joyce inflates its potential and reach to encompass all different voices and subject positions, so that narrative, no longer representational but synonymous with the voice of collective, transnational (not just English) culture, appears to occupy the transcendent subject position of the Name-of-the-Father.

Crucial is the fact that the text must incorporate "the great divide" (an Irish euphemism for death), the irreparable breach between pre-history and history, trauma and text, real and symbolic, into its own

---

[38] *SE* 23, p. 47.   [39] Caruth, *Unclaimed Experience*.

folds. Joyce's textuality must come to terms with "castration." As we shall see in the chapters which follow, *Ulysses* and *Finnegans Wake* are best understood as attempts to encrypt "castration," or the ontological void, *into* textual structure. Joyce's language of the outlaw which has no origin in a human voice, because like Moses' tables of the law, it is already written or engraved at the point of origin, uses its *materiality as a location in which to try and bury the threat of "castration" contained in death and sexual difference.* Thus the impetus of Joyce's later works is to encapsulate the lack of presence and self-identity of his *Dubliners,* and to incorporate the suggestion of trauma of *A Portrait of the Artist* into a more complex, transcendently self-conscious, fetishized form of textuality, without working the trauma through or transforming traumatic experience into memory. Joyce is like Woody Allen, flaunting the psychiatric interpretation of his symptoms while lacking the insight that will abolish them, but his work has a tragic dimension that Allen's lacks. Joyce invents a way of encrypting the traumatic wound of the moment of entry into a kind of language that transforms the pain trauma into a productive force, attended with a hilariously comic effect owing to the realization of a desperate mastery. Thus he stages the non-representability of the traumatic experience as the real condition of narrative – all narrative. This move is part of what Lacan speaks of as Joyce's "sinthome." Perhaps we should understand Joyce's identification with religious leaders like Moses, martyrs like St. Stephen, or even the figure of Christ himself, not as the symptom of narcissistic self-inflation, but as the indication of the pain involved in bearing the openness at the heart of the self. To me, Joyce represents an example of the inability to constitute a stable self-identity, without surrendering to despair, but attempting to transcend *sparagmos* by displacing it upon the text as an extension of the self, and transforming it into sovereign laughter.[40]

HIGH MODERNISM/POSTSTRUCTURALISM, AND THE DIFFERENCE OF JOYCE

How is this helpful in articulating the subaltern's voice? The inflation of narrative authority to coincide with that of the Name-of-the-Father would seem to deprive any voice of individual specificity and presence, and might be understood as the re-inscription of the stifling hegemony

---

[40] Robert Jay Lifton, *The Broken Connection: On Death and the Continuity of Life* (New York: Simon and Schuster, 1979), provides a description of the sense of inner death of survivors of historical cataclysms, and of psychiatric patients.

of English. To argue the specificity of Joyce's writing, it may best to establish a comparison with other postmodern works, because in such a comparison we may begin to hear the resonance of the "voice" and the "soul" of Joyce's affective investment in textuality, resonating with what Lacan spoke of as its "*jouissance.*" I have selected a passage from Donald Barthelme's *Snow White*, since it is a retelling of a traditional narrative like *Ulysses*, and it demonstratively flaunts its suggestion that language and representation are always already written. Also like "Cyclops," *Snow White* refuses to conform to the narrative convention that all linguistic signs in a text can be traced back to a definite point of singular origin:

Hubert wanted to go back to the dog races. But we made him read his part, the outer part where the author is praised and the price quoted. We like books that have a lot of *dreck* in them, matter which presents itself as not wholly relevant (or indeed, at all relevant) but which, carefully attended to, can supply a kind of "sense" of what is going on. This "sense" is not to be obtained by reading between the lines (for there is nothing there, in those white spaces) but by reading the lines themselves – looking at them and so arriving at a feeling not of satisfaction exactly, that is too much to expect, but of having read them, of having "completed" them. "Please don't talk," Snow White said. "Say nothing. We can begin now. Take off the pajamas." Snow White took off her pajamas. Henry took off his pajamas. Kevin took off his pajamas. Hubert took off his pajamas. Clem took off his pajamas. Dan took off his pajamas. Edward took off his pajamas. Bill refused to take off his pajamas. "Take off your pajamas Bill," Snow White said. Everyone looked at Bill's pajamas. "No, I won't," Bill said. "I will not take off my pajamas." "Take off your pajamas Bill," everyone said. "No. I will not." Everyone looked again at Bill's pajamas. Bill's pajamas filled the room, in a sense. Those yellow crêpe-paper pajamas.[41]

Beginning with an impersonal, seemingly third-person observation, the text reveals itself in the second sentence as narrated by a narrative instance who refers to itself as "we." One's first assumption is that we are dealing here with an individual who relates the experience of a group – one of the seven dwarves who voices the collective rejection of Bill's individualist leanings. Reading on, we soon note that the speaker of the word "we" cannot be any single dwarf, nor Snow White herself, since each of them is named individually in the third person in the ritual of their collective disrobing. Unless we assume that one of the dwarves, perhaps out of an exaggerated attempt at objectivity (as in Henry Adams' *Autobiography*) or narcissistic self-involvement (Mr. Duffy in "A

---

[41] (1967; repr. New York: Atheneum, 1984), pp. 105–06. The book appeared in slightly different form in *The New Yorker*.

Painful Case") composes and relates stories about himself in the third person, we are forced to the conclusion that the narrator is not one individual human agent, but the voice of a group, a collective consciousness which transcends or subsumes individual subjectivity.

Such a reading makes ironic sense, not only because of the theme of collectivity exemplified in the passage, but because it confirms Christopher Lasch's interpretation of *Snow White* as the product of a reductive linguistic democracy, American narcissism, mass-mentality, and consumer-culture.[42] I shall not argue for or against the aesthetic merits of Barthelme's text,[43] because my interest in it is different: the problem of the oddness of the "we." What to make of the passage "We like books that have a lot of *dreck* in them . . ."? Is this an interior group-monologue, or is it an extradiegetic comment to the implied reader? In fact, that is how the passage has been read.[44] The sentence about *dreck* has been taken as the author's metanarrative commentary on his own text.

The problem of interpretation is compounded when we look at the coherence of the text as a whole: in between narrative stretches we find a questionnaire to the reader, moral maxims printed in capital letters, a lecture on the Romantic poets, newspaper headlines and story titles. What Barthelme's montage of different forms of discourse suggests is that we can only find a unifying principle in this rag bag if we picture the text as the product of a collective entity, the mass-discourse of sixties' American culture; more precisely: *written* culture, its self-mediation in and as text. The communal language of the tribe would no longer seem a shared speech, but the "universe of *printed* disourse," to also appropriate a term the text itself provides. The thematics of the text also force us toward such an elaboration. To the dwarves reading *is* action, it is their daily activity. Their sexualization (the fabula relates the promiscuous access of the dwarves to the indifferent Snow White), is more properly a textualization. Just as to Snow White housekeeping has become "bookkeeping" (the dusting and restoring of expensive bindings), to the dwarves pajamas equal the dustwrappers of yellow (French? sexy?) books: "Bill's pajamas filled the room, in a sense. Those yellow crêpe-paper pajamas." Elsewhere we note that participation in

[42] *The Culture of Narcissism: American Life in an Age of Diminishing Expectations* (New York: Warner Books, 1979), pp. 74–75 ff.
[43] Robert A. Morace, "Donald Barthelme's *Snow White*: The Novel, the Critics, and the Culture," *Critique: Studies in Modern Fiction* 26 (1984): 1–10.
[44] Maurice Couturier and Régis Durand, *Donald Barthelme* (London: Methuen, 1982).

group activity is seen as "reading" one's "part," even if that part is merely the blurb: "the outer part where the author is praised and the price quoted." In the final, reductive analysis, Snow White with her white body, the great many beauty spots which Barthelme fetishistically displays in a vertical row on the first page as if they were the holes punched to bind the paper, may be taken as an image of the medium of print itself. Thus the novel becomes a deliberate dislocation of the assumption that narrative mediates presence, a personal voice, represents a fabula, or tells a story, however fictional. *Snow White* is a self-reflexive text which irreducibly narrates its own constitution as printed medium. As in "Cyclops," it becomes impossible to distinguish between mimesis and diegesis because everything is "already written." Not surprisingly, the book closes with an echo of Bloom's apotheosis:

> THE APOTHEOSIS OF SNOW WHITE
> SNOW WHITE RISES INTO THE SKY
> THE HEROES DEPART IN SEARCH OF
> A NEW PRINCIPLE
> HEIGH-HO

What we see here, I contend, is the ghostly voice of Joyce in late modernist and postmodernist writing (note the subtitle of Craig Hansen Werner's *Paradoxical Resolutions: American Fiction since James Joyce*[45]). Instead of taking my example from Barthelme, I could have turned to Sorrentino, Barth, Pynchon, or even Norman Mailer. What all these authors seem to associate with Joyce is "the usedupness of old forms, the difficulty of impressing readers who are all too familiar with conventional techniques, and perhaps most important[ly] that 'the old analogy between Author and God, novel and world, can no longer be employed unless as a false analogy.'"[46]

The paradox of late modernist or postmodernist self-consciousness about representation is that it destroys the communicative effectiveness of the medium. Narrative no longer constructs or mediates knowledge, but merely flexes its own operative principles, as does Barthelme's *Snow White* which fails to move, even fails to offend us. It employs language as empty gesture rather than as communication. It does not *speak*. Apparently, when the prospective hegemonic author looks into Joyce's cracked looking-glass with the intention of emulation and without the

---

[45] (Urbana: Illinois University Press, 1982).
[46] Beth A. Boehm, "Educating Readers," in *Reading Narrative: Form, Ethics, Ideology*, ed. James Phelan (Columbus: Ohio State University Press, 1989), p. 107. Boehm is quoting Barth.

protection of a radically distinctive style of his own, he freezes into
speechlessness as if he had been shown the head of the Medusa. As we
shall see in the next chapter, that is what Joyce does: revealing the site of
"castration" of language. But instead of the head of the female monster,
Perseus–Joyce's trophy may be the paralyzed face of Shakespeare. Thus
Joyce's writing places his successors in the position of the inhabitants of
Dublin as described in *Dubliners*: paralyzed. Like the boy in "Araby"
who must admit the futility of his attempt at romantic escape – at
"fiction" – the emulating reader of Joyce comes to "see" him/herself
through the disenchanting eye of the other (the repertoire of cultural
images), as a creature "driven and derided by vanity"[47] at the attempt to
wish to express an authentic self in a language which is always already
the property and instrument of a hegemonic collectivity. Joyce not only
writes out those effects of colonialism which nationalism refuses to
perceive or allow expression. He visits an intellectual form of its imprisoning self-consciousness on the white, male, Anglo-American
authors of the sixties and early seventies. Thus Joyce makes ghosts of his
successors as well as his precursors. Derrida has a point, after all.

INTENTIONALITY

There is a difference between Joyce's works and the novels of Barth,
Barthelme, Sorrentino, and others which resides in its emotional intentionality. There is more than one form of intentionality. When we ask:
"What did Shakespeare intend?" we refer to what the author meant to
say *by means of* his words. This is the construction of intention labelled
"the intentional fallacy" by Wimsatt and Beardsley.[48] There is another
form of intention, however. In our everyday experience in the world we
can immediately tell whether we are dealing with a "difficult" person, a
hysteric whose utterances are to be distrusted, a person who takes
himself or herself too seriously, or someone who just wants attention.
Here the intention of the language use does not formally reside in its
syntax or vocabulary, but in the social-psychological manner in which
the speaking subject is situated in language, expressed in tone, pitch, and
rhythm. Instinctively and unconsciously, we ask when we meet another
person: "You're telling me that, but what do you want with it, what are
you aiming at?" – the question epitomized by Lacan in "Che vuoi?"[49] A

[47] James Joyce, *Dubliners* (New York: Viking, 1967), p. 35. Hereafter *D* and cited by page number.
[48] "The Intentional Fallacy," *Sewanee Review* 54 (1946): 568–88.
[49] Žižek, *The Sublime Object*, pp. 87–130.

well-known demonstration of this gap between intentionality as we commonly use the term in the academy (enunciation) and the psychoanalytic variant I here propose (utterance), is to be heard in Mr Collins' proposal to Elizabeth Bennet in *Pride and Prejudice*. His true intention is not the expressed one to woo her – he departs from the foregone conclusion that she cannot but accept. His speech is a rhetorical demonstration of his own sycophantic self-importance. He seeks echoing confirmation. Any reader recognizes this immediately. Using the terms of speech-act theory, we might denote this gap between enunciation and utterance as the difference between locution and the illucutionary force of a given utterance.

Returning to the difference between Joyce and Barthelme from this perspective, it seems to me that Barthelme's fundamentally self-conscious irony generates an effect of futility; it lacks illocutionary force, appeal, affect. It is postmodern pastiche amputated of the satiric impulse, without any ulterior moral indignation – lacking the vision of a different and better order of things. The author is the ironic but nonetheless complicitous impersonal scriptor of the symbolic order, of a world of signs. He seems to close the gap between enunciation and utterance. Joyce on the other hand turns his alienated futility, his angry sense of lack into defiant anger and outrage with a Swiftian *saeva indignatio*. It is the fierce emotion behind the words which produces stylization and a dagger-like verbal precision which makes slapstick comedy out of "Literature" and its claim to the inscription of transcendent meaning. Thus it opens up an extra communicative but non-articulable dimension which Barthelme precisely forecloses.[50]

Not only is Joyce hilariously funny, his comedy rests in the suggestion that the symbolic order is itself structured around a lack, around an unclaimable, unassimilable moment just as Joyce's own traumatic texts. In his work this possibility is metonymized thematically as a fascination with the things people must repress in order to keep functioning, the things they cannot express for reasons of social acceptability, the things they cannot find ways of saying, or bring themselves to say. Joyce's stories are "peppered with ellipses" from end to end. Before I return to "Cyclops" to substantiate my suggestion, I should like to quote from Žižek's *The Sublime Object of Ideology*, which presents the late Lacan of the

---

[50] In "Humor" (*SE* 21, pp. 159–67), Freud points out that humor is by no means resigned: "The ego refuses to be distressed by the provocations of reality, to let itself be compelled to suffer. It insists that it cannot be affected by the traumas of the external world; it shows, in fact, that such traumas are no more than occasions for it to gain pleasure" (p. 162).

confrontation with Joyce on the subject of the lack in the other:

> Today, it is a commonplace that the Lacanian subject is divided, crossed-out, identical to a lack in a signifying chain. However, the most radical dimension of Lacanian theory lies not in recognizing this fact but in realizing that the big Other, the symbolic order itself, is also *barré*, crossed-out, by a fundamental impossibility, structured around an impossible/traumatic kernel, around a central lack. Without this lack in the Other, the Other would be a closed structure and the only possibility open to the subject would be his radical alienation in the Other. So it is precisely this lack in the Other which enables the subject to achieve a kind of "de-alienation" called by Lacan *separation*: not in the sense that the subject experiences that now he is separated for ever from the object by the barrier of language, but that *the object is separated from the Other itself*, that the Other itself "hasn't got it," hasn't got the final answer – that is to say, is in itself blocked, desiring; that there is also a desire of the Other. This lack in the Other gives the subject – so to speak – a breathing space, it enables him to avoid the total alienation in the signifier not by filling out this lack but by allowing him to identify himself, his own lack, with the lack in the Other.[51]

What brings Žižek, following Lacan, to this conclusion, is an argument beginning with the postulate of "castration." In the entry into language the body is submitted to a "castration" which evacuates enjoyment from it. The body lives on, "dismembered" and "mortified." This postulate in turn brings with it the conclusion that the symbolic order of the signifier is radically heterogeneous from that of enjoyment; "any accordance between them is structurally impossible":

> As soon as the field of the signifier is penetrated by enjoyment it becomes inconsistent, porous, perforated – the enjoyment is what cannot be symbolized, its presence in the field of the signifier can be detected only through the holes and inconsistencies of this field, so the only possible signifier of enjoyment is the signifier of the lack in the Other, the signifier of its inconsistency.[52]

As we noted, it was precisely the example of *Finnegans Wake*'s excessiveness which provided Lacan with an example of the penetration of enjoyment into the field of the signifier. Lacan's term for the kind of enjoyment which is excessive and inexplicable is *jouissance*. The term has a sexual connotation, and seems, in Lacan's work, especially related to the "otherness" of the feminine which is outside the other. Through that relation to the feminine, the term *jouissance* resonates with more meaning than just "excessive, climactic pleasure." Lacan's pun "j'ouis sens" [I hear meaning] implicates the sense of a meaning outside meaning in his use of the term *jouissance*.[53] Note the emphasis on "hearing," resonating

[51] *The Sublime Object*, p. 122.   [52] *Ibid*.
[53] Stephen Melville, "Psychoanalysis and the Place of *Jouissance*," *Critical Inquiry* 13 (1987): 348–71.

with Stephen's obsession with the ear. It is a "meaning" which cannot be formalized as such, which does not bear direct linguistic expression, but which rings in the laughter attending the pleasure of the symptom. In his reading of Bataille in *Writing and Difference*, Derrida points to Bataille's notion of laughter as: that which "makes the difference between lordship and sovereignty shine, without *showing* it however, and, above all, without saying it." The difference between lordship (Bataille is speaking of Hegel) and sovereignty resides in the latter's total otherness, its move outside dialectics. That move is possible and resides in its laughter:

Laughter alone exceeds dialectics and the dialectician: it bursts out only on the basis of an absolute renunciation of meaning, an absolute risking of death, what Hegel calls abstract negativity. A negativity that never takes place, that never *presents* itself, because in doing so it would start to work again. A laughter that literally never *appears* . . . And the word "laughter" itself must be read in a burst, as its nucleus of meaning bursts in the direction of the *system* of the sovereign operation ("drunkenness, erotic effusion, sacrificial effusion, poetic effusion, heroic behavior, anger, absurdity" . . .)[54]

Thus Derrida's articulation of Bataille shows affinity to Lacan's *jouissance*. Both ascribe to the pleasure of the symptom and the excess of laughter a non-formalizable meaning, which is somehow "sovereign" and opens up the notion of meaning outside the symbolic. Although Lacan's example is *Finnegans Wake*, my contention is that "Cyclops" also provides illustration of Joyce's sheer linguistic drive and *lust*. *Finnegans Wake* may seem to have totally succumbed to the peal of laughter, *Ulysses* inscribes laughter into what may, at first sight, have seemed representational narrative. The lordship of mimesis is transcended by the sovereignty of the loss of sense, to open itself up to "the (non-)base of the sacred, of nonmeaning, of un-knowledge or of play . . ."[55]

''*JOUISSANCE*''/THE SUBJECT WHO SHOWS

One of the more farcical moments in Irish history is Robert Emmet's failed escape from the country after a botched attempt to capture Dublin Castle – he returned to say goodbye to his secret betrothed. Emmet was publicly hanged in a ceremony which was also botched. His last words: "When my country takes her place among the nations of the

[54] Jacques Derrida, "From Restricted to General Economy," *Writing and Difference*, trans. Alan Bass (1967: University of Chicago Press, 1978), p. 256.   [55] *Writing and Difference*, p. 261.

earth then and not till then, let my epitaph be written. I have done,"
have become proverbial nonetheless. Immortalized as he is by Thomas
Moore in his *Irish Melodies*, Emmet offers a focus for Irish sentimentality.
"Cyclops" stages Emmet's hanging, mediated through the glossy lan-
guage of the society pages, as if it were the opening of the Olympic
Games, listing the attendance of foreign dignitaries:

> The delegation, present in full force, consisted of Commendatore Bacibaci
> Beninobenone (the semiparalysed *doyen* of the party who had to be assisted to
> his seat by the aid of a powerful steam crane), Monsieur Pierrepaul
> Petitépatant, the Grandjoker Vladinmire Pokethankertscheff, the Archjoker
> Leopold Rudolph von Schwanzenbad-Hodenthaler, Countess Marha Virága
> Kisászony   Putrápesthi,   Hiram   Y.   Bomboost,   Count   Athanatos
> Karamelopulos, Ali Baba Backsheesh Rahat Lokum Effendi, Señor Hidalgo
> Caballero Don Peccadillo y Palabras y Paternoster de la Malora de la Malaria,
> Hokopoko Harakiri, Hi Hung Chang, Olaf Kobberkeddelsen, Mynheer Trik
> van Trumps, Pan Poleaxe Paddyrisky, Goosepond přhklstř Kratchinab-
> ritchisitch, Borus Hupinkoff, Herr Hurhausdirektorpresident Hans Cuechli-
> Steuerli,   Nationalgymnasiummuseumsanatoriumandsuspensoriumordinary-
> privatdocentgeneralhistoryspecialprofessordoctor Kriegfried Ueberallgemein.
> (*U* 12.555–69)

Not only a parody of the inflated sentimentality surrounding Emmet
and the collusion of the media with spectacle and power, it attacks the
symbolic order of the signifier in its vital spot: the name. The zany list
proceeds as a cataloge which presents itself as a mimetic inventory of
attending foreign visitors, but in fact proceeds to make the names
resonate with our western cultural clichés about the distinctive phonetic
and morphological features of certain languages. Cliché leaks back into
the self-presence of the name. Thus Joyce voices and embodies as
"name" the peculiar resonance of a specific language. Its identity is its
sound, not its referent or signified. Taking up the seemingly naive
position of the uninitiated who cannot understand (a foreign) language,
Joyce turns the name into a voice. But even depriving the name of
presence to turn it into voice is apparently not enough to satisfy Joyce's
satiric instinct. In addition, he re-inscribes a form of oblique and
unintended meaning: "petitépatant" revives the prejudice about little
French men wanting to make a great impression; "athanatos
karamelopulos" seems to suggest the candy-sweetness of immortality;
"trik van trumps" puts pressure on the popular opinion of deceptive
Dutch trade-practises; the "grandjoker . . . pokethankertscheff" is put
down as a playboy, dandy or stuffed shirt; the "commendatore bacibaci

beninobenone" betrays the clichéd secret about dirty old Italian men; the name of the "archjoker" carries allusions to his private parts; and the final, long, seemingly German name seems to embody a paradox about German identity [both *"Krieg"* ("war") and *"Frieden"* ("peace")], and about scholarship (*"Ueberall"* / *"allgemein"* – "everywhere", "general"), to conclude with a parody of the German love of titles. Thus Joyce destroys *the name* by reading it as *voice* and inscribing into that sound a secondary (written) and subversive and clichéd meaning.

In addition to this reversal of the ordinary process of reading, in which we see words and spell them to make sense of them, Joyce, like Stephen Dedalus, proceeds by making sense from sound. Thus there is another force at work. The passage begins with presenting one name, that of the Commendatore, and explains who he his. Then it seems to gather speed, carried by its own momentum and incremental zaniness, to achieve a climax in the long German title of Kriegfried Ueberallgemein. The climax is a rhetorical figure, but as Fritz Senn points out, Joyce's typical gesture of long-drawn-out upping of rhetorical inflation until the balloon bursts is more than that. It would seem a compositional force in Joyce's texts based on visceral principle, "the graph of a recurrent, basic, Joycean motion," found again and again throughout the '*œuvre*: "augmentation, intensification, hypertrophy, amplification, and then, secondly, some divergence, a turn, a change, some divarication, shunting." Senn's name for it is "provection," and he defines it as an "exuberance or excess, an insistent drive out of – beyond – confines that had otherwise been largely taken for granted . . ."[56] Joyce's character, both in life and text, is literally e-normous. He always gets carried away.

In addition to being a rhetorical figure, provective climax borders on physical process. Tension builds until the body releases it as laughter. In Joyce's text, language and linguistic intention are grafted on the body and find pleasure in the mere building up of tension until the moment of release – seemingly scoring no other point than the play with its vehicle, the expressive power of language itself. But laughter effectuates a difference. "It entails a repetition that precisely is not a return of the same, but a movement of violent effraction. Its singularity consists in this return of alterity, of the excluded, or the repressed." As Samuel Weber suggests, "[i]n the movements of voice and body, the bond between 'what once belonged together but has been torn apart in the course of

---

[56] *Inductive Scrutinies* (Dublin: Lilliput Press, 1995), pp. 40 and 35.

[the ego's] development' is renewed."[57] I argue that in Joyce's laughter a space opens up between identification and rejection, a hybrid location "between" where, as Bhabha puts it "culture's double returns uncannily – neither the one nor the other, but the impostor – to mock and mimic, to lose the sense of the masterful self and its social sovereignty."[58]

Of course, linguistic versatility is a characteristic of subject people, especially city dwellers like Dubliners. Earlier we saw how Joyce's character Joe twisted Bloom's meaning in Kiernan's pub. Joyce also allocates to this character the privilege of "malapropism" which David Lloyd traces to another Irishman, Oscar Wilde, but which might also be referred back to Joyce's earlier countryman the playwright Sheridan. *The Rivals* introduces a Mrs. Malaprop who confuses the meanings of latinate words. Thus she accuses someone of being as "headstrong as an allegory on the banks of the Nile." Joe's "I, says Joe. I am the alligator" (*U* 12.1627), contains an allusion to Sheridan, as does his "Don't cast your nasturtiums on my character" (1040). But Joe's attack on the English language, however defiantly it may "fret," in the sense of "erode," its cognitive power, does not attack it as fundamentally as Joyce's zany lists do.

One more example: The list of Irish tribal heroes represented on the stones dangling from the Citizen's girdle, which I must quote at length to generate the sensible effect. The list begins innocently enough:

Cuchulin, Conn of hundred battles, Niall of nine hostages, Brian of Kincora, the ardri Malachi, Art MacMurragh, Shane O'Neill, Father John Murphy . . . Red Hugh O'Donnell, Red Jim MacDermott, Soggarth Eoghan O'Growney . . . Goliath, Horace Wheatley, Thomas Conneff, Peg Woffington, the Village Blacksmith, Captain Moonlight, Captain Boycott, Dante Alighieri, Christopher Columbus, S. Fursa, S. Brendan, Marshal MacMahon, Charlemagne, Theobald Wolfe Tone, the Mother of the Maccabees, the Last of the Mohicans, the Rose of Castile, the Man for Galway, The Man that Broke the Bank at Monte Carlo, The Man in the Gap, The Woman Who Didn't, Benjamin Franklin, Napoleon Bonaparte, John L. Sullivan, Cleopatra, Savourneen Deelish, Julius Caesar, Paracelsus, sir Thomas Lipton, William Tell, Michelangelo Hayes, Muhammad, the Bride of Lammermoor, Peter the Hermit, Peter the Packer, Dark Rosaleen, Patrick W. Shakespeare, Brian Confucius, Murtagh Gutenberg, Patricio Velasquez, Captain Nemo, Tristan and Isolde, the first Prince of Wales, Thomas Cook and Son, the Bold Soldier Boy,

---

[57] "The Blindness of the Seeing Eye: Psychoanalysis, Hermeneutics, *Entstellung*," in *Institution and Interpretation* (Minneapolis: University of Minnesota Press, 1987), p. 84.
[58] *Location of Culture*, p. 137.

Arrah na Pogue, Dick Turpin, Ludwig Beethoven, the Colleen Bawn,
Waddler Healy, Angus the Culdee, Dolly Mount, Sidney Parade, Ben Howth,
Valentine Greatrakes, Adam and Eve, Arthur Wellesley, Boss Croker,
Herodotus, Jack the Giantkiller, Gautama Buddha, Lady Godiva, The Lily of
Killarney, Balor of the Evil Eye, the Queen of Sheba, Acky Nagle, Joe Nagle,
Alessandro Volta, Jeremiah O'Donovan Rossa, Don Philip O'Sullivan Beare.
(*U* 12.176–200).

The straightfaced seriousness with which this catalogue begins soon
breaks down. First there is the odd juxtaposition of two names beginning
with "Red," then the anomalous presence of a "Village Blacksmith,"
deriving from the American poet Longfellow, followed by two captains.
From that moment the verbal eagerness of the inventory of cliché
overrides any attempt at seriousness. We might argue that the list
deflates the grandioseness of Irish purist-nationalist claims to a heroic
past. It is also a grand totalizing gesture of all-inclusive incorporation
which refuses to communicate and make sense: it indiscriminately
absorbs Dante, Napoleon, and Beethoven. But beyond this intention we
sense the sheer pleasure in inventing crazy combinations, unexpected
deflations, surprises, the introduction of anomalies, culminating in a
climax with "the Queen of Sheba, Acky Nagle, Joe Nagle" to wind
down to the end. The point of the passage is the linguistic inventiveness
with the clichés of the tribe itself. Joyce transforms the epic catalogue into
a sequence with a meta-mimetic structure of its own, which re-presences
the physical processes of breathing, pausing, climaxing, and relaxation,
which language – according to Freud and Lacan that is – superseded
and excluded at the moment of the entry into the symbolic order.

The game of *fort-da* serves to remedy the absence of and separation
from the maternal body. Joyce's text, however, recreates a sense of the
body *in* language, owing to the binding of pleasure onto the linguistic
utterance itself. We noted Stephen Dedalus' struggle with the *fort-da* of
language and his alienation from his body. Is Joyce, his author, engaged
in the subterfuge of re-inscribing physicality back into language? Does
he give language an extra, non-discursive layer beyond "the wall" of
traditional signification? If so, he does it with gleeful pleasure at the
voiding of conventional meaning. The diegetic content of "Cyclops" –
which, as we noted, itself slowly builds up to a climactic confrontation
and outburst of violence, to a "catastrophe" which shakes the earth –
functions as an allegory of its process and motive of enunciation. The
rhetoric of provection of the catalogues and interpolations is coextensive with the dynamic of the narrative. The length of the ritual litanies

of names and titles functions as a signpost to the reader of the impossibility of language's ever reaching the "nameless barbarity" of what the
chapter cannot "name."[59] It twists the *pathos* of the dramatic gesturing
of Myles Joyce at the bar into a destructive mimicry of representation.
The chapter "voices" not so much the relative positions in the debate
about the nation, as the build-up of tension surrounding the topic – a
traumatic topic which, owing to its constitutive unrepresentability,
cannot but lead to violence, as it still does today in Northern Ireland.
Like *A Portrait of the Artist*, "Cyclops" is a *Vorstellungsrepräsentanz*, in that it
is a representation which is offered in the place of what cannot be
represented. Here that is not the impossibility of the self-identity of the
artist, but the impossibility of the story of national identity in a recognized mother tongue. The rhetorical violence of "Cyclops" is the index
of that lack.

I suggest that a realistic set piece like the Christmas Dinner scene in *A
Portrait of the Artist* works in a similar way, but that we can only recognize
it in retrospect, after having learned to listen to Joyce's later works.
Stephen Dedalus hears the voices of the grown-ups argue about politics,
spoiling the peace of the occasion. Joyce's rendering builds up a rhetorical and emotional tension from which the child is excluded, but which
affects him to the core of his being, since the ideological rift threatens
his sense of integrity (beginning with Dante's two distinctly colored
political brushes at the beginning of *A Portrait of the Artist*). Indeed, the
child is the passive victim of the emotional violence of the adults. The
scene is played over his head, outside his power to interfere or participate – just as Myles Joyce is silenced by linguistic difference. This
realistic set piece in *A Portrait of the Artist* is also a "soundscript" of the
affective forces at work in Irish culture which preclude Christmas
peace. Here, the consciousness of the ideological rift at the point of
origin does not yet ring as laughter as it does in "Cyclops," but it echoes
with Dickensian comedy nonetheless. The dream-state of *Finnegans
Wake* dramatizes Stephen's (and Myles Joyce's) exclusion (dissociated
production) from the scene of rhetorical and emotional interaction – as
if they and we were overhearing voices in the next room. It presents the
psychodynamic of narrative – the emotional pattern of interaction and

---

[59] Note that Eugene Jolas' "Proclamation" of the "Revolution of the English Language" included
the following statements: "Narrative is not mere anecdote, but the projection of a metamorphosis of reality"; "The expression of these concepts can be achieved only through the rhythmic
'hallucination of the work'"; "The litany of words is admitted as an independent unit."
Transition: A Paris Anthology, intr. Noel Riley Fitch (New York: Anchor Books, Doubleday, 1990),
p. 19.

confrontation – without the semantic content. We only vaguely understand the meaning of the overdetermined words, but we can always tell
whether the voices are quarrelling, debating, gossiping, making love,
confessing, boasting, vying for attention, singing or crying, cross-
examining, etc. Joyce captures the affective rhythm of exchange, the
pitch of intonation, the pattern of altercation to mimic social discourse
without its content, as if we are listening to a foreign language we
cannot understand.

THE SOMATIZATION OF THE TEXT

Whereas *A Portrait of the Artist* manifested the impossibility of the representation and the memory of the original trauma through repetition
and the acting out of the impossibility of constituting the self, "Cyclops"
adds another dimension: through its rhetoric bordering on the body, it
tries to lend perceptible, acousmatic or aural presence to the non-
representable. It does not only point to the "original murder" of the
mother tongue, it attempts a filling in of its absence, by adding a gestural
dimension to written language which makes the absent mother tongue
"sensible" as a language of affect. The text "reverberates" with the
suppressed presence of a colonized body.

Joyce's interest in creating a language of "gesture," to use the words
from *Stephen Hero*, is well documented. Critics tend to point to Joyce's
keen interest in the theories of the Jesuit linguist Marcel Jousse who held
that the liturgy of the Church encodes a form of embodied knowledge
which the student can only acquire through memorization and identification with the combination of gesture and word. The student learns
to "eat" the Gospel; and in doing so releases the insight it encrypts. For
Jousse the Mass is a mime which constitutes the gestural re-enactment of
the communal memorization of Christ's death and resurrection.[60] Thus
the Mass combines voice, gesture, and word in a total concept of
language which would resemble Adorno's "true language" analogous to
the "figure for the divine name."

From Derrida's discussion of Artaud's concept of a "theatre of
cruelty," I get the impression that in addition to Jousse, Artaud provides
an analogue to help us understand Joyce's drive to transcend traditional

---

[60] Marcel Jousse, *La Manducation de la Parole* (Paris: Gallimard, 1975); and *L'Anthropologie du geste* (Paris: Resma, 1969). The critics who have paid most extensive attention to the influence of Jousse on Joyce are Lorraine Weir, *Writing Joyce: A Semiotics of the Joyce System* (Bloomington: Indiana University Press, 1989), and Jean-Michel Rabaté, *Joyce upon the Void: The Genesis of Doubt* (London: Macmillan, 1991).

notions of mimesis in rendering to representation an aspect of pure and concrete sensibility and materiality. If Artaud's program is carried out, speech and writing:

will once more become *gestures*; and the *logical* and discursive intentions which speech ordinarily uses in order to ensure its rational transparency, and in order to purloin its body in the direction of meaning, will be reduced or subordinated. And since this theft of the body by itself is indeed that which leaves the body to be strangely concealed by the very thing that constitutes it as diaphanousness, then the deconstitution of diaphanousness lays bare the flesh of the word, lays bare the word's sonority, intonation, intensity – the shout that the articulations of language and logic have not yet entirely frozen . . .[61]

What we note in Joyce's works is that from the early draft *Stephen Hero* on, there is in Stephen Dedalus's artistic aspiration a reversal of what we might commonly understand as poetic procedure. Instead of rhyth-micizing words, giving them pattern and metre as a poet does, Joyce shows Stephen attempting *to make sense out of rhythm and sound*: the "permut[ation] and combin[ation of] the five vowels to construct cries for primitive emotions" (*SH* 32); as if rhythm, as the nineteenth-century philologist Hans von Bülow claimed, were originary. As Laurent Milesi convincingly argues, throughout his career, Joyce proceeded to pro-gressively redouble this emphasis on the rhythmicization of language, feeding it into the writing itself, so that *Finnegans Wake* is a text which eventually "dances" its own "sounddance."[62] It is as if Joyce connects emotion with rhythm because affect and presence are not communi-cable through representational narrative. This privileging of rhythm is accompanied by an overvaluation of the sound of the voice, its music, as the instrument of presence. On the whole Joyce neglects the meaning of words for their rhythm and sound – together their "gesture." C. G. Jung disgustedly exclaimed that "worms write with their sympathetic nervous system for lack of a brain."[63] I hope my reader will conclude that Joyce's procedure does not derive from regressive primitivism, but from "cun-ning," as well as "silence" in his "exile" from the language of the tribe. The difference with Jousse's theory should be noted, however. If the ritual of the Mass is the re-enactment of a mystery which is from its institution attended with the words in which it can be re-enacted (the Gospels), Joyce's ritualization of language points to a moment which never was articulated semantically, and which can, consequently, only

[61] *Writing and Difference*, p. 240.
[62] Paper presented at the *Re:Joyce* Conference, Dundee, July 1996.
[63] "*Ulysses*: A Monologue," p. 194.

be conveyed by "cries for primitive emotions" invented by Stephen Dedalus or his author. Thus Joyce does not *recover* an original language or a primal speech, a Kristevan semiotic. He experiments and invents throughout his career in the hope that the repetitive act of utterance will eventually bring to life the voice of origin. In *Stephen Hero*, Stephen Dedalus, immediately after the narrative refers to a boy who "opened and closed the flaps of his ears while the noise of the diners reached him rhythmically as the wild gabble of animals" (*SH* 184), makes a claim to that effect, which is carnivalized in "Circe": "So that gesture . . . the gift of tongues render[s] visible not the lay sense but the first entelechy, the structural rhythm" (*U* 15.105–07). Only repetition as re-enactment keeps open the possibility that the void at origin will ever be filled by full discourse.

Perhaps the most flamboyant characteristic of Joyce's traumatized textuality is his demonstrative insistence that language will bring the body into words and undo the separation of body and discourse of subaltern subjectivity. In *Writing Degree Zero*, Roland Barthes articulates the modernity of Flaubert's style as an incantatory rhythm which appeals to a sixth, purely literary, sense. Joyce's rhythms do not just aim for the aesthetic, they ground that aestheticism in tone, word, timbre, resonance, and ritual gesture, the "grain" of the voice which signifies the presence of an articulating body. The term "grain of the voice" derives from Roland Barthes' *The Pleasure of the Text*, where he speaks of the text as an "anagram" of an "erotic body," where the word has become flesh. He names the process of articulating that incarnation "writing aloud":

Writing aloud is not phonological but phonetic; its aim is not the clarity of messages, the theater of emotions; what it searches for (in a perspective of bliss) are the pulsational incidents, the language lined with flesh, a text where we can hear the grain of the voice, the patina of consonants, the voluptuousness of vowels, a whole carnal stereophony; the articulations of the body, of the tongue, not that of meaning, of language.[64]

Again, it will be understood that Joyce's inscription of a "body" differs ethically and ideologically from Barthes': If Barthes allegorizes his own delight in reading as a sensuously erotic, self-pleasuring act, Joyce tries to body forth, to incarnate what has been excluded from language, reduced to meaninglessness under colonial rule. Both push representation "through the looking-glass," imitating God's act of incarnating

---

[64] Trans. Richard Miller (New York: Hill and Wang, 1975), pp. 66–67. Here Barthes himself seems to go back on his earlier claim concerning "The Death of the Author," even reviving a version of the voice.

the word as flesh; but Barthes' "new creation" is an attempt in the Symbolist tradition of Mallarmé to conflate book and world into a transcendent monism of textuality, whereas Joyce's "new creation" was a desperate attempt, by means of writing, to re-signify what history had reduced to insignificance. From this perspective, Joyce shares Albert Camus' notion of the specific task of literature as bearing witness to the body, thus countering the official version of history, the ideological-hegemonic version in which death has become invisible as it was in the Gulf War. "In a civilization where murder and violence are already doctrines in the act of becoming institutions," it is the artist who, owing to his vocation, is "'Freedom's witness' as far as he 'testifies not to the Law, but to the body'."[65]

Joyce may have or be a symptom, but that symptom contains the real reminder that spirit, art, technology, or culture are produced by the flesh, mediated by matter. When I first read the passage spoofing the style of the spiritist seance in "Cyclops," in which the heavenly abode of the spirits is equipped with 'tālāfānā, ālāvātār, hātākāldā, wātāklāsāt" (telephone, elevator, hot and cold, watercloset; *U* 12.359), I burst into laughter, not precisely knowing why. Now I can point out how economi-cally, by the simple means of a wide, horizontal, diacritical material mark imitating the obsession with Sanskrit of the Theosophical Society, the author deflates and counters our drive to repress the death of the body. Spirit, the idea of spirit, so the text would seem to say, is only viable and possible owing to our self-extended use of matter, writing – here the diacritical mark marking the vowels as if with a halo; but, however much spirit may deem to have transcended its physical nature, in Joyce all spirit is rewritten as the self-extension of matter. Joyce's spirits still need elevators and waterclosets.

Joyce's desperation to voice the body also "speaks" in the all-per-vasive and increasingly obsessive somatization of his texts. They try to articulate the unspeakable sensations of the body – an endeavor which is itself ironized by the text as in the unpronounceable sequences of letters voicing the respectively male and female ecstasy of Boylan and Marion in "Circe": "Godblazegrukbrukarchkhrasht!" and "Weeshwashtkis-sinapooisthnapoohuck?" (*U* 15.3809–13), which in turn may be seen as the final, ironic product of Stephen's "permut[ation] and combin[ation] of] the five vowels to construct cries for primitive emotions."

But beyond trying merely to speak the unspeakably physical, Joyce's texts spread a uniform layer of sexualization. Words like "metem-

[65] Felman and Laub, *Testimony: Crises of Witnessing in Literature, Psychoanalysis, and History*, p. 108.

psychosis" or "Plumtree's potted meat" – both terms bearing allusion to the death of the body – are charged with the overtone of *double entendre*. By a similar process innocuous, though spouted, objects like "teapot" (*U* 15.457–60) are pulled into the realm of panting desire. In fact, the passage in "Sirens" which describes the voice as an erecting phallus, "loud, full, shining, proud" (*U* 11.693) may serve as illustration: "Tenderness it welled: slow, swelling, full it throbbed. That's the chat. Ha, give! Take! Throb, a throb, a pulsing proud erect" (*U* 11.701–02). The sensation of the body is here displaced upon language, or more precisely voice. Not because Joyce sexualizes the voice, but because he uses the rhythm and drive of sexual excitement to create a textuality which ties language to physical process *per se*. Joyce's so-called "dirty minded" "phallopyrotechnic"'s (*U* 15.1495) are not sexual but textual, corporal, and betray an anxiety to undo the severance of language from body, speech from selfhood.

I shall not bore my reader by enumerating the many ways in which Joyce aims at fleshing out the text, an obsession which drives him to even turn words into speaking bodies, letting "[w]hispering lovewords murmur" (*U* 15.3797–98).[66] Joyce himself called *Ulysses* an epic of the body more "than of the human spirit,"[67] centering each of the chapters on an organ, and figuring the text as a whole as a human body; and, as Beckett first emphasized, Joyce's language itself conveys the rhythms of the body. It seems to germinate, maturate, and then to putrefy, imitating peristalsis, evacuation, tumescence and detumescence, meanwhile exhibiting somatic symptoms like stutters, lisps, palpitations, paralysis, yawns, hiccups, sneezes, snores, twitches, cramps,[68] contortions and convulsions.[69] His texts crow and whinny, they belch and fart, urinate and menstruate, sneeze and yawn, cough and laugh, swoon and ejaculate,[70] masturbate and fall asleep, all the while perfuming and deodorizing themselves heliotrope[71] in order not to kill our desire. "His writing is not *about* something; *it is that something itself . . .* When the sense is sleep,

---

66 Note Derek Attridge's *Peculiar Language: Literature as Difference from the Renaissance to James Joyce* (Ithaca: Cornell University Press, 1988), chapter 6: "Literature as Deviation: Syntax, Style, and the Body in *Ulysses*."

67 John Bishop, *Joyce's Book of the Dark: Finnegans Wake* (Madison: University of Wisconsin Press, 1986), p. 144.   68 Maud Ellmann, "The Ghosts of *Ulysses*," p. 115.

69 J.-M. Rabaté, *James Joyce: Authorized Reader* (Baltimore: Johns Hopkins University Press, 1991), p. 81.

70 E. L. Epstein, "James Joyce and the Body," *A Starchamber Quiry: A James Joyce Centennial Volume 1881–1982*, ed. E. L. Epstein (London and New York: Methuen, 1982), p. 92.

71 Margot Norris, "Joyce's Heliotrope," in *Coping with Joyce*, ed. Morris Beja and Shari Benstock (Columbus: Ohio State University Press, 1989), pp. 3–24.

the words go to sleep," Beckett said with pregnant meaning.[72] Perhaps we cannot take his words literally enough. "Oxen of the Sun" begins with the cry of students and midwife, but it also enacts the mother's rhythmic heartbeat as heard by the baby in the womb; then language enacts the rocking motion of the nurse's arms, while the unintelligibility of Joyce's latinate text suggests the lack of comprehension with which a newborn baby encounters the mystery of language.

Conversely, Joyce also demonstrates that the material letter kills the spirit of social hierarchy and the structure of pre-eminence. The "catastrophe" of the landing of the Citizen's missile at the end of "Cyclops" is reported in an interpolation in a neutral reportorial style, resembling contemporary journalistic practise. As in Swift's *A Modest Proposal*, the style itself does not betray its satirical mode. It is not until we get to the end of the description and the name of the rear admiral entrusted with the supervision of the work of salvage that we begin to feel the bite of Joyce's sarcasm:

H.R.H., rear admiral, the right honourable sir Hercules Hannibal Habeas Corpus Anderson, K.G., K.P., K.T., P.C., K.C.B., M.P., J.P., M.B., D.S.O., S.O.D., M.F.H., M.R.I.A., B.L., Mus.Doc., P.L.G., F.T.C.D., F.R.U.I., F.R.C.P.I and F.R.C.S.I. (*U* 12.1893–96)

Not only is there the hyperinflation of heroic personal names (both Hercules and Hannibal). The list of initials indicating titles, social functions and degrees, comically includes "S.O.D," which according to Gifford's annotation should be read as "sod": "a clod, a sodomite";[73] moreover, "P.L.G.," "Poor Law Guardian," evokes from the "Irish point of view an oppressor of the poor." But these undercover expressions of animosity are not my main object. The point of my citation is to show that the absurd exhaustiveness of this list of titles precisely undoes these titles from all possibility of marking distinction. The initial letters, instead of communicating the exclusiveness of a certain position or achievement, begin to lose their social referential function, and kill the possibility of seeing their owner as distinguished or in any way marked off or singled out from the commons. The rhetorical practice of "provection" foregrounds the fact that social distinction "is" no more than an arbitrary letter appended to a name; it robs the insignia of the differential system of their aura of authority.

[72] "Dante . . . Bruno. Vico . . . Joyce," *Our Exagmination* (1929; repr. New York: New Directions, 1972), p. 14.
[73] Don Gifford and Robert J. Seidman, *Notes for Joyce: An Annotation of James Joyce's "Ulysses"* (New York: Dutton, 1974), p. 311.

The same holds for the Church. A reference to prayer initiates a procession of all varieties of clerics, monks, priests etc., and lists half a page of names of Saints, including perversions: "S. Eponymous", "S. Homonymous," "S. Laurence O'Toole", etc. (*U* 12.1696–99), which precisely effectuates the emptying out of the prestige attached to these holy figures. Saintliness, the text would seem to argue, is just an arbitrary social matter of placing a capital "S" before the name. It is a form of linguistic differentiation; and the way in which Joyce writes this litany seemingly deprives the inscription of sanctity of any transcendental aura.

If we accept my axiom of trauma and its structural symmetry to the Irish situation of colonized subjectivity, this obsessive insistence on fleshing language out on the one hand, and reducing the aura of authority conventionally attached to print on the other, is not just a symptom of a particular form of anxiety (the traumatic threat of severance of language from body), but also an act of resistance against the violence with which Irish culture effectuates subjectivity. If subjectivity is constituted by a splitting of the self which facilitates self-reflection and self-correction by self-rejection, entailing the binding of the self to prevailing ideology, the refusal to permanently detach and separate is both an act of loyalty to the moment of trauma to which it is a witness, as well as an attempt to suggest what is at stake in its occurrence by obsessively entwining what culture wishes to separate. This insight offers a new perspective on the Homeric parallel of "Cyclops." As Horkheimer and Adorno point out in *Dialectic of Enlightenment*, the Homeric tale illustrates the triumph of a *ratio* which adapts itself to its contrary: the amorphousness of a Polyphemus who is a "consciousness that has not as yet developed any fixed identity." Odysseus triumphs by denying "his own identity, which makes him a subject, and keeps himself alive by imitating the amorphous. He calls himself Nobody because Polyphemus is not a self."[74] Joyce's littering of the letter, his somatization of the text and the perverse zaniness of his style, is, like the linguistic highjinks of Horkheimer and Adorno's Odysseus, a strategy of escape from an oppressive and cannibalistic giant – an "old sow" that "eats her farrow": colonial culture. So "familiar" yet so "foreign," Joyce's (post)colonial method of novelistic composition escapes from the hegemonic model of English example, to attempt and dislocate that tradition from its self-evident position of example and authority. Henceforward the English

---

[74] Trans. John Cumming (1947; repr. New York: Seabury Press, 1972), p. 67.

novel may have to understand its place and position in relation to the centrality of Joyce's *Ulysses*.

POSTCOLONIAL AGENCY

Thus it is owing to his sheer drive to wield the pen, letting a surplus of *quod* override the *quid*, and by means of the technique of representation as *Vorstellungsrepräsentanz*,[75] that Joyce inscribes into the symbolic order the surplus of intensity that eludes the field of hegemonic representation. He opens up a possibility for "the emergence and negotiation of those agencies of the marginal, minority, subaltern, or diasporic that incite us to think through – and beyond – theory."[76]

The structure of that possibility, which I earlier referred to by means of Žižek's postulate of an opening in the other, may now be more closely defined as that disjunction of meaning which opens up in the pun or *calembour*. Whether we understand the pun as a conjunction of different meanings in one graphic/visual symbol or in one phonological/acoustic unit does not matter, as long as there is the coincidence of divergent realities of meaning in one concept. The pun embodies the odd pairing we noted at the beginning of this chapter in Stephen Dedalus' words about the English language: "so familiar and so foreign." But if we listen closely, we can locate the beginning moment of the splitting of language at the moment of the trauma itself. Stephen's chiasmic repetition: "*Pull out his eyes,/ Apologise,/ Apologise,/ Pull out his eyes./ Apologise,/ Pull out his eyes,/ Pull out his eyes,/ Apologise.*" (*P* 8) negates command by appropriating it to aesthetic transformation while seeming to obediently repeat the "sentence." Homi Bhabha speaks of "writing outside the sentence" as if he were describing Joyce's praxis. Writing outside the sentence is "contiguous with the sentence, near but different, not simply its anarchic disruption." "The non-sentence is not before (either as the past or a priori) or inside (either as depth or presence) but outside (both spatially and temporally excentric, interruptive, in-between, on the borderlines, turning inside outside)."[77] The pun dramatizes or mimics the situation of subjection to colonization as the overdetermination of language by meaning; it also shows that meaning transcends and spills over the signifier and is not confined to the straightjacket of the official version. It is not surprising that Joyce had a life-long fascination with puns, and

---

[75] Note Lacan's definition of humor as "The spirit that lives as an exile in the creation whose invisible support it is, knows that it is at every instant the master capable of annihilating it." *Ecrits*, p. 60.   [76] *The Location of Culture*, p. 181.   [77] *Ibid.*, p. 182.

that *Finnegans Wake* should be written in a language and couched in a form which dramatizes the punning disjunction and surplus at the heart of the other. The interrogative agency in a catachrestic position of the pun re-"forges" the dualism of western ontology, the "bar" of the "occidental stereotomy" into a "coextensive, contingent boundar[y] of relocation, reinscription."[78] But the presence of the pun in itself does not constitute a new postcolonial agency; the pun must be voiced from the place of the void, the *locus* of impersonal authority of the Name-of-the-Father, which Joyce has appropriated – to ring with the laughter of recognition. To quote Bhabha once more:

The individuation of the agent occurs in a moment of displacement. It is a pulsional incident, the split-second movement when the process of the subject's designation – its fixity – opens up beside it, uncannily *abseits*, a supplementary space of contingency. In this "return" of the subject, thrown back across the distance of the signified, outside the sentence, the agent emerges as a form of retroactivity, *Nachträglichkeit*. It is not agency as itself (transcendent, transparent) or in itself (unitary, organic, autonomous). As a result of its own splitting in the time-lag of signification [Bhabha refers to what I call traumatic discursivity], the moment of the subject's individuation emerges as an effect of the intersubjective – as the return of the subject as agent. This means that those elements of social "consciousness" imperative for agency – deliberative, individuated action and specificity in analysis – can now be thought outside that epistemology that insists on the subject as always prior to the social or on the knowledge of the social as necessarily subsuming or sublating the particular "difference" in the transcendent homogeneity of the general. The iterative and the contingent that marks this intersubjective relation can never be libertarian or free-floating, as Eagleton claims, because the agent, constituted in the subject's return, is in the dialogic position of calculation, negotiation, interrogation: *Che vuoi?*[79]

It is as if Bhabha theorized Joyce's revolutionary example. Perhaps it is a pity that we need Bhabha to recognize what some of Joyce's contemporaries may have understood clearly. His younger countryman Arthur Power paints the following portrait of Joyce as "Fenian": "darksmiling, his wide hat, his light carriage, and his intense expression – a literary conspirator, who was determined to destroy the oppressive and respectable cultural structures under which we had been reared, and which were then crumbling."[80]

[78] *Ibid.*, p. 184. [79] *Ibid.*, p. 185.
[80] *Conversations with James Joyce* (London: Millington, 1974), p. 69.

CHAPTER 4

The primitive scene of representation: writing gender

"astronomically fabulafigured; . . . the last half versicle repurchas-
ing his pawned word"   *Finnegans Wake*

Joyce's mimesis of loss inscribes the "death-in-life" of trauma into his
text and vitiates the power of literature to incarnate truth and serve as a
mirror to sustain the reader's sense of coherent subjectivity. In the
discussion of "Cyclops" we noted that Joyce occupies the void hollowed
by the sense of lack of a mother tongue, from where he wages war on
hegemonic representation. The question remains: How could Joyce face
the terror of meaninglessness? In this chapter, I want to address Joyce's
strategy of coping with the "castration" which he inflicts on representation and the reader; and I shall argue that it is his fetishistic handling of
the possibility of diminishment, loss, or difference, which should be seen
in a historical perspective. The double relation to sexual difference of
the Irish male facilitates a double take on sexual identity. Identified as
the son of Mother Ireland – an ambivalent relation which locks the son
forever in the mother's womb as well as lending him a distinct, masculine social identity – Joyce invented a deconstructive strategy of *writing
difference* which styles itself feminine, and which is particularly modern,
because it anticipated the western drive to commodify sexuality, especially female sexuality, so characteristic of our own age. Thus this
chapter also addresses the modernity of Joyce; but it does not locate that
modernity in the content of his representations, his subject matter, but
in his fetishistic investment in the productivity of writing as production
and technology.

Joyce's writerly ambivalence is perhaps best understood if we first
scrutinize his protagonists. We already noted the contradictory inscription of gender/sexual difference at the beginning of *A Portrait*. The
father is feminized while the mother utters the command to apologize;
the son cannot model a stable identity on the father's example, while the

mother's music and the effect of her command transform language into echoing rhyme. Neither the father's nor the mother's "language" provides a stable grounding for a coherent identity. Moreover, although Stephen's sexual and social masculinity is emphasized, Stephen's ambivalent and inconclusive mourning of his mother in *Ulysses* testifies to his identification with her. He cannot separate from her, so that she pursues him, after her death, as a devouring "ghoul" or "hyena." This threat of being devoured, deriving from the absence of a boundary to a self which is partially identified with the feminine, contains the specter of pure materiality: the mother's body in death fragments into rotting parts. The identification with the mother, and we may extend the meaning of the figure of the mother to that of the nation, generates the fear of a reductive materialism in which man is nothing but corruptible flesh, in which the concept of a "soul" is meaningless. How to create the uncreated conscience if "womb" echoes "tomb" (*U* 7.723–24)? Stephen's hope is to use his writing as a non-fleshly material "womb of the imagination" in which "the word will become flesh." Appropriating female creativity to masculine *Geist* in "Oxen of the Sun," the chapter of *Ulysses* devoted to gestation, he claims: "Mark me now. In woman's womb word is made flesh but in the spirit of the maker all flesh that passes becomes the word that shall not pass away. This is the postcreation" (*U* 14.292–94). Through the materialization of art, and the transcendence of sexual difference in its genderized inscription, the contamination of death, the threat of death-in-life is to be contained in its postcreation.

Although Jewish, Bloom is Stephen/Joyce's mature *alter ego*. He suffers from a similar inability to separate the masculine self from a female/feminine other. This is highlighted in the "Circe" episode which presents the carnivalizaton of sexual difference, masculine and feminine reverting into each other. Here Bloom becomes the "new womanly man" (*U* 15.1798–99) who is "about to have a baby." As to Stephen, to Bloom the female sex represents the threat of apocalyptic death (the Dead Sea is the dead "cunt" of his world). It also figures as the antidote to the threat of annihilation in the form of warm, living human flesh.

In Joyce, then, indecidability also contains its own perverse resolution. As we noted, the mother in Joyce shares the treasury of the word. Joyce's women are portrayed as graphically authoritative; recipients or writers of letters, documents which may incriminate or justify the male. The point is that the means of escape from the threat of death and nihilism of the mother's tomb/womb also derives from what has been coded feminine: it is through writing, conflating the pen with the phantasmatic maternal phallus, that "castration" may be sutured. Thus writing, not in the "patriarchal" sense of a fixing of meaning, but writing (*écriture*) in the sense of an ongoing activity of self-inscription and self-materialization, is privileged as a syncretic technology which can cover up the traumatic rent opened up in the scene in *A Portrait*. In our western cultural heritage, writing participates in the masculine authority of the male author. At the same time, it may attenuate the threat of absolute difference, the threat of death, through its assimilation to the feminine other.

I suggest we understand Joyce's attitude to writing, which anticipates that of Derrida, as the product of its historical context and tradition: the double relationship to the feminine of the Irish male. As an individual, his maleness is oppositional to the female of the species; but as an Irish subject, he partakes in the collective projection of the self-identity of the cultural heritage as female and feminine (Mother Ireland, Mother Church, mother tongue).[1] Thus history itself provides Joyce with a strategy of "having it both ways," both denying difference and accepting it. "Having it both ways" may be the typical strategy of fetishism, the combination of avowal and disavowal, but in Joyce's case that strategy is suggested by cultural positioning. Thus it is the Irish cultural context which not only forced Joyce to confront the death-in-life of its heritage, but which also offered a strategy of survival.

It was the conception of "Penelope" in 1916, six years before the printing of *Ulysses*, which, using Joyce's own word, was the "clou" to his textuality which made the experimentation of the later chapters bearable and possible. It is his invention of "gendered writing" which allows the son to flaunt his "castration" in the act of disavowing it. The argument of this chapter does not aim to show that Joyce disavows sexual difference *in* the text. My point is that he fetishizes the act of writing and the materiality of textuality (by means of the attribution of gender-aspects *to* writing itself. Thus we are dealing with the more profound level of the gender *of* textuality rather than the gender *in* textuality). Not surprisingly, "Penelope," the concluding chapter of *Ulysses*, has provoked more critical discussion than any other part of Joyce's *œuvre*. Praised for its glaring realism, often performed on stage as a separate piece, this is the chapter which seems to lead an independent life – a necessary attribute to a fetish.

---

[1] See Richard Kearney, "Myth and Motherland," *Ireland's Field Day*, ed. Seamus Deane et al. (University of Notre Dame Press, 1986), pp. 74–78.

Looked at as fetish, this chapter may be understood as the substitute for the mother tongue. The contradictory soliloquy of silent but intensely expressive Molly Bloom, whose hardly punctuated stream-of-consciousness-between-sleep-and-waking is "recorded" as the conclusion of the text, becomes the odd, contradictory allegory fleshing out the lack which defies representation. As Joyce himself indicated, Molly Bloom is not to be understood as a "human apparition," but as the *Darstellung* of the "pre-human and . . . posthuman."[2] Molly's silence ambivalently "speaks" the mythic voice of origin, and her unstoppable abundance fills the traumatic lack which is the motor of Joyce's textuality. The feminine last word is thus theatrically staged and offered as a most original speech or language, and the speech of origin. Joyce's text seemingly gives epic form to what is operative through the structure of his narrative, and he embodies the unrepresentable as fully flowing inner speech.

As in previous chapters, I wish to bring out not just *what* Joyce paints, the content, but to analyze the structural and political function of this image of the feminine in the process of performing the fact of the inexpressibility of the trauma of origin of nation and narration. Thus my analysis does not hinge on the figure of Molly Bloom, but on the *chapter* entitled "Penelope," which functions as the umbilicus of Joyce's *text*.[3] I do not wish to collude with Joyce's fetishistic holding up of "Penelope" as a voice of origin or a new mother tongue. Therefore I shall analyze Molly's image as a structural function in Joyce's strategy of representation, an effect produced by and necessary to his *praxis* of writing from the place of the other, the Mosaic site of writing itself. "Penelope" is Joyce's means of incorporating or suturing the act of coming to terms with "castration" into textuality itself.

In order to perceive the place and informative function of gender in the totality of the construction of Joyce's novel, we must retreat from the immediacy of our involvement in the text to a perhaps unusual distance. In thinking about the Africanist presence in American fiction, Toni Morrison asks "How does literary utterance arrange itself when it tries to imagine an Africanist other?" Her conclusion is worth considering:

The fabrication of an Africanist persona is reflexive; an extraordinary meditation on the self; a powerful exploration of the fears and desires that reside in the writerly conscious . . . It requires hard work *not* to see this.

[2] *Letters I*, p. 180.
[3] Freud, *The Interpretation of Dreams*, trans. James Strachey (New York: Avon, 1965), p. 143, speaks of the navel as the "unplummable" point at the end of the process of interpretation, "its point of contact with the unknown."

It is as if I had been looking at a fishbowl – the glide and flick of golden scales, the green tip, the bolt of white careening back from the gills . . . – and suddenly I saw the bowl, the structure that transparently (and invisibly) permits the ordered life it contains to exist in the larger world . . . What became transparent were the self-evident ways that Americans choose to talk about themselves through and within a sometimes allegorical, sometimes metaphorical, but always choked representation of an Africanist presence.[4]

Underscoring the apparent lifelikeness of the image of the fish, Morrison describes the moment of the sudden perception of a different and wider perspective. The vividness of the image is due to the facilitating presence and containing function of a transparent, supportive structure, the glass bowl. "I came to realize the obvious: the subject of the dream is the dreamer."[5] I propose we transpose Morrison's perception of the structuring presence of authorial narcissism, and apply it to the figuration of the sexual other in deconstructive writing. In this chapter I hope to bring out the invisible, because ideological, but nonetheless coercive and constraining force with which the representation of Molly Bloom as simulacrum, and as allegory in Benjamin's sense of the word, holds *Ulysses* in place.[6]

The suggestion that my analysis does not just bear on Joyce but on deconstructive writing in general, forces us to return to the debate about Poe's *Purloined Letter*. Lacan's reading of Poe's story pointed out that the intersubjective scenario surrounding the letter (simultaneously denoting the phallus) prescribes masculine and feminine positions. In Poe's tale, as in Joyce, the queen is identified with the letter. Hiding the existence of the letter (the signifier which might tarnish the prestige of the king) from the king (the transcendent signifier as long as he is ignorant), the queen herself becomes the sign of subversion/castration. Every male who enters the letter's orbit (the Minister and later Dupin who try to restore the letter), is feminized. When the Minister who steals the letter (to gain power over the queen and contain the threat of castration) is forced to hide it in turn, he takes over "the curse of the sign he has dispossessed

---

[4] *Playing in the Dark: Whiteness and the Literary Imagination* (Cambridge, MA and London: Harvard University Press, 1992), pp. 16 and 17.   [5] *Ibid.*, p. 17.

[6] See Walter Benjamin, *Ursprung des Deutschen Trauerspiels* (Frankfurt: Suhrkamp, 1963), p. 95. "Der Allegoriker reisst ein Element aus der Totalität des Lebenszusammenhangs heraus. Er isoliert es, beraubt es seiner Funktion. Die Allegorie ist daher wesenhaft Bruchstück und steht damit im Gegensatz zum organischen Symbol." "The allegorical tears an element out of the texture of life. It isolates it and robs it of its function. Allegory is essentially fragment, in contrast to the organic embeddedness of the symbol." [Translation mine.] I do not use the term *Vorstellungsrepräsentanz* here, because I wish to reserve it for instances of the non-representability of trauma. As fetish, "Penelope" functions differently.

her of." When Dupin enters his office, the letter lies there "like an immense female body," which Dupin only needs to "undress."[7]. Having stolen the letter in turn, Dupin grows subject to "manifestly feminine" rage. Lacan's claim that "a letter always arrives at its destination" thus bears on the feminizing effect of intersubjectivity clinging to the signifier, which makes that "the sender . . . receives from the receiver his own message in reverse form."[8] The only place of escape from the letter's subversive feminizing effect is that occupied by the king who is outside the story. Derrida, resisting Lacan's proclamation of "the truth" of "castration," contested and contests Lacan's claim that the letter always arrives at its destination.[9] This chapter about the function of "Penelope" should also be read, I suggest, with this debate about Poe in mind. My intention is not to adjudicate or choose sides, but to demonstrate that the two perspectives are both already implicit in Joyce's syncretic and layered inscription of sexual difference.

The same goes for the feminist debate about this chapter, which offers two rivalling positions: one camp arguing that Joyce fails to do justice to women, the other arguing or even celebrating Joyce's assumption of a feminine position, however symptomatic.[10] In "'Beyond the Veil': *Ulysses*, Feminism, and the Figure of Woman," Jeri Johnson first pointed to the stereotyped scenario of this debate.[11] Taking Sandra Gilbert and Julia Kristeva as representatives of the two camps she concludes:

In the debate between feminisms about Joyce, the "figure of woman" mediates. What I would like to argue here is that Gilbert and Kristeva, anti-Joyce and pro-Joyce feminists, enact a debate which is repeated by anti-feminist and feminist Joyceans, even by feminist and post-feminist Joyceans. I would argue further that in so doing they replicate a debate already conducted within *Ulysses*, a debate presided over, and rendered undecidable by, the "figure of Woman." In becoming the ground of the struggle, "she" becomes the sign of divided, irresolvable meaning.[12]

---

[7] "Seminar on 'The Purloined Letter'," in John P. Muller and William J. Richardson (eds.), *The Purloined Poe: Lacan, Derrida, and Psychoanalytic Reading* (Baltimore: Johns Hopkins University Press, 1988), pp. 45 and 48.   [8] *Ibid.*, pp. 53 and 52.
[9] Most recently in "Pour l'amour de Lacan," in *Résistances: de la psychanalyse* (Paris: Galilée, 1996), pp. 51–72. In line with his argument elsewhere, e.g. in "Geslecht: différence sexuelle, différence ontologique," Martin Haar (ed.), *Martin Heidegger* (Paris: L'Herne, 1983), pp. 419–30, he implies that it might be possible to think of a sexual difference not barred by an absolute, oppositional division into two. Note that deconstructive writing resorts to the metaphor of sexual difference to style its own difference from the hegemonic tradition.
[10] "Joyce and Other Women Writers" is the title of part 5 of *New Alliances in Joyce Studies*, ed. Bonnie Kime Scott (Newark: University of Delaware Press, 1988).
[11] In: *Joyce, Modernity, and its Mediation*, ed. Christine van Boheemen (Amsterdam and Atlanta: Rodopi, 1989), pp. 201–28.   [12] *Ibid.*, pp. 207–08.

Divisive like Poe's purloined letter, *Ulysses* stimulates two mutually exclusive interpretations, neither of which is untrue, but each of which, standing by itself, is false because it elides the truth of the other. Instead of adjudicating truth, I want to show that it is the fetishistic doubleness of the function of "Penelope" itself which produces this effect. Joyce's "figure of woman" features uncannily as "the place onto which lack is projected, and through which it is simultaneously disavowed."[13]

To Joyce himself, muted but vocal Molly Bloom may have been significant as the allegory of the liberation of non-oppressed Irishness. In the participation *mystique* of traditional Irish culture, which experienced a representational tie between the single individual and the collective, the narrative of the individual is, at once, understood as the allegory of the nation.[14] If the rhetoric of Irish nationalism represented the nation as female, Molly Bloom also comes to stand for Irishness.

Whether Hibernia or Erin, whether appearing in political cartoons, paintings or engravings, historical or fictional narratives, songs, or even Yeats' play *Cathleen ni Houlihan* (1902), the collectivity of Irishness tended to be figured as female. Her specific characteristics may differ, however. Thus the mythic notion of Ireland found form in a variety of female characters: I note the ancient mother goddess "Mother Dana" (*U* 9.376) invoked by Stephen Dedalus. The eighteenth-century *aisling* typically depicts Ireland in a dream vision as a beautiful damsel in distress (James Clarence Mangan's "Dark Rosaleen" is a re-working of an older folk song). Especially important is the older Celtic goddess, the "Sovereignty," whose union with the king symbolized not only the prosperous tie of the soil with the extension of the reign, but especially the spiritual and juridical dominion of the king. Disasters and epidemics were taken as signs of an improper union between king and the Sovereignty – just as the plague in Oedipus' Thebes was related to his incestuous union with the mother.

Among the Irish contexts for Molly is the trickster-figure of the *puella senilis*, as Shann Van Vocht, the poor and ugly old hag who turns into a beautiful girl.[15] Note that *Ulysses* begins with Stephen's reflection of the "poor old woman" and ends with Molly. Secondly: the commanding warrior-figure of Medhbh in the epic *Táin Bó Cúailnge*, notorious for her

---

[13] Juliet Mitchell and Jacqueline Rose (eds.), *Jacques Lacan and the 'école freudienne'* (Houndmills and London: Macmillan, 1982), p. 48. Rose explains Lacan's theory of sexual difference.
[14] See Maria Tymoczko, *The Irish "Ulysses"* (Berkeley: University of California Press, 1994), who deals at length with the Irish backgrounds to Molly.
[15] The term *puella senilis* derives from Tymoczko, *The Irish "Ulysses"*, p. 100.

guiltless adultery. She captures Molly's quality as phallic mother who slays the suitors with the sharpness of her tongue. Finally, the great-bladdered Emer prefigures a Molly on the chamberpot, complaining about the quantity of fluid she exudes. Shape-shifting, victoriously adulterous and flowing with menstrual blood and urine, Molly Bloom incarnates all three at once.

It is important to understand that the representation of a female figure in the Ireland of Joyce's time may, almost automatically, have been taken as an allegory of national identity. It is even more important to recollect that, by the beginning of the twentieth century, the always already spiritualized female allegory of the nation, intensified by and linked with the puritanical ideal of Woman of Irish Catholicism, had grown into a sacred image and emblem of "purity." Even a seemingly innocent play like Synge's "Playboy of the Western World" created outrage because it was thought that no (pure) Irish girl could love a parricide.[16] As Richard Kearney argues, by the time Joyce began to write:

Woman [had become] as sexually intangible as the ideal of national independence became politically intangible. Both entered the unreality of myth. They became aspirations rather than actualities. Thus it might be argued that a sociological transposition of Irish women into desexualized and quasi-divine mothers corresponds somehow to an ideological transposition of Ireland from a Fatherland . . . into idioms connoting a Motherland. As the psychoanalysts remind us, the mother has always been a powerful unconscious symbol for one's forfeited or forbidden origins.[17]

In this light, Joyce's flaunting of "impurity," and the fact that he prided himself on the "obscenity" of Penelope, acquire a new context.[18] Indeed, he listed *Ulysses* among the important books of the world because of its "original" style, especially in "Penelope" and "Circe," the chapters he also considered most obscene; he boasted to Arthur Power that "[i]f we have a merit it is that we are uninhibited."[19] In a letter to Stanislaus he vituperated loudly against the "lying drivel about pure men and women" which "nauseated" him since few Europeans were free from the threat of syphilis.[20] In thus making his heroine an adulteress, Lloyd suggests, Joyce is making an argument in the name of truth

---

[16] See Stephen Tifft, "The Parricidal Phantasm: Irish Nationalism and the *Playboy* Riots," in *Nationalisms and Sexualities*, ed. Andrew Parker et al. (New York: Routledge, 1992), pp. 313–43, for a full discussion of the psychodynamic of Synge's play.

[17] In C. L. Innes, *Woman and Nation in Irish Literature and Society, 1880–1935* (Hemel Hempstead: Harvester-Wheatsheaf, 1993), p. 22.   [18] *Letters I*, p. 170.

[19] See Arthur Power, *Conversations with James Joyce*, p. 95.   [20] *SL*, p. 129.

against the falseness of the Irish allegory of the nation as pure woman; in writing her stream of consciousness, he is also trying to liberate the authentic mother tongue.

In order to understand the strange complication operative in the figure of Molly who is at once emblem of sexual "otherness" and original Irish womanhood, Mother Ireland and sexual object, we must get a grasp of the sleight of hand Joyce practises here: The idea of the "originality" of the nation travels under the banner of sexual liberation. The transgressive eroticism of Molly's thoughts makes up the distinativeness of her discourse as "mother tongue." In *A Portrait*, where sexual experience is privileged as the origin of the conscience of the race, Stephen had already constructed a countermyth to the notion of pure womanhood. This occurs when Stephen's friend Davin questions his nationalist loyalty, wanting to enlist Stephen in the cause of the Irish revival: "are you Irish at all?" (*P* 201) Refusing to accept the claim of a debt that must be paid in self-sacrifice and blood, in response he proudly points to his family tree in the office of arms (graphic-iconic inscription as warrant of identity), and turns the discussion towards sexual experience as the discourse of true liberation and self-identity. Davin retaliates by saying that he wishes that Stephen had not told him certain things. At this, "[a] tide began to surge beneath the calm surface of Stephen's friendliness." Davin's wish to *not know* and remain "pure" – indicating everything Joyce hated in his countrymen – provokes Stephen's recalcitrance:

–My ancestors threw off their language and took another, Stephen said. They allowed a handful of foreigners to subject them. Do you fancy I am going to pay in my own life and person debts they made? What for?
–For our freedom, said Davin.
–No honourable and sincere man, said Stephen, has given up to you his life and his youth and his affections from the days to Tone to those of Parnell, but you sold him to the enemy or failed him in need or reviled him and left him for another. And you invite me to be one of you. I'd see you damned first . . .
–The soul is born, he said vaguely, first in those moments I told you of. It has a slow and dark birth, more mysterious than the birth of the body. When the soul of a man is born in this country there are nets flung at it to hold it back from flight. You talk to me of nationality, language, religion. I shall try to fly by those nets. (*P* 203)

Stephen points to sexual experience, "those moments," as the origin of the *soul*, as he also does in the scene with Emma where he speaks of the birth of the *soul* of a girl at the moment of first menstruation (*P* 222).

Stephen insists that the soul is not (yet) tolerated by Irish culture: "Those moments" are precisely what Davin prefers not to become "conscious of." They cannot be admitted to discourse. Stephen's decision to go into exile is, therefore, a choice for free sexual expression in order to lift Irish repression (connoted "*omertà*" in Joyce's Trieste Notebook), and necessary to "forge in the smithy of [his] soul the uncreated conscience of [his] race" (*P* 253) as the freedom to speak of the ecstasy of the body in order to foster a *soul*. Moreover, Joyce's notes contain the following phrase in connection with "Dedalus": "He hoped that by sinning whole-heartedly his race might come in him to the knowledge of herself" (*P* 293). Thus the obscenity of "Penelope" may, to Joyce, have been liberational and utopian; and Molly Bloom seems to have been intended as countermyth to the contemporary figuration of Irishness as chaste, dutiful, daughterly, or maternal, because Joyce's writing of the words which Irish lips would not speak, would give material presence to what his culture repressed.

As the reader of *A Portrait* remembers, "those moments" are also the source of Stephen's poetry, and his "speech" is "the symbol of the element of mystery" (*P* 223). Thus writing and sexuality are bound up in each other in Stephen's mythology of the artist. In combination, they support Joyce's invention of the revolutionary signifier. I suggest we see "Penelope" as Joyce's attempt at *writing out* the repressed force of sexuality as an originary force and presence. The myth of sexual liberation fuses with the intention of writing, hence materializing the mythic, because as yet non-configurable "soul" of the nation, and by extension, the self.

However "original," "obscene," and revolutionary Joyce himself may have conceived his allegory of an unpure woman, paradoxically, Joyce remains within the Irish tradition – albeit the older Celtic one. As I said, Molly's flow of urine (and menstruation – the moment of constitution of the soul) may derive from the example of the great-bladdered Emer; her open sexuality from the phallic woman Medhbh; and her metamorphic function in the text of *Ulysses* (which I shall outline in this chapter) from the shape-shifting figure of Shann Van Vocht who embodies the concept of metempsychosis, and transforms herself from an old woman into a young girl. Moreover, like the Sovereignty, Molly eludes possession by one man.[21] Thus Joyce's myth of sexuality as the source of the soul remains expressed in images

---

[21] See Robert Welch, who emphasizes the mobility of the sovereign, and the men she finds acceptable as king, *Changing States*, pp. 272–82.

provided by Irish culture. It does not escape its nets. He repeats the Irish gesture of the participation of the image of the individual in that of the nation, one representing the other. In resorting to attributes of figures from ancient rather than nineteenth-century myths and history, he places himself as different and in reaction to the prevailing representation of the nation, but not as "other" or "outsider." Paradoxically, he transmits its cultural memory. In short: instead of behind the skirts of the pure, maternal image of contemporary tradition, Joyce, always the son of Mother Ireland, hides behind her sexy phallic precursor. It is from the safety of this position that he wages war upon the King's English and attempts to usurp the tradition of the English novel.[22] Let me make a bold and polemical claim: in cultural-historical retrospect it would seem to be that Irish-derived figure of Woman which, presented to the world in Paris, has also functioned as figure for the self-stylization of the otherness of deconstructive writing. Since, I argue, Derrida saw Joyce as emblem of his own style, we may claim that poststructuralism follows the trail blazed by Joyce's adaptation of the Irish allegory, which facilitated his revisionary use of the figuration of origin and identity as feminine. In the following pages I shall try to articulate how the discursive function of this figure of Woman encrypts the threat of castration it contains – making possible Derrida's denial of Lacan's one-sided ."truth." "Penelope," which allegorizes its own genesis, is, I argue, a representation which asks us to look beyond the rhetoric of "writing," and to enquire into the cultural-historical circumstances which facilitated the rise of a discourse which uncovers the limits of discourse. Its provenance dates from the precise historical moment when new technologies of representation like cinema, of special interest to Joyce, seemingly transcended the finality of absence and death. Early movies strike us as fantastic owing to the glee with which they exploited the power of the medium to create the illusion of the impossible. The fetishistic denial of deconstructive writing ought to be related to the cultural impact of these other technologies of representation, as well as the general tendency toward commodity fetishism of western capitalism. Joyce's modernity, I contend, rests in his early detection and appropriation of the cultural evolution of the twentieth century, owing to the specific determination of Irish culture and history.

[22] On the relation of modernist textuality to the fetish of writing and the skirts of the phallic mother, see Marcia Ian, *Remembering the Phallic Mother: Psychoanalysis, Modernism, and the Fetish* (Ithaca: Cornell University Press, 1993). Ian pays little attention to Joyce.

THE SUPPLEMENT OF ORIGIN

As Foucault pointed out, discourses may "circulate without changing their form from one strategy to another, opposing strategy. We must not expect the discourses on sex to tell us . . . what ideology – dominant or dominated – they represent; rather we must question them on the two levels of their tactical productivity (what reciprocal effects of power and knowledge they ensure) and their strategical integration (what conjunction and what force relationship make their utilization necessary in a given episode of the various configurations that occur)."[23] The closing chapter of *Ulysses* is unmistakably intended as a participation in the early twentieth-century drive to make sexuality discursive. Joyce wrote to Frank Budgen:

Penelope is the clou of the book. The first sentence contains 2,500 words. There are eight sentences in the episode. It begins and ends with the female word *yes*. It turns like the huge earthball slowly surely and evenly round and round spinning, its four cardinal points being the female breasts, arse, womb and cunt expressed by the words *because, bottom* (in all senses bottom button, bottom of the glass, bottom of the sea, bottom of his heart), *woman, yes*. Though probably more obscene than any preceding episode it seems to me to be perfectly sane full amoral fertilisable untrustworthy engaging shrewd limited prudent indifferent *Weib. Ich bin der* [sic] *Fleisch der stets bejaht.*[24]

Joyce's slip of the pen – gendering the flesh masculine instead of neuter – will prove telling. The discourse on sexuality is the linchpin of the book, the moment when language fuses with representation, and "female words" come "to be" "indifferent [neuter] *Weib*." In other words, "Penelope" is predicated upon Joyce's odd attitude to body and language. In addition to a representational function, "Penelope" has a performative function. It is language which makes present, like God's spermatic word in Genesis. Thus the chapter is seen as the presencing of pure materiality, affirmative *fleisch* (the opposite of the Goethean "*Geist*" [spirit] which always negates), while couched as the essence of disembodied voice – the *logos*. However impossibly double or utopian Joyce's conception may seem, Joyce underscores its importance. This "female" style is "the clou of the book."

Reductively essentializing the feminine as *Fleisch* and *Weib*, and assig-

---

[23] *The History of Sexuality, Volume 1: An Introduction*, trans. Robert Hurley (1976; New York: Pantheon Books, 1978), p. 102.

[24] Since Stuart Gilbert, the editor of Joyce's *Letters*, did not only omit a four-letter word, but silently corrected Joyce's gendering of the German word for flesh as masculine rather than neuter, I must quote from *SL*, p. 285.

ning it the role of "clou" to his text, Joyce seems to present a variant on the dual operation of an economy which devalues and abjects the feminine, placing her as different outside the self-image in order to safeguard self-integrity, but also maintaining an idealizing hypostasis of the feminine, making it the substitute image of the other of the self – the "other." The doubleness of this strategy manifests itself everywhere in the structure of Joyce's text. It is present in the image of Molly/Penelope who is at once silent and intensely loquatious, muted and vocal. She is both rooted and wildly wandering: her mind rambles illogically from present to past, Dublin to Gibraltar, but her body is fixed in bed and bedroom. The chapter supposedly approaches the dissolution of the dream-state, but it belies its oneiric quality in the garishness of its descriptive detail (the menstrual blood flowing in the chamberpot). Moreover, the placement of the chapter itself in Joyce's text is treated with ambivalence. Although in calling it the "clou" Joyce seems to place his female utopia as the *epitome* of his fiction, its actual embedding in the text and Joyce's own comments belie that distinction.

Joyce wrote to his Maecenas, Harriet Shaw Weaver, to inform her that not the last chapter of *Ulysses*, but the preceding "Ithaca" was "in reality the end as *Penelope* has no beginning, middle or end."[25] Thus Karen Lawrence concludes *The Odyssey of Style* with a discussion of "Ithaca" because "Penelope" does not add to fabula or story. A. Walton Litz also points to "Ithaca" as "the end of *Ulysses* as novel and fable." His comment is suggestive, because it forces us to rethink what we understand by "novel." Splitting *Ulysses* into two discourses: a book or text, and a "novel and fable,"[26] he forces us to see as separate what we conventionally conflate into one – the discourse/story on the one hand, and the text (the material and linguistic substrate, the screen upon which fabula/story appears) on the other. In narratological terms, "Penelope" stands by itself as a chapter of text (no longer a part of fabula and story), whereas "Ithaca" closes the fabula and story. Thus the "novel" *Ulysses* unravels into two layers together making up the embodied work of literature: one layer presents the father–son plot and abjects the mother; the other materializes and neuters the mother as the matrix of the text.

Joyce himself instructed the printer to place an oversize dot after "Ithaca." This dot functions as the point where one semiotic mode makes way for another:

[25] *L I*, p. 172.   [26] "Ithaca," in *James Joyce's "Ulysses: Critical Essays,"* ed. Clive Hart, p. 404.

When?
Going to dark bed there was a square round Sinbad the Sailor roc's auk's egg in the night of the bed of all the auks of the rocs of Darkinbad the Brightdayler.
Where?
■

(*U* 17.2327–32)

Squaring the circle of the riddle of human identity, the oversize period, in early editions sometimes even printed as a fat square mark on the page, provides a transition from fabula/story to the materiality of the text and its writing.[27] It is writing which squares the circle. The period also emphasizes "Ithaca's" masculine difference from "Penelope." The inky darkness of the square/round dot makes a window in the text through which the masculine protagonist transmigrates into the "other-world" of sleep and eternity.[28] Thus the siren song of "Penelope" is placed as feminine, and ek-static to the masculine fabula/story. Joyce commented on its function as: "the indispensable countersign to Bloom's passport to eternity."[29] The meaning of this use of the term "eternity" grows clear in Joyce's suggestion that Bloom and Stephen will become "heavenly bodies, wanderers like the stars at which they gaze."

In short, the end of *Ulysses* is split, blurred and recrossed; the ambiguity inherent in the Irish construction of masculinity coincides with the shimmering and oscillating redoubling of the boundary which marks the difference between narrative and text, inside and outside, fiction and the real, sign and the thing itself.[30] "Penelope" may be understood as a supplement in Derrida's sense: itself ambivalent, it is a surplus, a "plenitude enriching another plenitude, the *fullest* measure of presence." But,

[i]f it represents and makes an image, it is by the anterior default of a presence. Compensatory and vicarious, the supplement is an adjunct, a subaltern instance which *takes-(the)-place*. As substitute it is not simply added to the positivity of a presence, it produces not relief, its place is assigned in the structure by the mark of an emptiness. Somewhere, something can be filled up *of itself*, can

---

[27] Austin Briggs, "The Full Stop at the End of 'Ithaca': Thirteen Ways – and Then Some – of Looking at a Black Dot," in *Joyce Studies Annual: 1996*, ed. Thomas F. Staley (Austin: University of Texas Press, 1996), pp. 125–45, gives a full survey of the history of interpretation of this dot.

[28] Note that "circling the square" is the "last public misappearance" of the Derridean Shem-figure in *Finnegans Wake* (186.12).   [29] *L I*, p. 160.

[30] As Enda Duffy shows, it also affects the interpretation of Molly Bloom as postcolonial subject: "Molly Bloom is, therefore, both the image of the wholly interpellated subject, a type of the ideal colonial native, and simultaneously a shifting signifier that is at flash-moments deployed at a distance from the text altogether." *The Subaltern Ulysses*, p. 183.

accomplish itself, only by allowing itself to be filled through sign and proxy. The sign is always the supplement of the thing itself.[31]

Thus the ambiguity of the ending becomes an allegory of signification and writing itself. "Penelope," which stands outside the fabula, relates to it as the extrinsicness of the sign to the thing itself. It is the "clou" of *Ulysses* because its style "represents" the "thing itself," the fabula and story which it replays in memory-dream. More specifically, the supplement of the virtually unpunctuated flowing style of Molly's chapter is the "countersign" of the signature of Joyce's writing as a writing outside the sentence.[32] Thus "Penelope" is the literalized *personification* or *Darstellung* of Bhabha's "writing outside the sentence." But note that here the "outside the sentence" is enclosed *in* the sentence of the book/text seen as a representation. The supplement is outside, but also inside. *Thus it is the enclosure of the allegory of the otherness of its textuality within the covers of the text which elevates the text to the status and power of the phallus or a purloined letter: a signifier which surpasses the lack which it signifies, a signifier transcending a determinate signified.*[33]

The blurring ambiguity which we noted in the placement of "Penelope" as the final chapter of *Ulysses* also operates here. The functional presence of the feminine in the text of the masculine author engenders an oscillating blurring of the binaries of inside–outside, self and other, which at once comprehends and incorporates the other and disrupts the possibility of defining either self or other as self-identical. Here we have the mechanism of the invention of gender – sexual difference no longer thought of as an essential binary but as a discursive formation. Thus the clear line of demarcation between masculine and feminine, the thing itself and its supplement, begins to oscillate through Joyce's strategy of padding his fabula/story with an extra, appended chapter which stands outside fabula and story but which is part of the text, and which exemplifies the feminine. In fact, Irish Joyce participates

---

[31] *Of Grammatology*, trans. Gayatri Chakravorty Spivak (Baltimore: Johns Hopkins University Press, 1976), pp. 144–45.

[32] Laplanche, *Dictionary of Psychoanalysis*, pp. 176–77, calls this literalization of the flow of writing a "functional phenomenon" present in hypnagogic states and dream, the "transportation into an image" not of the "*content* of the subject's thought but of its present *mode* of operation." See also: Christine Van Boheemen, *The Novel as Family Romance: Language, Gender and Authority from Fielding to Joyce* (Ithaca: Cornell University Press, 1987).

[33] We must beware that we do not fall into the trap of blindly identifying speech and writing with political action, and claiming that Joyce articulates the Mother's desire, or succeeds in "Becoming Woman." Joseph Valente, *James Joyce and the Problem of Justice: Negotiating Sexual and Colonial Difference* (Cambridge University Press, 1995) points out that "Becoming Woman" does not entail speaking "for" women.

avant la lettre in what Alice Jardine, speaking of poststructuralist thought, has called "Gynesis": postmodernity's resorting to the use of gender to give figure to its own projective stepping beyond the logos or the fabula/story of western philosophy.[34]

THE CONFESSING VAGINA AND THE DARK CONTINENT OF FEMININITY

Let us return to Joyce's own epithet "obscene." Walter Kendrick's definition of pornography in *The Secret Museum: Pornography in Modern Culture*[35] does not address the common qualities of a group of texts or images, but their social determination. Pornography is what is, or once was, censored. Today, towards the end of the century, we may have become immune to the violent novelty of Joyce's obsessively voyeuristic representation of Molly Bloom. Television and video clips bring sexual phantasy into the sanctity of the home; and familiarity has attenuated the shock-effect of her polymorphous perversity. To us, "Penelope" seems hardly obscene; and our criticism tends to emphasize the positive values of Molly's affirmation and her endurance.

Contemporary reaction was markedly different from our polite acceptance. In February 1922, in a letter from Trieste, Stanislaus referred to "Penelope" as an "obscene ignorant scrawl"[36]; the *Daily Express* of March 25 found itself aggressively confronted with "all our most secret and most unsavoury private thoughts"[37]; the *Sporting Times* called it a "glorification of mere filth," ultimately "supremely nauseous," while *To-Day* concluded simply: "most disgusting." Modernist writers joined the chorus.[38] We cannot but believe that the censorship of *Ulysses* reflected accepted middle-class norms. Even the unsqueamish Stephen of *A Portrait*, who saw menstruation as woman's "strange humiliation" and "dark shame" (*P* 222), might have found the frothing stream of Molly's urine and menstrual blood intrusively garish.

In fact, my association of "Penelope" with pornography derives from Joyce himself. Not only did he give his heroine a name denoting

---

[34] Alice A. Jardine, *Gynesis: Configurations of Woman and Modernity* (Ithaca: Cornell University Press, 1985).   [35] (New York: Viking Press, 1987).   [36] *L III*, p. 58.

[37] *James Joyce: The Critical Heritage 1 1907–1927*, ed. Robert H. Deming (London: Routledge, Kegan and Paul, 1977) p. 191.

[38] See Margot Norris, *Joyce's Web: The Social Unravelling of Modernism* (University of Austin Press, 1992), p. 70 and *passim*; and Patrick Parrinder's "The Strange Necessity: James Joyce's Rejection in England (1914–30)," in Colin McCabe (ed.), *James Joyce: New Perspectives*. Parrinder documents contemporary charges of Joyce's "cloacal obsession" (Wells), the "record diarrhoea" of *Ulysses* (Wyndham Lewis), "obsessions arseoreial, cloacal" (Pound).

"whore," and emphasized the association through Molly's allusion to Moll Flanders as a "whore"[39]; in September 1921, in a letter to Frank Budgen he had asked his friend for "Fanny Hill's Memoirs (unexpurgated)."[40] This specific request allows me to shift from Kendrick's sociological perspective on *Ulysses* as pornography, to the rhetoric of pornography. "Penelope" belongs to an ancient tradition of texts in which women speak the secret of their sexuality, revealing its truth, staging its "true" nature. Molly Bloom confesses her pleasure in sexual intercourse, describing her physical response even more emphatically than John Cleland's Fanny Hill. Linda Williams begins her study of pornography in film with pointing to Diderot's 1748 fable *Les bijoux indiscrets* (*The Indiscrete Jewels*).[41] A genie tries to satisfy the Sultan's wishes to hear women speak of their experience, and gives him a ring which will facilitate this wish. The women will speak of their adventures loudly and explicitly, whenever he turns the stone of this ring. The genie adds that the Sultan should not be misled and believe that the women speak with their mouths. The astonished Sultan learns that they will instead use that organ which is most knowledgeable on the subject of sex, their "jewel." We might see "Penelope," in its sexual explicitness, as an avatar of *Fanny Hill* spoken not through the mouth, but through Molly's "jewel."[42]

Joyce, striving to create the Irish "soul," participates in the drive to speak about sexuality which, according to Foucault in *The History of Sexuality*, has been the discursive characteristic of western culture of the last century. Thus the drive to give a living habitation and a name to the non-presence of Irish discursive identity brings Joyce to consider the modern discourse of sexuality as the possible vehicle of his own project. Therefore, Joyce is even more specifically engaged in the effort to lift the hem of the secret of femininity which preoccupied not only pornographers but also medical science. From Charcot, through Freud to Lacan,[43] the impetus of the work of psychiatry seems to have been to fill

---

[39] Etymologically, "pornography" means "writing about whores."
[40] *L I*, p. 171. See also: Phillip F. Herring, *Joyce's Notes and Early Drafts for Ulysses: Selections from the Buffalo Collection* (Charlottesville: University Of Virginia Press, 1971), p. 63.
[41] *Hard Core: Power, Pleasure, and the Frenzy of the Visible* (Berkeley: University of California Press, 1989), p. 1. The fable is also mentioned by Foucault.
[42] Frances Restuccia, *Joyce and the Law of the Father* (New Haven: Yale University Press, 1989), p. 94, speaks of the chapter as a "womb of words."
[43] Lacan wrote his doctoral thesis entitled "*Aimée*" (1932) on a case of psychosis; in 1933 he published an essay on The Papin Sisters; and in the seventies he explicitly addressed woman's "*jouissance*." In addition to *Feminine Sexuality: Jacques Lacan and the "école freudienne,"* ed. Juliet Mitchell and Jacqueline Rose, see *De la psychose paranoïaque dans ses rapports avec la personnalité* (Paris: Seuil, 1975).

in the map of the "dark continent" of female sexuality, to answer its riddle. Thus the mystery of the feminine became the motor of textuality. The enigma of a living body – in contrast to the generic convention of the detective story which makes a corpse the engine of the plot – provides the hermeneutic drive for medical science. It might even be argued that a certain train of philosophy plays upon its priviliged insight into the "truth" of the feminine. Nietzsche's words in *Ecce Homo* suggest as much: "May I here venture the surmise that I *know* women? That is part of my Dionysian dowry. Who knows? Perhaps I am the first psychologist of the eternally feminine."[44]

Apparently, understanding this secret entailed social and cultural prestige, probably also for Joyce – who had always wanted to become a medical doctor himself. Thus he praised the venerated Ibsen for his portrayal of women. "[H]e seems to know them better than they know themselves" (*CW* 64). When he read Jung's comments on *Ulysses* he cannot but have taken pride in this confirmation of his own intellectual stature and avant-garde importance: "The 40 pages of non stop run in the end is a string of veritable psychological peaches. I suppose the devil's grandmother knows so much about the real psychology of a woman. I didn't."[45] Although Joyce vented his disappointment at Jung's unsmiling reading of *Ulysses*, he was eager to have this authoritative opinion of his superior insight broadcast. He must have taken it as a compliment.

More recently, we have come to query the truth-value of this filling in of the map of the other. Woman as the defining limit, the horizon of man, will remain and cannot but remain behind the veil.[46] As Stephen Heath writes in *Men in Feminism*: "All representation, we know, is transferential. Representation is at once an image given, an argument made and a deputation established, a construction of object, me and other. Representation, to put it another way, includes my position, my desire and its vicissitudes."[47] Heath's words recapitulate Morrison's lesson that the subject of the dream is the dreamer. This implies that "Penelope" can never be seen as the presentation of an objective truth about female sexuality (not even of Nora Joyce, who supposedly sat for this portrait). Nor is it the *Darstellung* of the conscience of the race or the

[44] *On the Genealogy of Morals and Ecce Homo*, ed. and trans. Walter Kaufmann (New York: Vintage Books, 1969), p. 266.   [45] *L III*, p. 253.

[46] Sarah Kofman, *The Enigma of Woman: Woman in Freud's Writing*, trans. Catherine Porter (Ithaca: Cornell University Press, 1985).

[47] "Men in Feminism: Men and Feminist Theory" in *Men in Feminism*, ed. Alice Jardine and Paul Smith (New York and London: Methuen, 1987), p. 44.

liberation of the mother tongue. Participating in the carnival of the redistribution of forces in the language economy of the beginning of this century, Joyce's style remains the projection upon the screen of representation of the unconscious content of a patriarchal mind.

In this context it is interesting to note that Joyce, according to Budgen, complained loudly about the "invasiveness" of women, and their "perpetual urge to usurp all the functions of the male."[48] The son, unable to extricate himself from the tie to the mother, accuses women of what he practices himself in his attempt at liberation: usurpation. This transposition betrays a homology to colonialism. It silences women as occupied territory, and lets men speak for them. Not surprisingly, the notesheets in the British Museum give us the following specification of Molly's "jewel": "her cunt, darkest Africa."[49] The organ which "speaks" "Penelope" is not only obscenely sexual, it is also explicitly named as the exotic dark continent. Joyce's orientalism may betray the ideological climate of the beginning of the century, but in emphasizing the "foreignness" of Molly's jewel, he also underscores his own magical powers. He can make this "heart of darkness" speak. Thus he demonstrates that he is capable of engendering the cultural domain,[50] by giving the world an apotropaeic image of femininity of such seeming naturalness, force and difference, that it can and will contain not only personal, but collective fears of extinction or "castration."[51]

This strategy of representation places Joyce in the context of what Hal Foster has called "modernist primitivism."[52] Foster's discussion moves from Freud's "primal scene" which riddles out the problem of origin, and its related scenarios (the fantasy of seduction, the trauma of

[48] *James Joyce and the Making of "Ulysses"* (1934; repr. Bloomington: Indiana University Press, 1960), p. 318. Also note the projective attribution of "woman's weapon" (*U.* 9.461).

[49] *Joyce's "Ulysses" Notesheets in the British Museum*, ed. Phillip Herring (Charlottesville, University of Virginia Press, 1972), p. 494. Note that Molly comes from Gibraltar (the point of Europe closest to Africa. Sheldon Brivic, *Joyce's Waking Women: An Introduction to "Finnegans Wake"* (Madison: University of Wisconsin Press, 1995), argues that Anna Livia, the figure of the female in *Finnegans Wake*, has African attributes.

[50] Luce Irigaray, in *Je, tu, nous: Toward a Culture of Difference*, trans. Alison Martin (New York and London: Routledge, 1993), p. 69, argues that "Men's appropriation of the linguistic code attempts to do at least three things: 1) prove they are fathers; 2) prove they are more powerful than mother-women; 3) prove they are capable of engendering the cultural domain as they have been engendered in the natural domain of the ovum, the womb, the body of a woman."

[51] See also Peter Brooks, "Nana at Last Unveil'd? Problems of the Modern Nude," in *Body Work: Objects of Desire in Modern Narrative* (Cambridge, Mass.: Harvard University Press, 1993).

[52] Hal Foster, "'Primitive' Scenes," *Critical Inquiry* 21 (1993): 69–103. See also: Mary Ann Doane, "Dark Continents: Epistemologies of Racial and Sexual Difference in Psychoanalysis and Cinema," *Femmes Fatales: Feminism, Film Theory, Psychoanalysis* (New York: Routledge, 1991), pp. 209–48.

castration), to the construction of masculinity in and by the "primitive scenes" in Gauguin, Kirchner, and Picasso – as in the latter's *Les Demoiselles d'Avignon* (a brothel scene involving African masks) which is seen as the founding moment of Cubism.[53] Foster writes: "On one level it concerns the founding of a *style*, often articulated around a specific work; this staging of a stylistic origin is a familiar trope in high-modernist manifestos and memoirs. On another level it involves the founding of a *subject*; in fact the stylistic founding often involves this subjective one. The ambiguity between these two origins is irreducible; often it is as if the stylistic founding structures the subjective origin retrospectively, even as the subjective origin impels the stylistic founding into being."[54] Using the primitive to exorcise the fear and threat of the primitive, modernist primitivism employs the "other," the uncontainable, against the fear of indistinction, and displays a classical ambivalence: "Picasso sees in 'the primitive' a recognition of the intimacy of the sacred and the defiled, of the potency of disorder and dirt. In this realm of pollution and taboo he locates the objects as agents endowed with fetishistic, even apotropaeic power (*intercesseurs*, shields, weapons), as 'spirits' to be used to defend against 'spirits'."[55] More pertinent still in connection with the function of "Penelope" as *monologue intérieur* placed outside the fabula/story: Studying Picasso's revision of *Les Demoiselles*, Foster points out how the painting was turned from a *narrative* mode:

perhaps an allegory of syphilis with a sailor seated at the center and a medical student on the far left . . . – to an *iconic* register, in which these surrogates for the Picassoid viewer are dropped out. The effect of this elision is to render *Les Demoiselles* a direct address. It becomes the encounter of the viewer. Indeed, the stare of the prostitutes for the Picassoid subject is like the stare of the wolves for the Wolf-Man. The look of the viewer is doubled, and he too is suspended between desire and identification, attraction and anxiety.[56]

"Penelope," like Picasso's painting, balances on the border between *ob*-scenity, where the object, without scene, comes too close to the reader, and the pornographic, where the object is staged for the viewer who is thus given distance enough to be its voyeur; and it is Joyce's

[53] John Golding, "Cubism," *Concepts of Modern Art*, ed. Tony Richardson and Nikos Stangos (New York: Harper & Row, 1974), pp. 53–82.   [54] "Primitive Scenes," 74.   [55] *Ibid.*, 91–92.
[56] *Ibid.*, 94. Foster refers to William Rubin's analysis in "From Narrative to 'Iconic' in Picasso: The Buried Allegory in *Bread and Fruitdish on a Table* and the Role of *Les Demoiselles d'Avignon*," *Art Bulletin* 65 (1983): 615–49. Foster's reading is supported by John Richardson, *A Life of Picasso, Volume 2: The Painter of Modern Life* (London: Cape, 1996).

invention of this literary style which, I argue, founds literary modernism just as Picasso's painting initiated Cubism.

"Penelope," like "The Dead," was a pivot in Joyce's work, but of a different order. If the completion of the short story facilitated the writing of *A Portrait of the Artist* and *Ulysses*, the flow of "Penelope" prepared the relinquishing of the representational imperative in *Finnegans Wake*. Just as Picasso's *Les Desmoiselles* of 1907 initiated the break-up of representation, "Penelope" marks the beginning of "the revolution of the word," as the belief that writing transforms the world and constitutes a new reality. Just as Picasso permanently changed our perception of visual space, "Penelope" added a new dimension to novelistic expression and the function of the literary sign.

THE THREAT OF AN ENDING

What unites "The Dead" and "Penelope" is their status as endings. They are conclusions to a body of text. If the ending of "The Dead" is notoriously ambivalent, Joyce himself was ambivalent about the ending of *Ulysses*. He sent "Penelope" to the printer before the completion of "Ithaca," and, as we noted, wrote Harriet Weaver that that episode was "in reality the end." It is as if finality generated a certain anxiety in Joyce, and had to be postponed and circumscribed by never declaring the work finished. Ending may have been related to the threat of death. In one of his letters to Harriet Weaver he refers to the writing of "Penelope," concluding: "Bloom and all the Blooms will soon be dead, thank God. Everyone says he ought to have died long ago . . ."[57] Even Molly herself seems identified with death. Ellmann relates Joyce's dream about Molly, in which she picks up a "snuffbox, in the form of a little black coffin" and throws it at Joyce with the words "I have done with you too, Mr. Joyce."[58] Here the term "snuff" bears associations with extinction, while Molly's "box" also has the shape of a coffin. Looking at the other dreams Ellmann mentions in these pages, it strikes me how many are associated with death: female mourners, the imprisoning effect of boxes, the threat of extinction by "little beast"'s, women in black clothes. Joyce's dreams seem to breathe a general tone of anxiety about death and the feminine. The pattern of association fits Freud's suggestion that the fear of death should be seen as analogous to the fear of castration.[59]

In Ellmann's biography, these dreams are immediately followed by a

---

[57] *L I*, 168.   [58] *James Joyce*, p. 549.   [59] "Inhibitions, Symptoms and Anxiety," *SE* 20, 128–29.

parodic ballad which fuses the characters of Molly Bloom and Anna Livia as "flowers" (both streams and blossoms related to Ireland: roses, but also the deadly flower of the potato blight). Interesting to me is not only the extreme promiscuity which it attributes to Molly, but its conjunction with a refrain echoing the threat of death: "She's left me on the doorstep like a dog for to die" and "O Molly, handsome Molly, sure you won't let me die?"[60] Note that Joyce's attribution of independence to his creature Molly Bloom confirms the auratic quality of the fetish as an object charged with a special power or force and independent life. The image of Molly Bloom carries two suggestions: rampant sexuality and the threat of extinction to her son–author. She has the power of the Medusa.

If Joyce saw Molly Bloom as a castrating female who threatens to "cut them off him so I would" (*U* 18.998), not so different in the end from the other female monsters (a Calypso, a Siren, a Scylla, a Charybdis, or the Circe) who had beset his Odysseus, he saw the figure of Molly also as the "clou" or instrument to take the sting out of this threat. The French dictionary suggests that the word "clou" can bear several interpretations: We can see "Penelope" as star turn of the novel, but also as the rivet of the text. Moreover, "*clouer*" means "fixing with a pointed instrument," such as a dagger (or a pen), and reducing to silence. As "clou," "Penelope" may have more than just a textual or formal function. In addition to ending the narrative, the chapter may have the psychosexual task of nailing the threat of finality, "fixing" the Medusa, and reducing to silence the fear of death generated by the act of ending. As "clou," "Penelope" transforms the anxiety related to a break in the forward flow of ink into a "passport to eternity" (Joyce's words about "Penelope").

The text of *Finnegans Wake* suggests as much when it refers to "Penelope" (in a passage voicing the narrator's weariness at the objections which had been raised to its obscenity, and highlighting the difficulty in ending):

and, eighteenthly or twentyfourthly,[61] but at least, thank Maurice,[62] lastly when all is zed and done, the penelopean patience of its last paraphe, a colophon of

---

[60] *James Joyce*, p. 550.

[61] Relating to the charge that *Ulysses* has eighteen episodes and the epic has twentyfour.

[62] This is not only the name of Darantiere, the printer (whose name ends the text, and whose decisiveness eventually forced Joyce to stop revising), but also of the (rival brother) character in *Stephen Hero* – the word "scrawl" which Joyce's brother Stanislaus had used to denote "Penelope," precedes shortly before (on *FW* 122).

no fewer than seven hundred and thirtytwo strokes tailed by a leaping lasso – who thus at all this marvelling but will press on hotly to see the vaulting feminine libido of those interbranching ogham sex upaninsweeps sternly controlled and easily repersuaded by the uniform matteroffactness of a meandering male fist? (*FW* 123.3–10).

In choosing the word "paraphe," Joyce denotes the chapter as the flourish added to a signature as a protection against forgery, labeling it supplementary, but also a safeguard against imitation (essentially authentic). The term "colophon" proves even more complex. The *Oxford Dictionary* gives "tail-piece . . . often ornamental." Joyce seems here at his ambivalent best. "Colophon" – which may be read as "culophone" ("cul" is French for "arse") in another variant of the "speaking jewel" – conflates the last part of a book (added as supplementary afterword and ornamental flourish) with the nether part of the body. But Joyce's favorite etymological dictionary *Skeat* tells us that "colophon" derives from the Greek word "*kolophoon*" which has the meanings "pinnacle" and "crown," suggesting rather the opposite. Thus the obscene afterpiece of "Penelope" is also the crowning star turn of the text. In fact, the "colophon" is the part of the book which inscribes the name of its maker; so that in choosing this word Joyce denotes this "speaking jewel" as the "passport to eternity" of his writerly immortality. Moreover, this "tail-piece" (also piece of tail) reconfirms the superiority of his masculine authority. It is "tailed by a leaping lasso" in 732 "strokes" (the number of pages of the first edition of *Ulysses*) thus containing the threat of the "vaulting feminine libido" through the agency of the writing, "meandering male fist." In short, "Penelope," stylistically a "leaping lasso" of a chapter, is characterized as the triumph of the writer's fist over feminine libido (personified as the unruly interlocking of the branches of the letters/trees of the Irish alphabet), constituting the imprint of its author's immortality. If there is a threat of death implied in the figure of Molly (or in ending a text in general) it is, and can (in Joyce's psychodynamic) be undone by his *writing the feminine*, just as Picasso had painted it.

Placing this passage about "Penelope" in its context in *Finnegans Wake*, it proves the conclusion of a long discussion of the *Tunc* page of the *Book of Kells*, where "Tunc" is the first word of the text of Matthew 27:38: "*Tunc crucifixerant XPI cum eo duos latrones*," "Then were there two thieves crucified with him." The Latin text differs from the English in that it clearly places Christ as object: "Then they crucified Christ and with him two thieves." Even this passage in *Finnegans Wake*, so seemingly concerned with writing and the representation of writing, predicates itself upon a dead body in a conjunction of death and signification. Here the ornamental elaboration of the large letter "T" provides an erect and flourishing scriptural-material antidote to the idea of the prostration of death contained in the meaning of the text.

One retrospective lesson from these pages in *Finnegans Wake* is that the writing of the feminine in "Penelope" should not be seen as performative of the feminine as "pure flesh." Molly is as already cast in the materiality of writing; her sexuality is already mediated through the letters of the Irish alphabet, which are, as is traditional, in turn named after trees – those "interbranching ogham sex upaninsweeps" (an image which transforms the snakes on Medusa's head into phallic symbols). Molly is the opposite of the "flesh-without-word" (*FW* 468.06); she is the "flesh-into-word," the flesh as *inscription* rather than decomposing maternal matter, graphic mark rather than a rotting corpse. Joyce triggers a spinning process of reversals of nature and culture, matter and sign, which turns around the dead body of Christ or HCE (the figure of the dead father in *Finnegans Wake*). This implies that it must have been the *act* of devising/writing "Penelope" itself which neutralized the threat of castration implied in her Medusan figure, and which made it possible for Joyce to move on from the threat of death of the feminine which haunts all of *Ulysses* obsessively, to the triumphant display of the prostrate presence of an unthreatening masculine-paternal dead body in *Finnegans Wake*. The writing of Molly Bloom was Joyce's "moly" (Odysseus' magic preservative guaranteeing survival) helping him to traverse the Scylla and Charybdis of submitting to the "sow that eats her own farrow" or self-annihilation. He traverses the great divide. Note that in the Irish alphabet the letter "I" is the yew tree, symbol of death.

WEAVING THE ASTRAL BODY

Joyce's notes for "Penelope" in the British Museum contain a suggestion. They read: "she weaves a deathshroud for *R* {Laertes which is Ul. coronation robe}."[63] Penelope's texture can reverse itself from a tissue enveloping a corpse into the token of royal power. Is "Penelope" itself the magic integument, the agency which transforms the penis into the crowning scepter of a phallus? At any rate, "Penelope," as conclusion of

---

[63] *Joyce's "Ulysses" Notesheets in the British Museum*, ed. Herring, p. 496.

the text, would seem to function as an apotropaeic strategy of coping with ending the flow and process of writing, in the act of writing the ending before the conclusion. But let us have a closer look at "Penelope" itself. The first thing which strikes me upon rereading it is its reversibility. On the one hand we have extreme obscenity: "if he wants to kiss my bottom Ill drag open my drawers and bulge it right out in his face as large as life he can stick his tongue 7 miles up my hole as hes there my brown part" (18.1520–22). This, as if by the flip of a coin, goes over into the lyricism which Derrida has called Joyce's "perfumative": "I love flowers Id love to have the whole place swimming in roses"; "I was a flower of the mountain yes so we are flowers all a womans body yes that was one true thing he said in his life and the sun shines for you today yes" (18.1557–58; 1575–88).

This flipping reversal of tone and mood seems related to another reversal having to do with age and youth. Joyce places in Molly's mouth a string of criticisms of older or ageing women – "sneezing and farting into the pots well of course [they are] old" (18.1083–84). She calls them "old faggot," "ugly," "vain" "filthy bitches"; notices the signs of age on their faces, accuses them of the desire "to be born all over again" (18. 1267–69). She worries that Bloom when he is out with "those medicals" will "imagine hes young again" (18.9260) and behave like the "old fool" he is. She notices that Bloom has a mid-life crisis: "all men get a bit like that at his age especially getting on to forty he is now" (18.50–51). She also tries to deny her own approaching sexual redundancy: "I suppose he thinks Im finished and laid on the shelf well Im not no nor anything like it well see well see" (18.1022–23). As all of *Ulysses*, Molly's soliloquy is suffused with the presence of death: she mourns Gardner who had died in the Boer War, Mulvey who may be dead or killed, thinks of the late Paddy Dignam, Nancy Blake, Mr Dillon, and especially her dead son Rudy. She has "heard the deathwatch too ticking in the wall" (18.1309); and senses the encroachment of nothingness as she lies awake: "I suppose theyre all dead and rotten long ago . . ." (18.977–79). When a thunderclap wakes her it is as if "the world was coming to an end" (18.138).

But just as obscenity can flip over to lyricism, so the cruel theme of old age and death reverses into youth and poetry, making the text "Bloom," letting its masculine subject return as a flower of rhetoric, immortal language, "the word that shall not pass away."[64] The central pivot in the

---

[64] In another sense, too, Bloom is already a flower of rhetoric. His father's name "Virag" (Hungarian for "flower") was somehow translated into English, although the name is the untranslatable sign outside the chain of substitution. Thus Bloom is already "Bloom," a sign, not a humanistic subject. Virag is also a circumcised virag(o) – without Molly's feminine "O."

text is the dot at the end of the fourth "period" where Molly herself makes a radical turn from evening to morning, old age to youth, old hag to attractive Shann Van Vocht:

but as for being a woman as soon as youre old they might as well throw you out in the bottom of the ashpit.
Mulveys was the first when I was in bed that morning . . . (18.746–49).

I am grateful to Hans Walter Gabler for restoring the period which concludes this middle sentence. Apart from the one following the final "Yes.", it is the only one in the soliloquy; and it marks the pivotal point of symbolic reversal where death turns into return and renewal, old age into blooming youth, and Shann Van Vocht returns as a young girl. Thus the significance of this dot seems related to the large dot at the end of "Ithaca," which marks the magical *locus* of Bloom's escape as heavenly body from text and print into eternity and starry night. In fact, the period within "Penelope" is its counterpointing confirmation, the repetition which seals and guarantees authenticity, its "paraphe." The repetition of the period sutures castration into the fold of the screen of the text.

If anything, it is the turning, recirculating movement of "Penelope," which according to its author traces the figure of the lemniscate, symbol of eternity, spinning "like the huge earthball slowly surely and evenly round and round," which would seem the "clou" to the resurrective power of the text.[65] It is its "spinning" in this sense (and not its "weaving") which takes the sting out of death, tracing a Moebius strip of renewal, rewriting "conclusion" as "metempsychosis." The movement of the heavenly body, the star, makes the femininity of Molly "prehuman" and "posthuman."[66] Thus "Penelope" incarnates what "Ithaca," in its association of Bloom and Stephen with stars and the fear of the cold of "interstellar spaces" had already claimed. "Penelope" is the performative of "Ithaca"'s constative.

Of course, on one level, this figuration of "Penelope" as instrumental symbol of eternal rebirth might be read as the displacing projection of Joyce's own concern with approaching middle age upon the screen of the text. He wanted the novel published on his fortieth birthday (as Molly's words suggest the typical age for a mid-life crisis at that time)[67]; and *Giacomo Joyce* records such a crisis between late 1911 and mid-1914, when Joyce was beginning *Ulysses*. *Giacomo Joyce*

---

[65] *L I*, p. 170.   [66] *L I*, p. 180.
[67] The protagonist of Italo Svevo's *Senilità* for which Joyce provided the title *As a Man Grows Older* is only 35! Joyce compared himself, at that age, to Dante beginning *The Divine Comedy*.

ends its dream of renewal through a dip in the adulterous fountain of youth, with renunciation: "It will never be. You know that well. What then? Write it, damn you, write it!" [68] At first sight this seems a different strategy of coping than that of "Penelope." *Giacomo Joyce* suggests sublimation, turning experience into art, drive into secondary process. But Joyce's words are not "write it down" in the sense of make a record of it, turn it into a story, he speaks of "writing it," where writing takes the place of experience and substitutes for it without the *Aufhebung* of sublimation. In this connection there is another aspect of *Giacomo Joyce* which draws our attention. If Joyce describes "Penelope" as a heavenly body, the earth turning indifferently and transcendently, there is in *Giacomo Joyce* a similar tendency to turn Amalia Popper into a heavenly body: "She speaks. A weak voice from beyond the cold stars"; she has "starborn flesh," and she is figured as a transcendent image of inhuman evil: "A starry snake has kissed me: a cold nightsnake. I am lost."[69] The similarity in gesture, transforming Molly and Amalia into "stars," astral bodies, suggests that this metaphor has special meaning, even more so because Joyce, in the dream referred to above, recounts a long speech to Molly which he ends on an "astronomical" climax, while the ballad compares her to "this gaily spinning earth of ours."[70]

How modern Joyce's revisionary inscription of the threat of the Medusa as her "astral" quality is, is perhaps suggested in Jean Baudrillard's *America*: "I went in search of *astral* America [*l'Amérique sidérale*] . . . the America of the empty, absolute freedom of the freeways . . . of desert speed, of motels and mineral surfaces. I looked for it in the speed of the screenplay, in the indifferent reflex of television, in the film of days and nights projected across an empty space, in the marvelously affectless succession of signs, images, faces, and ritual acts on

---

[68] *GJ*, p. 16. Note Joyce's inscription of this phrase in *Finnegans Wake*, playing on the "feminine O": (118.13–14): "wrote it, wrote it all, wrote it all down, and there you are, full stop. O, undoubtedly yes, and very potably so . . ."

[69] *Giacomo Joyce*, p. 15. Martha Fleischmann (his idol in Zurich around the time of beginning "Penelope," whose name takes on symbolic connotations in the context of this discussion), is also named a "star of evil, star of pain" in "Bahnhofstrasse," *PSW*, p. 62.

[70] Mario Praz and Bram Dijkstra show how the image of the Medusa proliferates in turn-of-the-century literature and visual art (see Praz, *The Romantic Agony*, trans. Angus Davidson [Oxford University Press, 1970] and Dijkstra, *Idols of Perversity: Fantasies of Feminine Evil in Fin-de-Siècle Culture* [Oxford University Press, 1986]). Praz gives a long analysis of iconographic manifestations of the phallic woman as Femme Fatale; and many of her qualities apply to Molly Bloom. In my perspective the importance of Joyce is that he moves from the iconography of the Medusa (which keeps textuality and representation distinct) to invent a kind of textuality which weaves the threat of the Medusa into its texture, and thus provides an antidote to it.

the road."[71] This evocation of the detachment from origin, and the transcendent rootlessness of modernity which Baudrillard sees exemplified in the United States, contains a suggestion with regard to Joyce. Joyce's emphasis on the astral detachment of Molly Bloom, and, in a literal sense, the "detachment" of "Penelope" from the body of the text, may derive from the ambiguity of gender inscription in Irish culture, but it prefigures the fetishizing trend of contemporary capitalism. "Darkest Africa" here turns into a "marvelously affectless" "America, my new-foundland." Gynesis meets with commodity culture.

FETISHIZED WRITING: PEN IS CHAMP

As several critics have suggested, Joyce's figuration of Molly Bloom seems implicated in the economy of fetishism.[72] The threat of castration is disavowed by the phallic attributes or qualities of the heroine. She seemingly denies the lack patriarchy projects upon women. As "heavenly body" or "star," Molly, indifferent, autonomous to the point that she can talk back to her creator and throw coffins at him, stands as "token of triumph over the threat of castration and as protection against it."[73] It is not accidental that Molly should be associated with Queen "Victoria."[74] But we are here not talking about Molly Bloom, a character in a fiction or a representation of womanhood, we are talking about "Penelope," a *chapter* in Joyce's work, and Joyce's strategy of defensive subject-formation. It is not just the figure of Molly Bloom, a phallic woman, which is pivotal, it is the existence of her soliloquy as text. The crucial question is: How can a piece of writing, a text *itself* function as fetish?

---

[71] Jean Baudrillard, *America*, trans. Chris Turner (London, New York: Verso, 1988), p. 5.

[72] Mark Shechner was probably the first: *Joyce in Nighttown: A Psychoanalytic Inquiry into "Ulysses"* (Berkeley: University of California Press, 1974).

[73] I take the words from Freud's essay "Fetishism," *SE* 21, 154. See also *A Portrait* where, in Stephen's delirious dream, the figure of Dante who first had presided over the inscription of language as trauma, walks like a queen by the water's edge in a "maroon velvet dress" and a "green velvet mantle" (*P* 27). Freud concludes the essay "Splitting of the Ego in the Process of Defence," *SE* 23, 275–78, with turning to the myth of Kronos, the old Father God, who swallowed his children. Only Zeus escaped with the help of his mother, to later castrate his father. Freud's text, once more, brings out the fear of engulfment.

[74] See Phillip F. Herring, *Joyce's Notesheets and Early Drafts*, pp. 45–46. Herring notes Joyce's ambivalence. Victoria is a triumphant queen and in this connotation a fit association for the phallic Molly; but Queen Victoria is also English, and *Ulysses* also refers to her as a "dead bitch." Since Queen Victoria was dressed in black, she would seem associated with the female figures in Joyce's dreams.

In his notes for "Penelope," Joyce had the habit of referring to Molly as "Pen"; also in *Ulysses* itself.[75] In "Aeolus" the Ithacans vow "PEN IS CHAMP" (7.1034). In the passage following, the text refers to "a book . . . which [takes] away the palm of beauty from Argive Helen and hand[s] it to Penelope" (7.1038–40). Since Helen was not only the incarnation of beauty, but the instrument of massive death, the shift from Helen to Penelope as "PEN" suggests that Joyce transfers his authorial favor from the beauty of mortal and lethal flesh to textuality personified as the (phallic) instrument of writing. The "clou" of "Penelope" is that it shifts the object of representation from the image which it creates to the process of writing itself. It favors style over message, textuality and code over a referent, the sign over the body, the masquerade of gender over the ontological difference of sexuality.[76]

In addition to notes like "Pen-stupid" or "Pen-remote" we find "odyss of Pen," as if the "true" epic plot of *Ulysses* were not the homecoming of its hero, but the transformation of the image of the heroine into a "pen" – mightier than the sword, and victorious over all the author's rivals, and triumphant like Queen Victoria. It is this "pen," as a maternal phallus, which produces the flowers of rhetoric which let the text "Bloom," and which generates the flow of textuality which in its endless circular movement guarantees immortality.

In a curious but not incomprehensible displacement, Joyce transferred the libidinal cathexis from sexuality unto the flow of writing, or, at any rate, refused to channel his energy solely as sexuality. Writing and sex are closely related throughout the *œuvre* not only in the "amplitudinously curvilinear" episode "Penelope."[77] Bloom thinks of sex as writing: "Blank face. Virgin should say: or fingered only. Write something on it: page" (11.1086–87) and in *A Portrait* the flood of language and soft liquid joy of sexuality are indistinguishable. The conflation of textuality and sexuality in *Finnegans Wake* needs no illustration. Even the pen is rendered in sexual terms as a "selfraising syringe and twin feeders" (*FW* 188.30), and the text is constructed as double entendre. The notoriously obscene letters to Nora are not only the substitute for her absence, they are also an expression of the sexiness of writing itself.[78]

---

[75] See p. 17 or 79 of *Joyce's Notesheets and Early Drafts*, and *Joyce's "Ulysses" Notesheets in the British Museum*, p. 494 or 504. Jean-Michel Rabaté, *Joyce upon the Void* also makes this point.

[76] For "Penelope" as a masquerade of femininity, see Kimberly Devlin, "Pretending in 'Penelope': Masquerade, Mimicry and Molly Bloom," *Novel* 25 (1991): 71–89.   [77] *L I*, p. 164.

[78] See also Philip Kuberski, "The Joycean Gaze: Lucia in the I of the Father," *Substance* 46 (1985): 49–67. Kuberski argues that "Joyce's desire for Lucia and his writing in the *Wake* is part of a refusal to segregate the energy of language and sexuality, to obstruct its libidinal exercise" (58).

Again I see a curious resemblance to Picasso. For Picasso painting *was* like sexual intercourse, the activity and rhythm of artistic expression would eventually even take the place of sexual expression; and a painting like *La Pisseuse* (1965) which gives us the shocking frontal image of a urinating woman, is the impotent product of his declining years. If "Penelope" is Joyce's "Pen," this suggests the extension of the *locus* of his vital selfhood from body unto text, the displacement of *cathexis* from the release of sperm to the activity of signifying, from penis to pen, from life to textuality, from the mortality of the body to the immortality of the signifier. *Ulysses* is a strategy of re-writing the self, giving it an immortal habitation and a name through its signature. Joyce here invents the "star system."

Only from the position of such a displacing extension can the text perform the metamorphosis of its author, penning his immortal body as words that "shall not pass away." In "The Unstable Symbolic. Substitutions in the Symbolic: Fetishism," Kristeva suggests that the writer, "[n]egating or denying the symbolic, without which he would be incapable of doing anything," "may imagine the thetic at the place of an object or partner. This is a fetishistic mechanism, which consists in denying the mother's castration, but perhaps goes back even further to a problem in separating an image of the ego in the mirror from the bodily organs invested with semiotic motility."[79] The only way to explain the transformative power of Joyce's textuality is to see it as an achieved perverse translation of the mortal self into the concreteness of the text, so foolproof that it can even allow what fetishism by definition cannot engage: the description of woman's genitals and the threat they represent. *Finnegans Wake* outperforms even "Penelope" in this respect. It drafts a geometrical ("geo-matric" as "earth-mother") diagram of the mother's vulva, thus exhibiting the secret of her "darkest Africa" as if it were the map to John Donne's "O my America! my new-found land." Similarly, it is only from the point of achieved transcendence of the threat of castration that Joyce can refer to his novel as *Ulysses* or "your bitch of a mother."[80]

But how did "Penelope" get transformed into a phallus? Let us focus on *Ulysses* as if it were a female body. Everywhere around us we see that the phenomenology of the contemporary female body is its demarcation and division in a subjection to its inscription as fetishistic sign. Whether in the theatre, advertising, fashion, or striptease: "the playscript of

---

[79] Julia Kristeva, *Revolution in Poetic Language*, trans. Margaret Waller (New York: Columbia University Press, 1984), p. 63.   [80] *L I*, p. 154. *SL* gives: "whore."

erection and castration" is all-pervasive. The high boots, the short skirt under a long coat, the horizontal line of the top of the stocking, belts, chains, the stripper's G-string,

> the scenario is the same everywhere: a mark that takes on the force of a sign and thereby a perverse erotic function, a boundary to figure castration which *parodies* castration as the symbolic articulation of *lack*, under the structural form of a bar articulating two *full* terms (which then on either side play the part of the signifier and the signified in the classical economy of the sign). The bar makes a zone of the body work as its corresponding terms here. This is not an erogenous zone at all, but an erotic, eroticised zone, a fragment erected into the phallic signifier of a sexuality that has become a pure and simple concept, a pure and simple signified. [81]

We have moved out of a world of real (even if sometimes invisible) presences into a textual realm where difference is no longer absolute or oppositional, but differential, relative, distributive, and variable, and where castration has lost its bite. Modern culture has substituted the stroke of demarcation between the elements in a sign-system for the absolute dividing line of castration. Thus the significant difference, the formal division between signs, has replaced "the irreducible ambivalence," "the symbolic split (écart)."[82] Consequently, the mark or the bar dividing the body transforms the nakedness of the thigh not into the frightening absence of the Medusa's face which threatens lack, but into sexual plenitude. "The naked thigh and, metonymically, the entire body has become a *phallic effigy* by means of this caesura, a fetishistic object to be contemplated and manipulated, deprived of its menace."[83] What makes the fetish functional is this phantasmatic cut that lends it the quality of erection, the bar which makes it autonomous and phallic. "Everything beyond this bar is the phallus, everything is resolved into a phallic equivalent, even the female genitals, or any gaping organ or object traditionally listed as a symbol of the feminine."[84] Moreover, any part of the body may take on this structural function, provided it is "as closed and smooth as possible";[85] and this, to Baudrillard, is modern culture's "real castration" of the feminine.

From this point of view the ritual of striptease is the slow ritual transubstantiation of the body into a simulacrum of the phallus. Instead

---

[81] Jean Baudrillard, *Symbolic Exchange and Death*, trans. Mike Gane (London: SAGE Publishing Ltd., 1993), p. 101.
[82] Jean Baudrillard, *For a Critique of the Political Economy of the Sign*, trans. Charles Levin (St. Louis: Telos Press, 1981), p. 95.   [83] Baudrillard, *Symbolic Exchange*, p. 102.   [84] *Ibid.*, p. 110.
[85] *Ibid.*, p. 102.

of revealing depth, a hidden truth, a "darkest Africa," the process of revelation proves a construction of a simulacrum. There is no depth. Every piece of clothing which falls increases the constructive transformation of body into phallic autonomy. Hence the striptease must not only be slow, the best stripper is herself as transcendently aloof and "astral" as a goddess, a star. From this perspective, Joyce's "detachment" of "Penelope" from the body of the text, his insistence that this chapter does not belong to its story, and that it be marked off by the dot at the end of "Ithaca," in combination with its oddly unpunctuated, "smooth and closed" textual structure, makes the detachment function as the horizontal mark of the top of the stocking. It transforms the chapter, and by extension the whole text, all of *Ulysses*, into the plenitude of the phallus instead of the symbol of lack.

In addition to calling it "the clou" to *Ulysses*, Joyce also called "Penelope" "*le dernier cri.*"[86] That he was fully aware that this expression related to the world of fashion, proves its occurrence in *Ulysses* in the following context: "Henry and James's wax smartsuited freshcheeked models, the gentleman Henry, *dernier cri* James" (10. 1216). Even if we did not know that in his later years Joyce pronounced himself more interested in women's clothes than their bodies, we might come to the conclusion that Joyce was not unaware of the fashionable implications of his fetishistic textuality, which fuses the imaginary with the symbolic, as do cinema, glossy magazine, glamor photography, soap opera and fashion show. Like Joyce's textuality (which, I argue, transforms the irreducible ontological difference between the sexes into the slippage of the difference between signs of gender), fashion transforms body or clothing into sign or image, depriving it of presence or depth, and linking it into an infinite chain of substitution. In calling "Penelope" "*le dernier cri,*" Joyce signals his consciousness of the modernity of his own procedure of understanding sexual difference as if it were a system of signs. In using it in turn as a model of signification, creating an object which frustrates the search for symbolic meaning and depth, fixing the gaze to the glaring details of the aesthetic surface, Joyce practices the opposite of what Carlyle, in *Sartor Resartus*, had called his "clothes-philosophy." If Carlyle pointed to the illusion of appearance, Joyce emphasizes the impact of the simulacral image, the power and presence of appearance. It is as if Joyce, living in the age of the rise of cinema and the flowering of photography, saw his own textuality in the light of

[86] *L I*, p. 169.

those art forms. The photographic image is iconic-indexical in relation to its object of representation. It exudes an aura of presence (albeit past), and allows the order of language and objective reality to coincide.[87] Moreover, it seems transcendently autonomous, seemingly freed from the historical conditions of time and space which constrict it. It does not "represent," it "re-presences." Its semiotic status of iconic index suggests that it does not just resemble the world, but that it partakes of the world owing to the objectivity of its registration of an authentic slice of life on a reel of celluloid. The extreme – "obscene" – overvalued realism of "Penelope" would seem to have a function in this constitution of the chapter as the *dernier cri* – a piece of literature which approaches the power of the new media owing to its seeming vividness and extreme concreteness of representation. In another way, too, the creation of the figure of Molly Bloom as "star" would seem related to the world of cinema. Like Marlene, Mae, Marilyn, or Madonna after her, Molly is an image of the transcendently feminine, a female (bitch) goddess, a fetishized heavenly body made to seem immortal by the optical illusion of the screen of representation. Even more pertinently perhaps, Molly incarnates the qualities of the consumer fetish, she is infinitely available (indiscriminatingly willing to engage any passer-by in Joyce's ballad), and infinitely desirable (even to herself, so that she vicariously identifies with men who have the privilege of making love to such desirable creatures as women).

As we know, the fetish is an object of fascination in order not to see, not to look. In the Freudian version of fetishism, what had to be avoided was the look at the wound of castration. Almost a hundred years after Freud's essay, fetishism would no longer seem limited to individual psychopathology; modern consumer culture, turning everything into sign, skating on a void of meaninglessness without daring to look down, thrives on the fetish of the female body as its propelling mechanism. In relating Joyce to the new media-technology of his age, I am trying to suggest that Joyce's fetishistic construction of "Penelope" should be seen as the reflection of his crucial participation in this modernity of our century, propelled by the drive to give figure to the trauma of the non-figurability of his subaltern Irish origin, and facilitated by the ambivalent inscription of gender in the Irish situation. Joyce, in attempting to liberate the "soul" of his race, invented the collusion between

[87] See André Bazin, "The Ontology of the Photographic Image." in *What is Cinema?* 2 vols., trans. Hugh Gray (Berkeley and Los Angeles, University of California Press, 1971).

gender and writing, long before philosophy caught up with it, or consumer culture and the power of the media made the fetishization of femininity into the driving force of culture. This conclusion, however, raises a question about our modernity. If Joyce radicalized the situation of the subaltern subject, and if his strategy is typically modern, how do we distinguish between the two? I shall return to this question in the next chapter.

Concluding this chapter, I shall refrain from attempting what Nietzsche, Freud, Jung, or Joyce did: claiming "the truth" or "clou" of "the feminine" – a "truth" which Joyce might have missed or denied in his revisionary rewriting of sexual difference as a triumph over castration and a protection against it, or a "truth" which might return after repression has been lifted. As Baudrillard cautions: "There is nothing behind this succession of veils, there has never been, and the impulse which is always pressing forward in order to discover this is strictly speaking the process of castration; not the recognition of lack, but the fascinating vertigo of this nihilating substance. The entire march of the West, ending in a vertiginous compulsion for realism, is affected by this myopia of castration."[88]

Instead of asking what is behind the veil, I would like to conclude with pointing to what is on this side of it, to the *effect* of Joyce's "postcreation." The name of Molly Bloom has itself entered the chain of signification as signifier for adulterous dalliance. In an ad in the "Personal" column of the *New York Review of Books* of February 1, 1990, we note the following text:

YES I WILL YES. Male Molly Bloom, fit fiftyish, married, wants to go Blazes in afternoon with male friend. Box 165, 1202 Lexington Avenue, NY 10028.

The affirmation of Molly's surrender to life, "yes I will," is here trivialized into consent to both extramarital and homosexual activity, motivated by mid-life panic ('fiftyish" but "fit"). The name of Molly Bloom as signifier refers to afternoon escapades. It is used in a transsexual manner, and functions to bring together two men. We seem to be back at the familiar structure of kinship in which a woman (deprived of subjectivity) is only the *trait d'union* between male subjects (long before Joyce called his Penelope "Molly," the "molly house" was the eighteenth-century name for the clubs where sodomites met). Inadvertently,

---

[88] Baudrillard, *Symbolic Exchange*, p. 102.

the advertisement in the *New York Review of Books* would seem to reveal the ideological effect of the cultural inscription of gender. The chapter heralds the continuity of the hegemony of the universal but generic "he"for the writing subject.[89] (A "Molly" is also a transvestite.)[90]

[89] See Naomi Schor, "Dreaming Dissymetry: Barthes, Foucault, and Sexual Difference," in Elizabeth Weed (ed.), *Coming to Terms: Feminism, Theory, and Politics* (New York and London, Routledge, 1989), pp. 47–58.   [90] Gifford and Seidman, *Notes for Joyce*, p. 291.

CHAPTER 5

Materiality in Derrida, Lacan, and Joyce's embodied text

> It must be supposed that after the parricide a considerable time elapsed during which the brothers disputed with one another for their father's heritage, which each of them wanted for himself alone.
>
> Freud, *Moses and Monotheism.*

Poussin's well-known painting *Et in Arcadia Ego* shows us the surprise discovery of death in a landscape of seeming eternal spring. A kneeling figure traces the writing on a tomb, and spells out the letters which symbolize its meaning to his companions. The question Poussin's representation brings into this inquiry is not just the reminder of our mortality, but the relation between representation (writing or reading) and death/castration. As the reading figure traces the letters, his arm throws a shadow on the tomb which takes the form of the traditional symbol of the scythe which cuts human life. Thus the very act of reading – and by extension the act of writing – itself brings the shadow which denies the permanence we traditionally attribute to the medium: *ars longa vita brevis.*

Joyce's strategy of encrypting the discursive trauma, which, as I argued in the previous chapter constitutes his (post)modernity, may be understood as writing's perverse attempt to overcome the shadow thrown by the writing or reading hand. It is, however, also that strategy which lends the shadow uncanny, concrete materiality. As always, Joyce's strategy is ambivalently double. In this chapter, after bringing out the defiant perverseness of *Finnegans Wake*, I shall argue that the phantasmatic scenario of the authority of *"écriture"* in Derrida and Lacan, Shemlike and Shaunlike, respectively reflects one side of Joyce's writing strategy. The question which this discussion revives is: What do we mean by "writing" and by the "materiality" of the letter?

Let us first think of *Ulysses* again, not as a rendering of Dublin, but as Joyce's discursive strategy of projecting an unbroken writerly subjec-

155

tivity. The concluding words of the text, "Trieste-Zurich-Paris/ 1914–
1921," link the disjunctive *peripeteia* in space with the linearity of time.
Such a juxtaposition suggests coherence and teleology in its projection
of an unbroken development which culminates in the moment before
publication in Paris. It is as if the realization of the work as material
object becomes the fulfillment of the nomadic exodus of Joyce's life. The
dispersal of physical displacement (Joyce apparently moved sixteen
times in that period) ends up in the unity and wholeness of the tangible
object which founds its maker's authorial subjectivity: the transformation of the anonymous Irishman Joyce into "Joyce" the world-
famous author. It is the concrete existence of the book which supports
and corroborates Joyce's identity as "genius," just as contemporary
stardom is an effect of the globalizing power of the media. Thus material
inscription countersigns and embodies authorial subjectivity.

Still, the disjunction which the postscript reveals and covers is not
fully healed by the text. As we learned from the critics' reactions, the
thematic and narratological unity of the text (in contrast to the material
unity of the book) remains undecidable. In fact, there may be a split in
the text itself. The large round/square dot after "Ithaca" marks a break
in the body of the text, which identifies the first and largest part of the
text as masculine, because the dot symbolizes Bloom's spiraling away
"into orbit,"[1] and makes the last chapter into the feminine supplement.
The dot has a double function: demarcating the intersection between
two separate but not wholly separable parts, it both denotes difference
and continuity. My suggestion that the period in the middle of
"Penelope" is the countersign of this dot reinforces that ambiguity. The
squared-circular mark on the page, the ultimate reduction of writing,
also functions as the linchpin of the text as fetish. It fills the hole to make
the text (w)hole; it negates the threat of an ending as a *"fin-negans"* to
speak with Jean-Michel Rabaté.[2] After this dot follows *Finnegans Wake*.

If we understand *Ulysses* as Joyce's attempt to undo the non-figurability of Irish origin, the dot takes on an uncanny nature. If the text itself is
the (impossible) attempt to encrypt the death-in-life of Irish experience
into symbolization, the black dot becomes the uncanny material reminder of that impossibility and of that experience. The "death instinct," or discursive trauma, cannot be inscribed. "[W]hat is excluded
from reality reappears as a signifying trace (as an element of the

[1] See Clive Hart, *Structure and Motif in Finnegans Wake* (London: Faber and Faber, 1962), p. 113 *passim* on the cycles of Stephen and Bloom and Shem and Shaun.   [2] "Lapsus ex Machina," p. 79.

symbolic order: a name, a teabrand on the very screen through which we observe reality," to return to Žižek's words.[3] Inscribed here, in this dot as a non-signifying stain on the page, is the materiality of trauma – the fact that it is recorded in the body or in the text – which insists on manifestation as "a signifying trace." If fetishism allows the subject to seemingly avow the possibility of his or her own effacement, its inescapability insists in making itself present in the form of a black blot on the screen of the representation. The period on the page is the material reminder of the blackening of consciousness and discourse at the moment of trauma, and is suggestive of the obliteration of the self under the fracturing pressure of the violence of linguistic inscription in an already hysteric symbolic. It is the point in the text when signification and writing return to the indistinctness of black fluid: pure undifferentiated matter. "[G]iving body to the unspeakable," it is this "psychotic stain"[4] which marks the division of the text.

What Joyce's text demonstrates graphically and non-discursively is the ineluctability of the insistence of trauma. The stain inexplicably appears on the page, though there is no memory or history, no story of which it is the known correlative.[5] Thus the text, instead of the psyche of the authorial subject Joyce, enacts the "splitting of the ego" (*Ich-Spaltung*) with which, according to Freud, a child may react to a threat entailing real danger which requires it to give up instinctual satisfaction. Instead of either giving way or disavowing the threat, the child chooses neither, that means both courses. "On the one hand, with the help of certain mechanisms he rejects reality and refuses to accept any prohibition; on the other hand, in the same breath he recognizes the danger of reality, takes over the fear of that danger as a pathological symptom and tries subsequently to divest himself of the fear."[6] Freud describes a form of having your cake and eating it.[7] The text acts out the construction of the

<hr>

[3] *Everything You Always Wanted to Know about Lacan*, p. 238.   [4] *Ibid.*, p. 239.
[5] As Jacqueline Rose puts it: "Although Freud abandoned the particular event of paternal seduction as either likely or, more important, causative, he retained the notion of an event, pre-historical or actual. Something intruded from without into the child's world. Something that was not innate but came from outside, from history or prehistory. This 'event' was to be the paternal threat of castration" (p. 13).
[6] "Splitting of the Ego in the Process of Defence," *SE* 23, 275.
[7] In *Finnegans Wake*, this splitting becomes self-conscious and fetishistic. Note Joyce's parody of the discourse of psychoanalysis: "*Zweispaltung as Fundemaintalish of Wiederherstellung*" (*FW* 296.L1). As Elizabeth Grosz suggests, "The fetishist is midway between neurosis and psychosis; he preserves himself from psychosis by representing the maternal phallus through fetishistic substitution, yet he is saved from neurosis by his repression of the castration threat." "Lesbian Fetishism?," in *Fetishism as a Cultural Discourse*, ed. Emily Apter and William Pietz (Ithaca: Cornell University Press, 1993), p. 108.

subject as the splitting of the ego under the threat of physical harm, as well as providing a disavowing antidote. The advent of the dot between "Ithaca" and "Penelope" is one more suggestion that Joyce's text, seen as the screen of representation, is constructed as the displaced extension of the authorial "self."

Finnegans Wake, Joyce's unreadable final work which occupied him from 1922 to 1939, is best understood as the next step in Joyce's self-dialectical trajectory of attempting to catch up with the non-figurability of the moment of trauma. It inhabits the darkness of the stain on the text of *Ulysses,* and inscribes its discursive death on the history of western culture as an "event" subverting cultural history. If *Ulysses* elaborates the forward flight of exile and wandering, *Finnegans Wake* is the triumphant literalization of the meaning of the dot after "Ithaca": staging itself in the locus and as the locus of inscription *per se,* as liminality, between life and death, dream and waking. It "litters" the letter of representation, smearing the signifier with the darkness of non-meaning, non-differentiation and obscenity (an intention staged *in* the text as the pricking of holes in the letter, burying it in a dungheap, staining it with tea, etc.), as if to give a *location* and presence to the non-figurability of discursive trauma. But Joyce's text also *possesses* and *owns* this location. The text not only attempts to stage the impasse from which it originates, it claims to inhabit its point of trauma; and it is marked by a jubilant self-consciousness. Thus Joyce's drive to make language "constitutive of reality" as Seamus Deane put it,[8] eventually forces him to try and stage its trauma in his text for all to see. *Finnegans Wake* is "apocalyptic" in the literal sense of the word of "disclosing a secret," but also in the sense of the ultimate littering destruction, the "literalization" of the letter and meaning. Instead of giving the world a *magnum opus* revealing truth, Joyce kills the authority of writing and desacralizes the meaning of art. He points to the fact that our illusions of transcendence have a materialist base: ink on paper, the concreteness of the medium, just as the skeleton supports our flesh. *Finnegans Wake* holds a baroque fable for our age of self-aggrandizement.

The instance on which I focus is suggested by its evocation of the "original" scene of trauma in *A Portrait of the Artist*:

–**O**, Stephen will apologise.
Dante said:
–**O**, if not, the eagles will come and pull out his eyes. (*P* 8)

In *Finnegans Wake,* this scene uncannily returns in the "geomatric"

8 "Joyce and Nationalism," p. 173.

revelation of the mother's genital zone, which offers itself as the location and the moment of self-engenderment of the text.[9] The earlier scene of trauma becomes the textual site of the inscription of the auto-genesis of the work, highlighting the apparent overcoming of trauma through graphic inscription.[10] It crows its triumph over "castration" as the reduction of writing to iconic graven images, while the material generativity of the mother is appropriated for the materiality of the medium itself.

The letter "O" (of "provocative gender" [*FW* 251.31]) which featured prominently as the symbol of Molly Bloom's female physique,[11] and the double "**O**" (also the lemniscate of "Penelope" and the graphic figure of "noughty times **oo**" [*FW* 284.11]) become the location of the figuration of the nullity and naughtiness of its own procedure, as well as its source of "originality." Toward the center of the book, the place of chiasmic return and the dark crevice of the crack in the mirror, we find, inscribed upon the double "O," the triangular Delta (Δ) of the mother-figure Anna Livia Plurabelle, both river and female,[12] displayed by one twin to the other through a "pudendascope":

You, you make what name? (and in truth, as a poor soul is between shift and shift ere the death he has lived through becomes the life he is to die into, he or he had albut – he was rickets as to reasons but the balance of his minds was stables – lost himself . . .

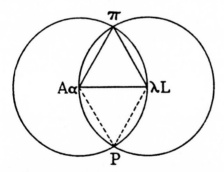

[9] On the representation of the external feminine organs as the locus of the phantasy of self-engenderment of avant-garde textuality, specifically Robbe-Grillet's *Projet pour une révolution à New York*, see Susan Suleiman, *Subversive Intent: Gender, Politics, and the Avant-Garde* (Cambridge, MA: Harvard University Press, 1991).

[10] See also Michael Kaufman, *Modernism, Postmodernism, and Print* (Lewisburg: Bucknell University Press, 1994). That *FW* is "cluttered with visible symbols" was first pointed out by Clive Hart, *Structure and Motif in "Finnegans Wake"* (London: Faber and Faber, 1962), p. 32.

[11] Penelope is demonstratively littered with the apostrophic "O" which Joyce used as graphic symbol for the feminine; cf. also: "M Bloom . . . looking blooming" (*U* 18.843–44).

[12] Joyce used sigla, diagrammatic ciphers to denote character in *Finnegans Wake*. He presents a list in the same passage in the *Wake*.

Vieus Von DVbLIn, 'twas one of dozedeams a darkies ding in dewood . . . A is for Anna like L is for liv. Aha hahah, Ante Ann you're apt to ape aunty annalive! Dawn gives rise. Lo, lo, lives love! Eve takes fall. La, la, laugh leaves alass! Aiaiaiai, Antiann, we're last to the lost, Loulou! Tis perfect. (*FW* 293.1–23)

The marginal annotation of this scene of reading, which is already a parody of a scene of academic writing, provides the following commentary: "*Uteralterance or the Interplay of the Bones in the Womb*," and "*The Vortex. Spring of Sprung Verse. The Vertex.*" (*FW* 293.L1–4). The text then immediately passes to a view of the "Modder ilond," "With Olaf as centrum": "O, dear me! O, dear me now! Another grand discobely!" This discovery is attended with the marginal comment: "*Sarga, or the path of outgoing*" (*FW* 294.4–13).

Announcing itself as the (re)turning-point of the whirling text ("vortex" turning into "vertex"), this projection of the view of the mother's delta ("uterus" but also the mouth of the river Liffey or the "muddy/mother island")[13] turns the upright letter "A" of Anna Livia Plurabelle upside down (the alterance of the uterus), to redouble the figure of the triangular delta, and to make the "A" into a "V" ("Vieus Von DVbLIn" [also remember Molly Bloom as Victoria]). The lowercase Greek "π" (here also pronounced "pee") doubles over into Latin capital "*P*"; and the "uteralterance" (also the alterance of uttering) redoubles the *locus* of origin, counterpointing the origin of feminine creativity with the mud and *sarx* ("*Sarga*":"saga" but, in Greek, "flesh") of uncreated matter (according to Domenichelli the "grotesque creation of the opus itself as dead, anal matter" ["*popo*" instead of the flow of "pee"]).[14] This doubling over sets up a pattern of babbling repetition: "Lo, lo" and "La, la," shading into a "laugh." Hereafter, the text phrases its own echoing repetition as "Olaf" "O-laugh" (uniting the female "O" with "joys/Joyce".) Thus the infantile phantasy of anal procreation, neuter in the sense of ne-uter, which is "perhaps the material, unsublimated root of the opus itself,"[15] leads to the triumphant jubilation of laughter.

---

[13] The geomater diagram is "the locus of identity-shifting and -questioning." The Greek capital Delta is "the graphic representation of an allegory of cosmos . . . from which the discourse system as a whole may be generated in performance" whether as the revelation of the secret beneath the mother's apron, or "the reader's programmed enactment of the *Wake*'s performative discourse." Lorraine Weir, *Writing Joyce: A Semiotics of the Joyce System* (Bloomington: Indiana University Press, 1989), p. 74–75.

[14] Mario Domenichelli, "Implosion, Hyperreality and Language in *Finnegans Wake*" in R. M. Bosinelli (ed.), *Myriadminded Man: Jottings on Joyce* (Bologna: CLUEB, 1986), p. 284. Also see Jean-Michel Rabaté, "Lapsus ex Machina."

[15] Domenichelli, "Implosion, Hyperreality and Language," p. 285. Also see Henry Staten, "The Decomposing Form of Joyce's *Ulysses*," *PMLA* 112 (1997): 380–92.

In addition to this redoubling, or better, the drafting of the *dark and muddy shadow* as the totalized hence neutered location of origin which becomes the *locus* from which the book "speaks," what should be noted is the curious *graphic* encrypting in this linguistic reductiveness. The place of the delta of ALP is obtained by pushing two gigantic "**O**"s so close in juxtaposition that they overlap. This is the figure of the lemniscate doubly invaginated to cover the point of its crossing and redoubling – as if to hide the navel of attachment, to eradicate the gap between the identical feminine letters – the gap over which the castrating Aunt **D**ante holds sway (the passage above resonates with aunt "Ante" "aunty" "Antiann" Dante, whose name also begins with the letter "**D**elta" [Δ]). But this gesture of invagination also creates the *location* for the inscription of the redoubling of the Delta which removes the threat of castration through the projection of the Delta as the *neutral* of the feminine between two gigantic "melons" (Molly's buttocks in *Ulysses*).[16] The phantasy which offers itself as the core of the text is placed in between the two "**O**'s which had already marked the threat of physical harm expressed in *A Portrait of the Artist*. Thus this primitive scene and nodal point of the *Wake* seems a remedial elaboration of the moment of inscription of trauma of the earlier work; and it inscribes the subject as "**O**laf" (O-laugh): the hilarious effect of elaborating the phantasy space between the feminine "**O**'s.

What the above seems to suggest is that the triumphant laughter, the *jouissance* of Joyce's later work, is based on the phantasy of the primal and undifferentiated (anal) materiality of writing, the redoubling of the flow of ink ("**p**ee")[17] as graphic mark ("**P**opo"), which creates a location for the inscription (the **P**en) of the alienation of self-identity. What we must not overlook, however, is the dramatizing self-consciousness of all this. Joyce is not betraying an unconscious phantasy. In fact, he is defiantly up against the tenet of castration of psychoanalysis. He holds up the mirror to those of us who are "yung and easily freudened" (*FW* 115.22–23), and believe that there is a truth or reality behind, underneath, or above the text in terms of which it might be explained, or to which it might lend presence. Joyce's "*graphocentric*," demonstrative enactment of this primal phantasy destroys the limit to the logic of representation

---

16 In Joyce's notebook VI.B.5, the delta not only indicated the figure ALP, but also his wife Nora. See David Hayman, "'I Think her Pretty': Reflections of the Familiar in Joyce's Notebook VI.B.5" *Joyce Studies Annual* (Austin: University of Texas Press, 1990), p. 42.

17 It seems unnecessary to point out that Molly's flows of urine and menstrual blood in *Ulysses* have been understood as analogous to the "language of flow" of her author.

which Freud's postulate of the unconscious still held in place. The sheer materiality of this cartoonist "doodling" (Joyce's own word) betrays a magical belief in the presence of inscription as such. From the bourgeois western point of view this may seem almost psychotic, but if placed in the light of postcolonial writing elsewhere, this nullification of the Word may also be understood as a strategy of defense.

A further elucidation of the resisting force and specificity of *Finnegans Wake* may be provided by linking the words of Joyce's marginal commentary, "the bones in the womb," to Žižek's discussion of "The Spirit is a Bone" in *The Sublime Object of Ideology*. Žižek argues that:

> the limit of the logic of representation is not to "reduce all contents to representations," to what can be represented, but on the contrary, in the very presupposition of some positive entity (Thing-in-itself) *beyond phenomenal representation*. We overcome phenomenality not by reaching beyond it, but by the experience of how there is nothing beyond it – how its beyond is precisely this Nothing of absolute negativity, of the utmost inadequacy of the appearance to its notion. The suprasensible essence is the "appearance *qua* appearance" – that is, it is not enough to say that the appearance is never adequate to its essence, we must also add that *this "essence" itself is nothing but the inadequacy of the appearance to itself*, to its notion (inadequacy which makes it "[just] an appearance").
>
> Thus the status of the sublime object is displaced almost imperceptibly, but none the less decisively: the Sublime is no longer an (empirical) object indicating through its very inadequacy the dimension of a transcendent Thing-in-itself (Idea) but an object which occupies the place, replaces, fills out the empty place of the Thing as the void, as the pure Nothing of absolute negativity – the Sublime is an object whose positive body is just an embodiment of Nothing. This logic of an object which, by its very inadequacy, "gives body" to the absolute negativity of the Idea, is articulated in Hegel in the form of the so-called "infinite judgement," a judgement in which subject and predicate are radically incompatible, incomparable: "the Spirit is a *bone*," "*Wealth* is the Self," "the State is *Monarch*" . . . [18]

Joyce's sublimity – Hegelian rather than Kantian – is to have made a location for the presence of the Nothing to which colonial culture reduces the subaltern. Moreover, he clearly inscribes the traumatic incomprehensibility of such experience. In contrast to the Kantian or Romantic experience of the sublime, triggered by the overwhelming impact of natural phenomena such as thunder or lightning, for Hegel the sublime is the irreducible material "little piece of the Real": "the Spirit *is* the inert, dead skull; the subject's Self *is* this small piece of metal that I am holding in my hand . . . God who created this world *is* Jesus this miserable individual crucified together with two robbers." Žižek

[18] *The Sublime Object of Ideology* (London: Verso, 1992), pp. 206–07.

goes on to call this Hegelian notion of the sublime the "last secret," explaining that "this very negativity, to attain its 'being-for-itself' must embody itself again in some miserable, radically contingent corporeal leftover."[19] *Finnegans Wake*, then, is not just the location of the mimicking inscription of the narratives, myths, and debates which make up Irish culture; it inscribes the text as that which, as graphic object, occupies the place of the void of signification: it is the metonymic materialization of the dissolution of meaning which history perpetrated on Irish culture.

This dissolution of meaning goes beyond a semantic unmooring, an opening of the self-identity of the signifier to "dissemination" or the inscription of "*différance.*" Joyce seems to convey a Lacanian point when he turns writing into a non-signifying activity of material productivity, the product of doodling with a pencil: black matter on white paper, dark ink on a virginal page, excrement on the foolscap of the body. In doing so, Joyce makes visible the abyss of meaninglessness and dissolution which we so easily skate over if we redefine writing as "dissemination." The stain which the dot after "Ithaca" makes on the narrative text of *Ulysses* may be understood as a *memento mori*: *Et in historia ego*. *Finnegans Wake* becomes that dot and stages its meaning in littering the letter of the signifier with the materiality of inscription, setting the visuality of the inscription against the auditory perception of meaning, as the "literal" reminder of its possibly meaningless materiality. In his text, Joyce stages the trauma of "castration" as the "castration" of writing and discourse, depriving it of meaning-making. How Pyrrhic a victory is this?

Here we need to turn to Lyotard's notion of the postmodern and its relation to the sublime because it takes "Joyce" (no specific work is named) as the vehicle of that version of the postmodern which "puts forward the unpresentable in presentation itself." Moreover, this postmodernity transgresses existing practises, "[i]n order to formulate the rules of *what will have been done.*"[20] This is the logic of the retroactive constitution of meaning which inheres in the attempt to narrate an unclaimed experience of trauma. Elsewhere, in *The Differend*, Lyotard spoke of Joyce as "waging war among the genres of discourse" and classified him as an author who puts the genre of literature itself at stake.[21] Perhaps because the essay: "What is Postmodernism?" in *The Postmodern Condition* ends with a call to "wage war on totality, to witness

---

[19] *Ibid.*, p. 207.
[20] *The Postmodern Condition: A Report on Knowledge*, trans. Geoff Bennington and Brian Massumi (Minneapolis: University of Minnesota Press, 1984), p. 81.
[21] *The Differend: Phrases in dispute* (Minneapolis: University of Minnesota Press, 1988), p. 151 and p. 139.

the unpresentable and to activate differences," Lyotard's comments on Joyce are all too easily aligned with the narcissistic sublime. The "unpresentable" is sometimes misunderstood as a form of presence because the prepositional "*in* presentation" is explained as denoting place rather than expressing the quality of unpresentability as an attribute *of* (re)presentation. Thus the extra dimension which Joyce adds is flattened to refer to something *on* the canvas rather than to something attending the medium itself. The precise meaning of Lyotard's use of Joyce in the definition of the postmodern becomes clearer, however, when we turn to his address to the International James Joyce Foundation in 1988, which contained a discussion of filiation and return in *Ulysses*.

Alerting us to several versions of incommensurable difference, Lyotard concludes that the text's "question of return" centers on one unanswerable philosophical question about difference: "is sexual difference not ontological difference? Is it not from this that the temporalizing separation of consciousness from itself is engendered, and the unconscious takes shape as a past without memories?"[22] Unable to either answer or escape this question, the one which divided Derrida and Lacan, the ambivalent text traces "the crack or the flaw that Judaism, (the Irish condition), produces on the beautiful vase of the Homeric periplus."[23] Its language is always oriented backward, turned elsewhere, to the moment of the origin of textuality and consciousness. If we accept the correctness of Lyotard's perspective and my reading, it also grows possible to think of *Finnegans Wake* as the perverse enactment of the impossibility of the attempt to "solve" the problem of incommensurability of colonial thinking (the symptom of the fact that hegemonic western thought is unable to think of difference in other terms than as "otherness"; or, in other words, that origin, in order for sense to be preserved, must always be singular and preferably self-identical rather than hybrid or syncretic). Instead of either ignoring or scarring over and escaping the crack of the flaw, *Finnegans Wake* inhabits this wound in the Symbolic, and enforces it upon western history as a traumatic "event." Endlessly recirculating itself ("Finn-again"), Joyce's text perversely never stops tracing the pattern of the flaw.

Seen thus, a part of Joyce's practice resembles Derrida. Derrida, who read Joyce when at Harvard in 1956–57, confessed himself more than indebted to his textual precursor Joyce. In *The Postcard* he noted that:

[22] "Going Back to the Return," in R. M. Bosinelli, Carla Marengo, and Christine van Boheemen (eds.), *The Languages of Joyce* (Philadelphia: John Benjamins, 1992), p. 208.   [23] *Ibid.*, p. 202.

"He has read all of us plundered us, that one."[24] The earlier performativity of Joyce deprives Derrida of the title to originality and self-presence. Derrida's texts enact the circular structure of Joyce's writing which supports its elusive ambivalence. A recent instance is his meditation on skepticism, *Memoirs of the Blind* of 1990, subtitled "The Self-Portrait and other Ruins," which links the last words to the first like *Finnegans Wake*. Nevertheless, the priority of the literary text does not seem cause for real concern; nor need it be if authority is seen as only a function of discourse. If, however, the peculiarity of Joycean textuality is understood as pointing to a specific historical embedding, there may be reason to examine the relationship more closely. Like Derrida, Lacan is endebted to Joyce. *Finnegans Wake* gave Lacan material proof of the insistance of *jouissance*. Joyce's textuality seemed to him a defensive demonstration of a "castration" turned inside out so that style protrudes where masculinity is lacking, and where, in its littering of signification, the "Real" insists. Lacan eventually imitated Joyce's punning in his year-long seminar on Joyce. Although it must be said that Lacan and Derrida never expressed a rivalry regarding Joyce, it seems curious that one literary *œuvre* should be so present in two disciplines which hotly disagreed on the subject of "castration." Did Lacan and Derrida read the same Joyce? What was the function of literature for what we have come to call "theory'?

In the essay "What is an Author?" Foucault set out to draw the full implications of the "death" of the author, because notions like "the work" or "writing" ("*écriture*") "suppress the real meaning of his disappearance."[25] Foucault thus hoped to clear the way to a full understanding of the function of discourse in the positioning of subjectivity. But his suggestion carries additional meaning. The "death of the author" was also the death of authority, its prestige and privileged access to truth. The "linguistic turn" of philosophy and psychoanalysis as we see it in Derrida and Lacan, also brings with it a question about the authority of the discipline. Not only were their versions of the profession feminized because they placed themselves as different from the mainstream tradition, their own theoretical position implied that authority is the effect of *writing*. How to establish the authoritativeness of the new field through *écriture*? Here the epigraph to this chapter comes in: "It

---

[24] *The Postcard: From Socrates to Freud and Beyond*, trans. Alan Bass (University of Chicago Press, 1987), p. 148.

[25] Michel Foucault, "What Is an Author?" in *Textual Strategies: Perspectives in Post-Structuralist Criticism*, ed. Josué V. Harari (Ithaca: Cornell University Press, 1979), p. 143.

must be supposed that after the parricide a considerable time elapsed during which the brothers disputed with one another for their father's heritage, which each of them wanted for himself alone."[26] Freud's words in *Moses and Monotheism* have relevance for the rivalry of Derrida and Lacan concerning the claims to truth of their respective disciplines involving them in a written debate that replayed the *crux* of "the two and the one": castration "yes" or "no," the distinctive nature of the "death instinct" in relation to the "pleasure principle," sexual difference, etc.[27] In their attempt to establish authority, they turned to the literary text as an earlier form of writing to support their own textual strategy of authorization, both as example and resource. The appropriation of the passive literary text in the service of the truth of theory bothers me. Disregarding its affective origin and effect, literature is reduced to abstraction and conceptualization and effectively/affectively muted because theory has purloined its power in redefining it as "textuality."

In a discussion of Lacan's and Derrida's response to Joyce, I want to show that the phantasmatic primal scene of theory's *écriture*, its projection of its own identity as "writing," remains caught in the ambivalence of the crack or flaw which Joyce painted on the Hellenic vase. I moreover argue that the literary text, which manages to hold two positions in one perspective, escapes the reductive definition of writing as pure inscription, because it communicates affect which, as Mikkel Borch-Jacobsen argues in *The Emotional Tie*, eludes inscription and narrative. It is not the articulation of what had hitherto remained unconscious, or the revision of the earlier narrative of the self which causes the patient to change, but narrative attended with affect. Inscription by itself does not constitute subjectivity. Joyce's language, even when it destroys signification, always maintains its affective appeal. As I noted earlier, that is its difference from postmodernist writing of the fifties. Joyce's inscription is also always addressed to an implicit other, even if only a future imaginary "conscience of the race." In Joyce's postcolonial case the intangible non-presence of the other (Lacan's universal of human culture) coincides with the historical situation of the void of the lapsed language. Thus Joyce does not betray a personal pathology; he participates in the larger symbolic situation of his culture. His littering of the letter remains meaningful, however obscurely, because it testifies to the "feeling" (Lyotard's term) or affect which history

[26] Sigmund Freud, *SE* 23, p. 82.
[27] See, for instance, Derrida's "Speculations – On Freud," *Oxford Literary Review* 3 (1978): 78–97, where he points to the necessarily ongoing nature of the debate.

threatens to obliterate and forget, and to which Joyce can make the reader respond, albeit non-intellectually. Joyce's fetishized writing is best understood as the attempt to keep alive the affect of the repression of the native language. He visits castration on his reader to make the reader share the emotional situation of the Irish subject born around the turn of the century. Joyce's *writing*, then, seems to partake of a different affective mode, that of witnessing and testifying (rather than significa-tion) – and it more closely follows a phenomenological outlook, al-though it seems to confirm the "truth" of either Lacan or Derrida.

THE LETTER IN LACAN

What fascinated Lacan in Joyce was the latter's play with writing as graphic inscription – the "littering" [Lacan's term] of the letter, its brinkmanship and virtual destruction of meaning. However "psycho-tic," Joyce's text keeps a *modicum* of meaning beyond its nonsensicality. It communicates something which defies paraphrase but which generates laughter, perhaps some kind of unconscious recognition about our dependence on language. It especially intrigued Lacan how Joyce could destroy the symbolic without disintegration. What satisfaction did he derive from his painful, laborious, and almost blind lonely writing? Finally, what generates the hilarious effect of *Finnegans Wake* which sets the reader's body resonating spasmodically with laughter?

Lacan's suggestion, at the conclusion of the essay on the mirror stage, that succesful analysis may teach the patient to undo the illusion of wholeness and cohesion derived from the reflected image, helps me to articulate a similar function for Joyce's text as the reader's mirror. *Finnegans Wake* places the reader as patient, forced to continually recog-nize the lack of unity of the signifier, the dispersal of meaning, the refracted elusiveness of truth. The reader must be able to tolerate a certain measure of frustration in order to engage with the text. The question is, then, does Joyce's writing effectuate, however attenuatedly, what Lacanian psychoanalysis aims for? This seems especially relevant in connection with Lacan's fascination with Joyce, which was extraor-dinarily intense. Lacan may have had his own transference on the case of Joyce.

One of the ways in which the foreclosed returns as an element *in* representation is in the guise of the Lacanian *objet a*. This object of phantasy contains a fascinating appeal for the beholder, because it embodies the object that the subject is in the phantasy scenario which directs his desire. Lacan compares it to a Moebius strip at times (the structure of *Ulysses* and *Finnegans Wake*), because this object has "no definable, fixed border; indeed its structure seems to *be* that of such a twisted border."[28] I suggest that the materiality of circular yet splitting inscription in *Finnegans Wake* was the *objet a* of Lacan's *theory*. It was the confrontation with *Finnegans Wake* which led Lacan to revise the hierarchy of his topography (hitherto the Symbolic had been the *locus* of the other circumscribing and hiding the "Real," now the three are on one level, bound by the "sinthome"). Joyce's littering proved the material "reality" of the fourth order which insists through the pleasure it gives, the affect it generates. Thus it is "Joyce" who effectuated that in this later structure the Symbolic no longer hides the Real as the "impossible."[29] The "Real" is also no longer seemingly privileged as that which seems to transcend the Symbolic or the Imaginary, but falls into line as one of the three registers which are held together by the symptom. Their consistency is detectable in the Imaginary – in the diagrams of knots expressing their interrelationship which Lacan makes visible on the page, but also in the littering writing of the "sinthome" – in the scriptural insistence of the letter, Joyce's doodling.

Lacan focuses on the odd inscription of and in *Finnegans Wake* as the *graphic* truth of the existence of the "sinthome" and the Real persistence of pleasure as *jouissance* (elsewhere in his theory related to the feminine and outside the Symbolic). It is important that we understand that this is not because *Finnegans Wake* repeats the same *story* over and over again like the patient in interminable analysis, a story of falling and rising which never becomes quite clear although the reader senses a blurred gist through the endless repetition and redoubling. That may be Derrida's version of "the letter." It is because of the self-conscious perverseness with which the text joyously defies meaning through inscription. Charged with: "Can you not distinguish the sense, prain [brain], from the sound, bray [pray]? You have homosexual catheis . . . ,"[30] the accused answers: "I can psoakoonaloose myself anytime I want . . ." (*FW* 522.29–33) I choose this example of a splitting of the self into two opposing voices, an insistent strategy of Joyce's text, because it offers the

[28] Samuel Weber, *Return to Freud: Jacques Lacan's Dislocation of Psychoanalysis* (Cambridge University Press, 1991), p. 158. Weber goes on to quote Lacan: "This is a remainder, in the sense of a division, a residue. This remainder, this ultimate other, this irrational [number], this proof and sole guarantee, finally of the alterity of the *Other*, is the *o*. (11.21.62)."
[29] See Jacques-Alain Miller, *Joyce avec Lacan*, p. 12.
[30] The annotation is from Roland McHugh, *Annotations to "Finnegans Wake"* (Baltimore: Johns Hopkins University Press, 1980).

occasion to articulate more exactly the splitting of *inscription* that occurs in *Finnegans Wake*. If the text of *Ulysses* splits between "Ithaca" and "Penelope," *Finnegans Wake* which keeps splitting the text into multitudinous reamalgamating fragments, also splits *writing* itself while seemingly preserving the unity of the recirculating text.

Seamus Deane argued that Joyce wanted to counter the calamitous history of Ireland with fiction; and that to do so, Joyce had to deprive fiction of the "traditional affiliations with history: Plot and theme, those elements which produce the story, are to be subdued, even abolished, and replaced by language."[31] Since the term "language" is not precise enough for my purpose here, I should like to redefine Deane's terms. In *Ulysses*, as we saw, fabula and story were embedded in a matrix of text, and the novel could still be read as about Dublin in 1904. In *Finnegans Wake*, the autonomy of fabula and story have dissolved into textuality, and referentiality has become precarious too. We might say that the text has become a floating "signifier" loosened from the signified but moored to the inscription on the page. Thus Joyce unties the signifier from the signified, and blurs the horizontal bar which separates the signifier from the signified in the diagram in the linguistic textbooks. Moreover, for him, unlike de Saussure, it is not the acoustic expression which is the signifier, it is the written version always simultaneously played off against its sound and against similar sounds and graphemes in other languages. Thus Joyce introduces the difference between the visual and the auditory perception of the word, between spelling and pronunciation, into the signifier itself, as a displaced return of the repressed of the bar which (before *Finnegans Wake*) marked the gap between signifier and signified. We must conclude that *Finnegans Wake's jouissance* hinges on the exploitation of the incommensurability of the divide separating the visual and the auditory, the graphic and the spoken (even if merely articulated mentally during reading). Again, Joyce is not just blurring sound and sense in the pun. He exploits the visual element of graphic inscription of language, its spelling (the Imaginary), at the expense of its Symbolic function: the transmission of discursive meaning. Moreover, he does it so insistently and repetitively, that the text becomes the location of the Real bound by the "sinthome." Obviously, Joyce's perverse procedure leads to a process of dispersal which we may at times find liberating and witty, but, as I argued above, it also gives an additional, self-conscious turn to the screw of the

---

[31] "Joyce and Nationalism," p. 169.

non-discursivity of the trauma of the absence of the native language. Joyce's "sinthomatic" materialization of writing is not – and given the premise of this book it cannot be – a lifting of the lack of recall, or the articulation of unconscious material, it is its "mother tongue-in-cheek" inscription as the power of the medium of print which encrypts the trauma.

The oddity in Lacan's seminar on Joyce is his enthusiastic imitation of Joyce's punning and graphic experiment.[32] Punning had always been a significant feature of Lacan's discourse. In "Eat Your *Dasein*: Lacan's Self-Consuming Puns," Françoise Meltzer takes Lacan's phrase from the seminar on Poe as an example. She argues that Lacan's reliance on this rhetorical figure relates to his attempt to "'rupture' the (male) economy of totality by means of a phantasy of supplementarity – precisely as he argues, in 'The Woman,' when describing the woman's *jouissance*. I will propose that we see the pun in Lacan as an attempt to overcome analogy (totality) with supplementarity – an economy of contiguity which will, ultimately, allow for moments of 'grace.'" Indeed, Meltzer implies that for Lacan the pun is the "voice of the unconscious," which sets up "a trembling which rescues him, through the very notion of supplementarity, from the sterility of the totalizing 'One', and from the seduction of etymology." She concludes with the suggestion that Lacan's idealism, not monist but Dadaist in origin, "seeks a politics of breaking out from within . . ."[33]

This suggests an analogy between Lacan and Joyce. Lacan shares Joyce's interest in supplementarity. Both attempt to extend the range of language in articulating within it an echo or uncanny redoubling which suggests that the circumscription of language, the limit to discourse, is eluded. Lacan sees Joyce as the prime example of the insistence of *jouissance* in binding the other registers in the "sinthome." But that insight also brings a problem of which Lacan seems unconscious. Joyce's style, I argue, is not the expression of an unconscious. It does not bring into discourse what is excluded from it. It tries to fill in a gap between foreign and familiar which opened up in discursivity itself. This means, in effect, that what Lacan sees as Joyce's "unconscious" should be located on this side of the barrier which separates discourse and consciousness from an unconscious. What may have stared Lacan in the face without his conscious realization, is the anamorphic effect of Joyce's

---

[32] I choose an example which is still easily reducible to a French sentence: 'LOM, LOM de base, LOM cahun corps et nan-na Kun." *Joyce avec Lacan*, p. 31.

[33] In *On Puns: The Foundation of Letters*, ed. Jonathan Culler (Oxford: Blackwell, 1998), p. 157 and 163.

textuality on the truth of his own discipline. If the unconscious, or its effects, may originate within discourse, the unconscious is historical, a product of history. This would mean that the Oedipus Complex need not be universal; it also raises questions with regard to the rise of psychoanalysis. If it is the history of colonial rule which produced the death-in-life of Joyce's trauma, is the unconscious perhaps the effect of the trauma of history?

Another aspect of Lacan's interest in Joyce also needs attention. Especially in connection with an understanding of Lacan's difference from Derrida, the use of the term "the letter" needs scrutiny. His essay "Agency of the Letter in the Unconscious or Reason since Freud," delivered for an audience of philosophers, begins with a play on the difference between the disciplines, and states as the intention of his discourse the mediation of that difference: "its sole object encounters the collusion of their common training, a literary one, to which my title pays homage."[34] Lacan proceeds to stress that Freud had always insisted on literary training as the "prime requisite of the formation of analysts."[35] Lacan situates this discourse on the literariness of the discipline in the frame of the gap between writing and speech, fixity and fluency, dogma and self-revisionary becoming, truth and knowledge. He berates the dogmatic seriousness of some recent developments in pychoanalysis, and seems to claim a literary truth for psychoanalysis – a paradoxical and ambivalent truth. Thus it seems that the meaning of the word "letter" in the title of the essay refers to the literary, "letters." The French edition of the *Ecrits* begins with a Preface opening with the sentence "The style is the man himself" ["*Le style est l'homme même*"] referring to Buffon – both renowned as scientist and as author of a treatise on style which represents the classical ideal of orderly presentation and a firm intellectual grasp. Lacan intends to reopen the question of subjectivity and its relation to style, and he does that by means of a reference to his "Seminar on Poe" which is given the opening position in his work. Thus Lacan takes Freud literally, and, in his competition with philosophy, moves the medical discipline in the direction of literature.

Is psychoanalysis a form of literature, then? Lacan, to avoid that conclusion, introduces the science of linguistics to shore the specificity of his academic discourse; and he begins a discussion of "the letter" which

[34] For a reading of Lacan's essay, which articulates Lacan's ambivalence, as well his identification of truth as *aletheia* with truth as *homoiosis*, see Jean-Luc Nancy and Philippe Lacoue-Labarthe, *Le Titre de la lettre (une lecture de Lacan)* (Paris: Galilée, 1973).   [35] *Ecrits*, p. 147.

is marked by semantic sliding. While psychoanalytic practice is grounded in "speech" (the language produced by the patient in the closely circumscribed setting of the psychoanalytic session), Lacan's scientific contribution to analytic experience is that it "discovers in the unconscious . . . the whole structure of language." The name he reserves for this is the "letter." Aware of the possibility of confusion, Lacan raises the question: "But how are we to take this 'letter' here? Quite simply, literally [*à la lettre*]." Then he adds "By 'letter' I designate that material support that concrete discourse borrows from language."[36] After an exposition of the nature of the symbolic, he resorts to the metaphor of lower-case typefaces to "render validly present what we call 'the letter.'"[37] Thus the "letter" in Lacan turns out to be the materiality of the signifier as symbolized by the medium of print – spelling, typeface, layout – which in turn symbolizes the support the body lends to the effect of human subjectivity. This is just as in Joyce's fetishized writing which encrypts trauma.

This argument about the "letter" as the material support upon which subjectivity rests involves him in a reflection on the tenet that "the letter killeth while the spirit giveth life," which concludes with "the pretensions of the spirit would remain unassailable if the letter had not shown us that it produces all the effects of truth in man without involving the spirit at all."[38] Here Lacan's theoretical formulation comes close to Joyce's practice of writing in *Finnegans Wake* which belabors the signifier without the meaning (spirit) of a signified, and puns on having "[n]either a soul to be saved nor a body to be kicked" (*FW* 298.F2). But Lacan comes also close to the evaporation into non-sense of Joyce's text.

There is also an important difference. Inscription takes place on the page in Joyce and in the body in Lacan. When Lacan speaks of the "agency of the letter in the unconscious," he specifically does not refer to recorded, written language or literature, but to the effect of the systematicity of language upon consciousness, which he sees as the effect of its inscription on the body. His argument, however, that the "letter always arrives at its destination," introduces an ambiguity. He means that the truth of the unconscious always re-insists; but he offers that suggestion by means of analogy with the trajectory of a concrete letter in Poe's story. The difference between speech and writing, psychoanalysis and literature is here ignored. I suggest that in seeing Joyce as the embodiment of the "sinthome," this ambiguity in the meaning of his use

[36] *Ibid.*   [37] *Ibid.*, p. 153.   [38] *Ibid.*, p. 158.

of the term "letter" is given additional pressure. Not only does a material object (a letter or typeface) serve to allegorize the truth of Lacan's figuration of the unconscious, but literature becomes the passively docile body of psychoanalysis, the place of its inscription as theory and medical science. But there is a difference between inscription in consciousness and in matter.

Apparently, Lacan's involvement with Joyce grew so intense that he had trouble in "free[ing] himself from the quandary in which the Joycean text had imprisoned him," needing "nothing less than the cord of his chains and knots" to "displace the reading."[39] What the words of the French psychoanalyst Tardits imply is that the confrontation with Joyce, resolved through the "cord of [Lacan's] chains and knots," may have entailed a confrontation with the ultimate implication of the necessity of the material example and the concrete letter in the claim to truth of deconstructive psychoanalysis. Let us return to the *object a* as that object in which the subject identifies him or herself, but without being able to recognize it. "The scopic *objet a* . . . has the remarkable property of making appear, in imaginary space, precisely what escapes in principle from every specular identification and objectification. There, in that nonspecular image – namely, the gaze (or painting, or stain) that 'stares at me' (or 'concerns me') before I see it – I am present in my essence; I identify myself in my nonidentity, in my perpetual distance from myself: *ego sum alibi.*"[40]

My suggestion is that the cracked looking-glass of the Joycean text reflected "the essence" of the non-self-presence of Lacanian analysis in a number of ways. First of all, its reliance on the priority of literature as the location of its inscription of the truth places psychoanalysis as neither literary nor scientific, notwithstanding its linguistic orientation or preoccupation with algorisms and graphs.[41] Perhaps we ought to say that psychoanalytic writing with "philosophical" aspirations – psychoanalytic texts which aspire to present the truth of psychoanalysis in rivalry with philosophy – must fall into an unconscious relation with

---

[39] Annie Tardits, "Joyce in Babylonia," in *The Languages of Joyce*, p. 230. Tardits is a former member of "L'Ecole de la cause freudienne." She wrote this essay when a member of the psychoanalytic association "Dimensions freudienne."

[40] Mikkel Borch-Jacobsen, *The Emotional Tie*, pp. 172–73.

[41] In *The Subject in Question*, David Carroll writes: "What is repressed by Lacan as it is for the most part repressed by Freud . . . is that psychoanalysis has always-already been made into an example of fiction by the very process of making literature into an example" (University of Chicago Press, 1982), p. 42. See also Derrida, "Le Facteur de la vérité," *Poétique* 21 (1975): 96–147, which begins with raising the question about the effect of the self-conscious literary example upon the truth of psychoanalysis.

literature, owing to its transferential self-definition over against philosophy, "the genre presumed to know." Using the material presence of literature as naturally as if it were annexing a colony, or as naturally as patriarchy arrogates the voice of women, it makes "literature" the symptom of psychoanalysis, just as the Woman is the symptom of the Man in Lacanian psychoanalysis. Perhaps it reveals the unconscious negative *imago* of psychoanalysis as "not-whole" and "not-true." Lacan is noted for his joke that, a "perfect hysteric," he only made mistakes in *"genre"* (both "gender" and "genre").[42] Seen thus, *Finnegans Wake* is the *alibi* or the symptom of late-Lacanian psychoanalytic theory.

In order to rationalize the uncanny of Joyce's literary text, Lacan resorted to the figure of the knot, because knots, like numbers, best serve to illustrate the supposed abstract universalism of the psychic. However, this reliance on knots, graphs, schemas, algorisms, as if to create a mathematics of the operations of the psyche, seems to me a perilously close analog to Joyce's fetishistic reliance on graphic inscription of the feminine "**O**"s in *Finnegans Wake*. What appears to support Lacan's theory as "theory" (and let me emphasize that there is a crucial difference between theory and the practice of psychoanalysis), is this dependence on the fetish of representation by and as abstract, scientific inscription. It is as if inscription as cipher (which has perhaps a remote iconic resemblance to its object left, but which reduces its flesh and blood to the skeleton of a letter or diagram), giving magic control over the object, performs two activities at once. It contains the material threat of meaninglessness and rotting decay which clings to the "letter which kills,"[43] and it illustrates Lacan's theory of our dependence on the material. Yet, whereas Joyce's fetishized literalness is the desperately reductive decreation of the oppressive hegemony of the English language, Lacan is fighting a battle to establish the authority of his revision of psychoanalysis and make a name for himself as theorist. My suggestion is that Lacan's involvement with Joyce ought to alert us to an implicit fetishism in his academic discourse.

Another suggestion: "Joyce sets himself up in the very locus of 'what is written per se: that which leaves its trace after a breakup of being'," as Tardits points out.[44] What her words bring home is that the Lacanian

[42] The seminar of November 16, 1976, *Ornicar?* 12–13 (1977): 12.

[43] Lacan began his address to the International James Joyce Foundation in 1975 with defining "man" as a creature which "rots in hope." *Joyce avec Lacan*, p. 21.

[44] Annie Tardits, "Joyce in Babylonia," p. 244, quoting from *Le Séminaire XX: Encore*, published during Lacan's Joycean phase, in 1975.

engagement with Joyce may also have had a function in the self-stylization of theory as transcendent and non-contingent. In particular the French intellectual tradition values the principle of universality; and Lacan seems to share that assumption. Though Lacan's text contains occasional references to Joyce's Irishness (puns like "sint'home rule"[45]) the historical background of Joyce as an Irish writer is not addressed. In the context of a psychoanalysis which claims to be linguistically oriented, that seems strange. In fact, Lacan seems to have co-opted Joyce as almost a fellow Parisian. He mentions meeting him in Paris – emphasizing the shared material location. Writing during a period in history when the drive for independence of nations around the world (think of the Algerian War of Independence) ought to have made anyone aware of the significant importance of nationality and language, Lacan ignores the historical specificity of Joyce's writing. Though he regards the phenomenon "Joyce" as unique, he never stops to wonder whether that uniqueness relates to anything other than the symptomatic structure of his individual psyche. To Lacan the topography of the psyche is universal and non-contingent. The occasion of Joyce's "sinthome" and the feelings of pathos and anger it ought to evoke are never addressed; nor need they be on Lacan's terms, since the peculiarity of Joyce (according to Lacan) is precisely his resistance to treatment, the self-consciousness of his symptomatology. Thus the historical specificity of Joyce's work, its power as witness to the pain and suffering which official history cannot convey, is denied.

At the same time, that symptom is given an important place in Lacan's later theory. Since Slavoj Žižek's work, which has become influential in Cultural Studies, is in turn based on the late Lacan, we may claim that Joyce's trauma plays an important but implicit function in contemporary theory, perhaps precisely because his "sinthome" has not been understood for what it is: the product of a specific set of historical circumstances and a defensive strategy of coping with them. Perhaps theory's fascination with Joyce is a way of colluding with *Finnegans Wake*'s defensive literary presentation of the pain and despair of *sparagmos* as laughter and *jouissance*, without affective opening up, and *reading* the work and engaging the meaning of its castrating effect. In fact, I am implying that Lacan himself never accomplished the task he set his readers in the Preface of the *Ecrits*, of delivering Joyce's letter at its destination. Thus Foucault's suggestion that the notion of *écriture* may function to ward off the full realization of the "death of the author" gathers new meaning.

But perhaps Lacan did deliver the manner in an oblique manner; perhaps we should see Lacan as Joyce's ideal reader. Joyce had expressed the hope of keeping the professors busy for centuries with his enigmatic textuality. What greater success than finding that academic theory formalizes the insights of the literary work? But this manner of delivering the letter colludes with its symptomatic nature. In fact, the "sinthome" as the limit of psychoanalysis may also be the symptomatic indication of what the theory of psychoanalysis cannot engage or address: the affect of the trauma; or, in words abusing Lacan's term: the suffering encrypted in the "letter in sufferance."[46]

DERRIDA'S IMMATERIAL LETTER

Like Lacan, Derrida partakes of Joyce's fetishization of the signifier. Derrida resorts to material inscription to coin new words, uses metaphor derived from the art of printing (the tympan), or locates the referent of his theory in the human body (the hymen, invagination); yet his emphasis on materiality is different from Lacan. In contrast to Lacan's littering "letter," that of Derrida does not hammer primarily on the physical aspects of death, rot, and decay. It is the use of the image of the tympan in *Margins of Philosophy* – an object which, narcissistically or autogenetically, "punctures" and "grafts itself" . . . which alerts me to the oddness of Derrida's materialization of the letter: Whereas Lacan understands consciousness as engaged in the denial of our existence as matter, and sees Joyce as the non-repressed reminder of that truth, Derrida takes the opposite direction. He conflatingly suspends the difference *between* letter and "spirit," turning writing into an act of emotional survival. In taking as his model the abstractness of the systematicity of language as an endlessly performative act of signifying,[47] he implicitly defines materiality as permanence rather than decay. The hypostasis of "writing" is placed as the continuum of cultural representation which transcends the truth of "castration." Derrida's letter does not perish, nor does it come to a stop at a destination, although it perpetually flirts with its own impossibility and the threat of non-signification. It seems as if the persistence and insistence of this flirtation

---

[46] See also Mikkel Borch-Jacobsen, *The Emotional Tie*, for a discussion of the place of affect in the psychoanalytic cure, and the inability of Lacanian psychoanalysis in giving it a place in the termination of treatment. My play on the *lettre en souffrance* derives from Lyotard's *The Differend*, p. 195.

[47] *Margins of Philosophy*, trans. Alan Bass (University of Chicago Press, 1972), pp. xxvii–xxviii.

itself serves as a protective ritual precluding consummation. To use an analogy: just as circumcision may be seen as an apotropaeic gesture which, in paying a small but painful tribute of flesh, protects against the major loss of power, Derrida's brinkmanship and his fixation on the edges of the *chora* (the unnamable matrix of signification as well as its vanishing point) seem to be protective gestures which pay verbal tribute in the hope that the ongoing act of symbolization will shore up consciousness of a *terminus ad quem.*[48]

The metaphor of circumcision is not arbitrary. In his autobiographical account in Geoff Bennington's *Jacques Derrida*, Derrida situates himself as perpetually fixated to the traumatic moment of that painful ritual, locked in the scene of inscription just as Joyce's character Stephen Dedalus is locked in the scene of naming. But such a fixation also has the effect of precluding the necessity of emotionally accepting diminishment. Like trauma, fixation practices a sleight of hand with temporality. The future is blocked out by an emphasis on the repetition of the present. This makes Derrida's word an affirmative Word, trembling with the self-inscription of the negative, liberated from its harness of beginning or end in uninterrupted inscription, and clothed in stylistic elegance. At the same time, the stubbornness of the attachment to writing seems to affirm the threat which it denies.

One of the things which seems to interest Derrida most in Joyce is the latter's seeming strategy of radical *Aufhebung* and transcendence. Joyce lifts himself by his own bootstraps. Joyce's exponential self-reflexiveness (which comes to include the universe), also swallows the dark stain of history, or the materiality of the letter which Lacan reinscribes, and it locates the negative as an echoing repetition within the self. In fact, Derrida himself, for all his verbal tribute to the presence and power of death or blindness, may be projecting a perversely enlarged subjectivity, based on the conflation of death and the permanence of the medium. At any rate, Derrida is transferentially involved with an ambivalent, Shem-like Joyce who laughingly eludes the split between signifier and signified, and endlessly makes signification its own signified in the act of signifying. This is the ahistorical Joyce of the forward flight of the subject celebrated in *Post-Structuralist Joyce.*

Derrida's most recent comments on Joyce date from Derek Attridge's interview in *Acts of Literature*. Here he mentions Joyce often, names him an "event," and speaks of literature as a "force." Of continued impor-

---

[48] See my *The Novel as Family Romance: Language, Gender, and Authority from Fielding to Joyce* (Ithaca: Cornell University Press, 1987), chapter 7.

tance to Derrida is the fact that Joyce consciously planned the transferential chain of translation and commentary which will keep his texts
alive.

Joyce dreamt of a special institution for his oeuvre, inaugurated by it like a new
order. And hasn't he achieved this, to some extent? . . . I did indeed have to
understand and share his dream too: not only share it in making it mine, in
recognizing mine in it, but that I share in *belonging to the dream* of Joyce, in *taking a
part* in it, in walking around in *his* space. Aren't we, today, people or characters
in part constituted (as readers, writers, critics, teachers) *in* and *through* Joyce's
dream?[49]

Gone from Derrida's view is his earlier emphasis on Joyce's design to
"compute," "control," and "program" us. What remains is the lack of
demarcation within Derrida's construction of "history" as an echo-
chamber of intertextuality, an archival universe of textuality. Joyce's
priority, Joyce's death, makes us the figures in his "dream." It seemingly
deprives the successor of life and presence. But Derrida's willingness to
share the death-in-life of the *Wake*, to be a *ghostly* son of Joyce, also
suggests an ambivalently defensive strategy of affiliation which wards off
the necessity to draw the line of distinction and difference. First of all, it
keeps the precursor alive so that he need not yet be mourned or
commemorated in witnessing narrative. Moreover, Joyce's enduring
presence provides the ghostly son with a new kind of paternity, achieved
within the realm of textuality, which circumscribes material incarnation
in or as flesh. Like Stephen Dedalus in *Ulysses*, whose theories about art
hinged on the escape from death, materiality, and the mother in a
"postcreation," Derrida imagines and projects a post-material world in
which filiation is passed on through the word: "In woman's womb word
is made flesh but in the spirit of the maker all flesh that passes becomes
the word that shall not pass away. This is the postcreation" (*U* 14.273–
74). Stephen's words anticipate Derrida's program. Perhaps Stephen's
meditations on the meaning of the navel, as the sign of the spirit's
indebtedness to mother nature are also relevant here. What Stephen
dreams of and Derrida projects is the concept of a belly without blemish,
a subject without a navel jumping from the pages of a book rather than
the mother's womb.

Indeed, the presence of Joyce in Derrida's *œuvre* ought to alert us to
the central role of the phantasy of textual filiation in its mapping of
modernity. The author of the work of philosophy or literature takes his

[49] *Acts of Literature* (New York: Routledge, 1992), p. 74.

place in a textual genealogy, transcultural, globalized, not sexualized but "neuter" since mediated through writing and rhetoric. Note the beginning of *Psyche* which allegorizes Derrida's thematic of authority and relates the transmission of rhetoric and translation to Cicero's relationship to his son.[50] Most important, because this constitutes Joyce as model for Derrida, is not the question of sonship, however, but of a paternal generativity without recourse to mother nature or brute materiality. How does the author create sons in the spirit? The anxiety of procreativity leads to Derrida's emphasis on the importance of translation, commentary, and response – the demand pre-programmed in Joyce's texts. While Derrida notes the admixture of negativity in Joyce's laughter, his essay on *Ulysses* is a celebration of its affirmative dissemination and self-conscious manipulation of the medium to ensure intellectual progeny. The reading of the work should generate writing and commentary in order to propagate it and keep it alive. The author's rhetoric insures that his letter is not lost, but will arrive at its destination. In his analyses of literary texts, Derrida tends to focus on strategies of auto-constitution or the doubling self-inscription of writing as textual weaving.

Relevant is Jacques Derrida's curious joint publication with Bennington, *Jacques Derrida* of 1993. Split into two layers of text, the upper half of the page presents Bennington's articulation of the content of Derrida's teaching. The lower half gives us Derrida's autobiographical commentary which in turn dwells upon a number of splits: the split within the text itself, but also the split between the past and the present, and between the maternal and paternal. This latter split is figured in Derrida's shifting back and forth between the imminent death of his Jewish mother and his involvement with St. Augustine's *Confessions*. St. Augustine, born in Algeria where Derrida was also born, serves as a father *imago* for the mediating activity of the text which shifts from language to language, Jewishness to Christianity, the death and physical decay of the mother to the paternity of the word. The split in the text suggests that the mediation proclaimed is only thinkable owing to its fetishized inscription.

The central theme of this autobiographical account is a meditation on the traumatic impact of the Jewish ritual of circumcision, which seems to account for Derrida's intense cathexis both to the knife of the priest threatening virtual castration, and the arms of the mother which

---

[50] *Psyché: Inventions de l'autre* (Paris: Galilée, 1987), pp. 11–13.

hold the child up for this sacrifice. Instead of accepting diminishment or splitting, the text makes this threat into the occasion of its structure, and weaves back and forth between maternal and paternal *imago*. As in Joyce, it is as if the *act* of weaving-writing lends substance and presence to a traumatized split-subjectivity which remains fixated on the occasion of that single traumatic moment. But also as in Joyce, the reader is wisely counselled not to underestimate the self-consciousness of this performance.

For all my admiration and gratitude for what I learned from him, what disturbs me is that Derrida should only begin to publicly address his personal history as marginalized Jew in Algeria this late in his career, and then not explicitly enough. It is as if Derrida's war on "Western metaphysics" had first to be won as if from within the hegemony before the difference or marginality of his own situation could be made explicit. In his earlier publications, especially *The Postcard*, Derrida's projection of the transnationality of the postal condition conflates the globalization of technological modernity with a universal subjectivity which elides national and cultural differences. In its choice of metaphor it also betrays a notion of culture as a rootless circulation of disembodied signifiers, and opens the illusionary perspective of the post-materiality ("postcreation") of a purely abstract "writerly" world.

Most telling, perhaps, is Derrida's failure to respond to the history of literature's sometimes traumatic occasion, as in his comments on Joyce and Celan. Is it because the truth comes home too closely? At any rate, Derrida confesses that he does not like reading narrative, which, in *Acts of Literature,* he calls "gripping"! He looks to literature as a discourse which "teaches us more, and even the 'essential,' about writing in general, about the philosophical or scientific . . . limits of the interpretation of writing."[51] Thus literature is seen purely formally, as a manipulation of the self-inscriptive power of the signifier, not as an inscription of knowledge and experience by means of a relationship between signifier, signified, and referent. What Derrida's strategy of understanding literature – which may go back to Jakobson's definition of literariness as a writing which calls attention to itself as such[52] –

[51] *Acts of Literature*, p. 72.
[52] This is owing to literature's stitching (redoubling enfolding) of the activity of the choice of words from the storehouse of the vocabulary into the text itself. This is what Jakobson spoke of as the projection from the axis of selection onto that of combination. Jakobson's definition of literariness is, it seems to me, the model for Derrida's understanding of textuality as such, not just literature.

effectuates, is the total elision of the affective meaning of the literary text through its excision of the referential function and its power as gripping narrative. It should be noted that Derrida steadily ignores *what* Joyce says. He splits the literary signifier into style and message. Privileging style, he ignores literature's narrative packaging of knowledge, the work of conceptualization and subjectification implied in plot – as Hayden White and Peter Brooks have taught us to see it. If, as Felman pointed out, literature is the unconscious of psychoanalysis, it is even more so of Derridian philosophy.[53] If I am permitted the metaphor, I should like to say that literature is "castrated" because the definition of literature as performative "writing" represses its intersubjective function as the cultural *locus* of affect. Nevertheless, and at the same time, Derrida's philosophical commentary on literary texts allies itself to the cultural value those texts have acquired. Thus the emotional "work" of Celan or Joyce is the labor upon which his master discourse builds its house of speculation. Need I point to the structural similarity between this relationship and that of colonial rule or sexual division? Homi Bhabha's reminder seems pertinent here: However "impeccably the content of an 'other' culture may be known . . . it is its *location* as the closure of grand theories, the demand that, in analytic terms, it be always the good object of knowledge, the docile body of difference, that reproduces a relation of domination and is the most serious indictment of the institutional powers of critical theory."[54]

DERRIDA AND FILIATION

Derrida's approach to Joyce, in its repression of the affective meaning of the fabula, acts out the phantasy of origin of *Ulysses*. Since my discussion of *Ulysses* only discussed two single chapters, the paternity theme which Joyce inscribes upon the Odyssean quest for return received no mention. Many early commentators considered this superposition of the Jewish problematic on to the Greek quest ("Jewgreek is Greekjew" [*U.* 15.2097] also quoted by Derrida), the main point of the novel. Stephen Dedalus, the Telemachus figure, son of a father who cannot function as father because he lacks a coherent identity-model, is looking for a

[53] "To Open the Question," *Literature and Psychoanalysis*, p. 10. In addition, Derrida's postmateriality raises another question. Does theory's claim to intellectual preeminence, its attachment to the *cogito* however marginal, imply that it opts for its becoming "ghostly" (liminal like *Finnegans Wake*) rather than becoming literature and suffer the passage of writing through the flesh and blood of witnessing narrative or personal confession?   [54] *Location of Culture*, p. 31.

spiritual father.[55] Bloom, the supposedly Jewish father of a dead son, is looking for a masculine object to continue the line in the spirit at least. The two men meet and find each other in the activity of parallel urination (a physical form of *graphesis*, analogic to "writing"). This communal production of flow constitutes their bond; and the text ridicules the reader's expectations of resolution and traditional affiliation. It refuses to suggest an enduring relationship between the two men. Instead, rather than their joint image, the text lets the face of Shakespeare, figurehead of writing or textuality, appear in the mirror. In other words, *textuality is the consubstantiality of father and son.* The looping flow of the signature doubles the winding of the umbilical cord as proof of true origin (also note the difference with Lacan's interest in looping knots in connection with Joyce). A long analysis of the "Scylla and Charybdis" chapter in *Ulysses*, which presents Stephen Dedalus' discussion of Shakespeare as the author of *Hamlet* in the context of the problem of spiritual filiation, would substantiate my claim that Derrida's theoretical stance enacts the views there articulated by Stephen Dedalus. But such an analysis of how the "unliving son" becomes the "ghost" of the "unquiet" father, would also bring us back to the historical circumstances of Joyce's traumatic textuality.

What precise experience or psychodynamic force moves Derrida's writing we may never know. We do know he was excluded from secondary school owing to his Jewishness; he mentions his entry into a French-speaking school as a rude shock to a virtually Arab-Algerian youth. Moreover, *Acts of Literature* confesses that his career was a strategy of eluding both familial and ideological pressure. Am I permitted to see a deep affinity between Joyce's self-projection as the Stephen Dedalus who appeals to a mythic (textual-cultural) father named Dedalus in order to effectuate his exile from the old sow that eats its farrow, and Jacques Derrida who negotiates the Scylla and Charybdis of "the metaphysics of castration" versus the "denegation of modern Rousseauisms," through the tracing of the configuration of the "Hegelian wound" "to give birth, from the lesion without suture" to a subjectivity which is grafted on the Name as signature?[56]

Earlier I argued that Joyce's creation of Stephen Dedalus was an

---

[55] Asked what his father is – an important issue in *A Portrait* – Stephen Dedalus provides a "provective" list of identities: "–A medical student, an oarsman, a tenor, an amateur actor, a shouting politician, a small landlord, a small investor, a drinker, a good fellow, a story-teller, somebody's secretary, something in a distillery, a tax-gatherer, a bankrupt and at present a praiser of his own past." (*P* 241).

[56] *Margins of Philosophy*, trans. Alan Bass (University of Chicago Press, 1972), pp. xxviii and xxvi.

effect of the inability to express discursive trauma, as well as an attempt to cope with the split-constitution of Irish subjectivity which offers two rivaling "languages." Since there is no fabula or story to convey "unclaimed memory," as Caruth calls it, the counterfeit narrative of the self-constitution of Stephen Dedalus as artist-author must come in the place of the representation of an integrated self. As we noted, with this replacement, language is severed from the direct expression of affect. Thus the presence of the *Vorstellungsrepräsentanz* allegorizes the underlying condition which itself cannot be represented. Moreover, this inaugural severance keeps generating new splits. One of these splits is *Ulysses*' severance into two differently gendered plot-lines (one staging the search for father/son, the other dealing with the double figure of the feminine). Thus we also have two "endings," just as we have two sexes and two "languages." *Finnegans Wake* will eventually inscribe splitting into the fabula, story, and text itself, dramatizing its own *praxis* of hybridizing signification. The ongoing debate between Shem and Shaun locked into fixed and repetitive opposition may thus be understood as the allegory of the split condition of the text's discursivity – its fetishistic denial of pain. We may extend the opposition between Shem and Shaun to that of Lacan and Derrida. Derrida's Shem-like response to just the scriptural aspects of Joyce colludes with the forward movement of the splitting repetition of the non-representability of the moment of trauma, whereas Lacan's Shaun-like hammering on materiality fetishizes the concreteness of its textuality. In avoiding story, narrative, or the pain behind the words, both Derrida and Lacan escape the engagement with the full totality of literary writing.

Perhaps as a consequence, their theory enacts the double phantasy of Joyce's text. Derrida's writing *enacts* Stephen Dedalus' formula of textual paternity as the implicit narrative of self-constitution in and of his own *œuvre*. Deftly dodging the tenet of gender difference as castration, it links to the plot of (mythic) paternal filiation inscribed in the fabula-story of *Ulysses*. Unlike Stephen, he seems to do so without guilt or *agenbite of inwit*, and Derrida takes pride in his pro-feminist intentions. It may be that his deafness to the "other voice" of the text, the baroque voice from the mother's tomb heard by Lacan, is predicated on his heritage. In Jewish patriarchy, the link to the mother *guarantees* the continuity of the race. The mother's lap, which holds the son up to the threat of the knife, also provides the security and material support which guarantees survival. The Jewish mother's flesh does not hold the threat it does in Joyce. The mother's voice does not call upon the son to "apologise"; nor does she contaminate him with death from beyond the great divide. Lacan, on the other hand, in his insistence on the truth of castration, would primarily seem to relate to that layer of Joyce's text which engages the question of materiality. This question does not reside in the fabula of paternity and filiation. It is located in the screen of the text upon which the story is inscribed, and which allows what Lacan named the foreclosure of the Name-of-the-Father to return as black dots, doodling and the littering of writing. Thus Derrida and Lacan collude with the "materiality" of the "letter" in a different way. In Shem-Derrida, the materiality of the letter, "writing," proves to be the incessant activity of textual production which generates a disembodied textual memory, transcending individual existence and location like the Internet. The writing pen becomes a transcendently generative phallus. For Shaun-Lacan (especially the Lacan of the "Seminars on Joyce"), the letter is the material "inscription" of language in the clay of the body, and its symptomatic appearance in Joyce as materialized litter (generating physical effects such as laughter and *jouissance*). Lacan's materiality of the signifier is more reductively materialist than that of Derrida, and far more threatening to our *vanitas*.

THE MATERIALITY OF THE MOTHER IN THE VOID OF RELIGION

At first sight my linking of Derrida with patriarchy and Lacan with the materiality of Stephen's mother may seem to contain a surprising injustice. Is it not generally known that Derrida advocates emancipation, whereas Lacan is held to relegate "Woman" to a Gehenna outside the Symbolic?[57] In order to clarify this seeming contradiction, we must return to Lacan and the mother. Instead of supporting Derrida's claim that Lacan's truth rests on the absolute fixity of the maternal body as the place of the return of the letter – which would mean siding with Shem the Derridian Penman against Shaun the Lacanian Postman – I turn aside to Henry Staten's discussion of Lacan in *Eros in Mourning* which historicizes Lacan.[58] Staten's argument is that Lacan projects an absolute, Platonic level transcending or voiding the Symbolic and Imaginary, where our destiny, the "empty-yet-full *particularity* of the own-most"

---

[57] Jacqueline Rose, in *Feminine Sexuality*, points out that Lacan constructs the woman as an absolute category excluded and elevated at the same time, and as warrant of the unity on the side of the man. p. 47 *passim*.
[58] "The Bride Stripped Bare, or Lacan *avec* Plato," in *Eros in Mourning: Homer to Lacan* (Baltimore: Johns Hopkins University Press, 1995), pp. 166–185.

is determined.[59] From my discussion of Joyce, the reader will recognize that Staten is referring to the place hollowed by the experience of linguistic alienation, from which, in Lacan's view, the "sinthome" issues. Staten refers to this place as the "transcendent void" (Joyce's "woid," the absolute void transcending the word). It is this void which is the *locus* of what Lacan in Seminar 7 called "the Thing" (*Das Ding*), and to which Julia Kristeva gave such prominence in her discussion of depression and melancholia.[60] Staten's definition is:

> The Thing is the transcendent or transcendental non-object, the negative of the Platonic Idea in whose place it nevertheless stands, at the summit of the hierarchy of desires. Since "this Thing will always be represented by emptiness," the function of the symbolic as route of access to authentic desire involves fundamentally the annulment of the particularity of all empirical objects of desire. This annulment reveals the Thing for which objects can be only the stand-ins or reminiscences and thus reveals as well the unspeakable particularity of the subject.[61]

Staten's main point – here remember our analysis of "Cyclops" – is that Lacan postulates the presence of the negative drive to destruct in the same place as the *locus* of *jouissance*. This apocalyptic or transcendent negativity, which aims at destroying even the cycles of nature, is, via Melanie Klein, in Lacan related to the figure of the mother as the mediator-occupant of the place of "the Thing." "*Das Ding* itself is absolutely inaccessible, a reminiscence like that of immortality; it is 'the prehistoric other that it is impossible to forget'. The law of the father comes to save us from the 'choking pap' of the mother's love so that the transcendental form of desire may be revealed behind the empirical beings that stand in for it."[62]

Again, it is a literary text which substantiates the truth of the existence of the place of "the Thing" to Lacan. By means of a discussion of a Troubadour poem about courtly love which reduces the mark of gender of the mother's genitals to the neutrality of the "*transsexual* hole" the anus (as in *Finnegans Wake*), Lacan argues the special aptitude of the mother as occupant of the place of "The Thing." Staten's demystification of this identification (the inverse, incidentally, of Lacan's alleged conflation of the phallus with the penis) points to the unacknowledged neutralization of gender difference in the service of warding off the threat of death. What is at issue is not the nurturing maternal body,

---

[59] *Ibid.*, p. 173.   [60] See *Soleil noir: dépression et mélancolie* (Paris: Gallimard, 1987).
[61] "The Bride Stripped Bare," p. 174.   [62] *Ibid.*, p. 177.

but "the body of dissolution, ultimate formlessness as the hidden secret of the form of the body":[63] the mother as image of death. As Staten points out, death, however, is beyond gender; it is indeed the very principle of the undoing of difference. What reveals itself here as a semantic sliding from the figure of the female genitals through the image of the anus to the neuter of death, is the strategy of containment of death through its projection onto the feminine. The traversal of this "radical phantasy" and the full realization of the nullity of the subject is apparently the ultimate aim of Lacanian psychoanalysis. Staten concludes: "Truth of the nullity of the subject and the object: In some ways Lacan's is a very traditional truth, as we have seen . . . [But] [i]t may be that for Lacan . . . the price of authenticity is confrontation with the *absolute* nothingness of the self, and thus with something never before approached in the tradition, the frustration of all desire for self-presence." He names this a "platonic desire disabused of the illusion of self-presence and nevertheless obeying its imperative of self-propriation, where self-propriation means the return to itself of a nothingness."[64]

This (Lacanian) confrontation with the absolute nullity of the self through the maternal imago, is, just as the (Derridian) strategy of spiritual filiation, a major thread in the texture of *Ulysses*. Joyce's text combines them. Stephen Dedalus mourns his recently deceased mother whose memory haunts him and whose spectre threatens to drag him with her into death. Called a "Ghoul! Chewer of corpses! No, mother! Let me be and let me live" (*U* 1.278), Joyce presents the appearance of this orientalized vampiric spirit on one of the first pages of the text. Stephen's preoccupation with her is so intense that her hallucinated presence overtakes reality, flipping inside outside: The bowl-shape of the landscape prospect before him turns into the deathbed basin into which she spit up her innards, "[h]er hoarse loud breath rattling in horror." May Dedalus is presented in the full horror of physical decay, bile trickling from her mouth, spitting up her rotting liver. She returns from the grave in "Circe," and "*raises her blackened withered right arm slowly towards Stephen's breast with outstretched finger.*" "*A green crab with malignant red eyes sticks deep its grinning claws into Stephen's heart*" (*U* 15.4217–21). In the text, Stephen "traverses" this apocalyptic phantasy (the color green relates the mother to the nation) by means of the acceptance of absolute annihilation: "*Nothung!* (*He lifts his ashplant high with both hands and smashes the chandelier. Time's livid final flame leaps and, in the following darkness, ruin of all*

---

[63] *Ibid.*, p. 181.   [64] *Ibid.*, p. 185.

space, shattered glass and toppling masonry)" (*U* 15.4242–46). This moment, a turning-point in the relationship between "son" Stephen and "father" Bloom, suggests in its dramatization that the threat of the materiality of the mother is only to be laid to rest by the accepted risk of an Absolute Nothing beyond materiality, giving presence to death-in-life: in short, transcendental mourning.

It is not only the son-figure in the novel who encounters the spectral effect of the maternal *imago* as transcendent nullity. The father-figure Bloom is similarly visited throughout the day with apocalyptic sensations related to the feminine, but his response is not transcendental mourning, but return to the womb and the warmth of the fleshly presence of the generative female:

> A cloud began to cover the sun slowly, wholly. Grey. Far.
> No, Not like that. A barren land, bare waste. Vulcanic lake, the dead sea: no fish, weedless, sunk deep in the earth. No wind could lift those waves, grey metal, poisonous foggy waters. Brimstone they called it raining down . . . A dead sea in a dead land, grey and old. Old now. It bore the oldest, the first race . . . The oldest people. Wandered far away over all the earth, captivity to captivity, multiplying, dying, being born everywhere. It lay there now. Now it could bear no more. Dead: an old woman's: the grey sunken cunt of the world.
> Desolation.
> Grey horror seared his flesh. (*U* 4.218–30).

Bloom's antidote to the spectre of materialist entropy is the memory of Molly's warmth: "To smell the gentle smoke of tea, fume of the pan, sizzling butter. Be near her ample bedwarmed flesh. Yes, yes" (*U* 4.238–40). Thus *Ulysses*, splitting its protagonists, both masculine and feminine, in old and young, provides a syncretic strategy of coping with the specter of nothingness. Stephen, whose shape cannot be changed, lives the terror of annihilation, while the older Bloom places genital Molly Bloom as counterimage to the neutered death of the mother (the "turfbrown mummy" *FW* 194.22). Since Bloom's "yes" is repeated by Molly as the conclusion of the text in the double affirmative which Derrida made so much of, the novel as a whole presents itself as a strategy for countering the specter of a reductive materiality which it raises, through its weaving of the recurrent and reversible material/textual web, the feminine letter. In *Finnegans Wake* the spectre of the castrating mother pursuing her firstborn son will return, but here the son, become a Christlike figure owing to the successful strategy of writing *Ulysses*, clearly triumphs over the threat of death. Instead of lifting a stick, "He lifts the lifewand and the dumb speak. –

Quoiquoiquoiquoiquoiquoiqquoik!" (*FW* 195.5–6). Self-parodying the nonsense of *Finnegans Wake*, Joyce turns the tongue associated with the mother (here the mother as the possessor of the letter) into the meaningless quacking of ducks, or a croaking and stammering French question delivered as exclamation. Does Joyce imply that the "original" language cannot be recovered? Is he alerting us to his strategy of encrypting the nullity of the void into writing? Is he just pulling our leg? It may be significant to add that 1904, the date at which *Ulysses* is set, was the year in which Joyce wore mourning for his mother, wrote the sketch for a self-portrait which became *A Portrait of the Artist*, and met his later wife Nora Barnacle. Perhaps some phantasies can never be traversed.

What we may conclude, however, is that Joyce's literary text interlaces in its syncretic body the rivaling views on the nature of the letter of Lacan and Derrida. Joyce's works incorporate, embody, and engage both positions, just as they pair Shem and Shaun, Jew and Greek without *Aufhebung* – without mending the crack between them. Its embodied textuality stages the implicit phantasy-scenario's and family romances underlying theory – just as the dream provides a screen for unconscious content. This turns literature into the screen upon which the "unconscious" of theory is projected, rather than its passive and mute location. Joyce's ambivalent textuality, which functions as the rhetorical figure of the hendiadys (Gr. *hendiaduoin*) which predicates two as one, is also the seemingly passive "other" of theory whose passivity comes to reveal the self-projection of its commentator.

To some it might seem as if Joyce, in *Finnegans Wake*, becomes more Lacanian. Here we read that the letter was "Hers before his even, posted ere penned" (*FW* 232.16–17). Such an impression, however, ignores the Derridian performative drive which propels *Finnegans Wake*. Nor is Joyce's specter of ultimate materialism linked to his later work. The constellation of woman, death, and language is replayed from the early manuscript pages of *Stephen Hero* to *Finnegans Wake*. *Stephen Hero* ends with the scene of a "thing," a female corpse, stiff, lifted from a canal, and covered with a brown sack, a woman escaped from a madhouse. Stephen is transfixed, gazing "near the feet of the body, looking at a fragment of paper on which was printed: The Lamp a [mazn] magazine for . . . the rest was torn away and several other pieces of paper were floating about in the water" (*SH* 252–53). From Joyce's textual beginning, the woman is related to the missing signifier, the lacking meaning, the absent word (as in Lacan). But also from the beginning, print offers itself as the medium of keeping subjectivity "afloat" (as in Derrida). In *Ulysses*, Stephen will cry out to the spectre of the mother to "[t]ell me the word, mother, if you know now. The word known to all men" (*U* 15.4191–92). The mother's death, the spectre of the ultimate voiding of material presence, is also related to the possibility of her knowledge of the word – an absent mother tongue. In *Finnegans Wake*, it is the possession and possible origin of the *letter* (the Word become print) which is always related to female figures, from Biddy the Hen to Anna Livia herself – whose dying monologue concludes and recycles the text through the "article" "the" (note Joyce's pun on materialism. Language and subjectivity become "thing.") But this letter is not only littered (Lacan's "sinthome"), it re-inscribes death in each stroke of the pen, as does Derrida, and keeps itself never-endingly "afloat" while doing so. It is as if Joyce insisted on incarnating an impossible and "crazy" (because outside discourse) mother tongue which he pursues and which pursues him, defying the annihilation of meaning and subjectivity to do so.

There is one moment in Joyce's work where the mother tongue sounds: In the story of Eveline in *The Dead*. Imprisoned like a helpless animal in the abusive structure of family and ideology, and contemplating an impossible escape, her memory of the mother's voice in the lapsed language irrupts:

> As she mused the pitiful vision of her mother's life laid its spell *on the very quick of her being* – that life of commonplace sacrifices closing in final craziness. She trembled as she heard again her mother's voice saying constantly with foolish insistence:
> –Derevaun Seraun! Derevaun Seraun!
> She stood up in an impulse of terror. Escape! She must escape! . . . But she wanted to live. (*D* 40, italics added)

Decades of Joyce criticism have not been able to establish the definitive meaning of these Gaelic-sounding words.[65] Perhaps that was Joyce's point. As Joyce himself suggested, a thin sheet separates his writing from madness. The phantasy of the recovery of a lapsed language, the traversal of the phantasy of apocalyptic death through the dissolution of the maternal body, are projects which can never be completed. They may, perhaps, only be engaged as self-consciously as Joyce does, if one invents a strategy of scriptural survival which can balance the engagement with the deadly letter of Lacan with the forward flight of

---

[65] John Wyse Jackson and Bernard McGinley (eds.), *James Joyce's Dubliners: An Annotated Edition* (London: Sinclair-Stevenson, 1993), p. 32 provide a number of possible meanings.

writerly subjectivity of Derrida, "P"ater Daedalus with *"M"ater(ia prima,* and speak the "S"plit text with a forked tongue.[66]

This pairing of theory and literature may hold relevance to the concerns of contemporary culture. The problem of the transcendental void, according to Kristeva connected with the unmourned pre-Oedipal mother, and in Martin Jay's "The Apocalyptic Imagination and the Inability to Mourn"[67] related to our loss of mother nature, is placed by Joyce's postcolonial narrative as the effect of placing the mother-imago in the void which colonial rule hollowed. In Joyce, "the Thing" and the notion of a transcendental void are figured as related to the construction of the mother in a colonized Catholic culture. The power of the mother-figure in *Ulysses* depends not just on her maternal qualities, but on her unusual, (post)colonial symbolic double function. She also up-holds what is left of the paternal function. It is she who wants Stephen to "apologise," to return to the Church, do his Easter duty, and confess. Her transcendent hand outstretched from the grave is powered by the higher authority of God and Eternal Damnation. If the Irish tradition tended to represent itself in the figure of a woman, now we also see that in the colonial Dublin of Joyce's *Ulysses* the alignment of the feminine with the Church, a patriarchal institution *par excellence,* works to "woid" the location of the maternal *imago.* The paternal principle is of little corrective use in Joyce's colonial Dublin. As we saw, Joyce fights his perpetual battle to maintain a textualized subjectivity by means of the splitting substitution and exchange of one female image for another – young for old; carnal for spiritual; affirmative for castrating; emphati-cally secular for religious. It is the split-off and excluded or abjected image of the mother-of-spiritual-authority, rather than the mother-as-nurturing-agent which ends up being transformed into the black hole of the transcendental void as the place of the absoluteness of nullity. "The Thing" in Joyce acquires its power through the (post)colonial linkage of the threat of absolute materiality to the lingering concept of transcen-dence. Joyce's myth of sexual liberation was projected as counter force.

A suggestion which seems to follow is that Joyce's text allegorizes both Derrida's and Lacan's placement of the sexual other, owing to his splitting of the representation of the feminine. Derrida's supplemen-tarity is given figure in the ambivalent placement of "Penelope";

---

[66] The Joycean reader will think of the trinitarian division of the text of *Ulysses* by means of three capital letters: "S"on or Stephen, "M"olly, and "P"oldy.
[67] *Forcefields: Between Intellectual History and Cultural Critique* (New York and London: Routledge, 1993), pp. 64–99.

Lacan's exclusion of the woman from the Symbolic is to be seen in Stephen Dedalus's abjection of the mother (and repeated in Molly's vicarious triumph over older women and Aunt Dante). In *Tristes Tropiques* Claude Lévi-Strauss defines two attitudes toward madness practiced to maintain social health. The "anthropoemic" (cf. "emetic") one is to spit out the undesirable entity; the other, "anthropophagic" method incorporates and digests the alien(ated) object. Joyce syncretically practices both. In one novel, *Ulysses*, the respective strategies of Lacan and Derrida of handling castration seem paired.

I might go on, but I hope enough has been said to show that some of Lacan's and Derrida's contributions to the discussion of postcolonial textuality have their grounding in the Joycean text. Différance, dissemination, supplementarity, *jouissance*, the Thing, these abstract concepts might have made less impact if the literary work and the lived experience to ground and illustrate them had not existed. I do not make this point to suggest that the truth of theory is corroborated by the literary text or resides in it. My claim is different. To begin, it seems to me that theory owes a historical debt to the postcolonial experience of the literary text which it fails to acknowledge sufficiently. Joyce created *in* his works the marginal space which presents, stages, and allows strategic resistance. His text is *both* symptom *and* the locus of ongoing survival. His text was designed as a location where the anxiety of postcolonial existence could find embodied existence, *and* as an anamorphic mirror which returns to the reader the experience of traumatic insufficiency characteristic of colonial experience. Most important is that concepts which derive from the *experience* of the colonial situation as lived by Joyce are inserted into western writing as universal features of textuality and consciousness. Thus they are separated from their roots in Joyce's struggle against the hegemony of the English language and its canon.

As I said, there is a difference between the presentation of an insight as theory and its presentation as narrative. Theory, projecting a "universe of discourse," communicates rational insight and abstract conceptualizations. It promotes intellectual understanding. Even Lacan, although many of his rhetorical strategies are aimed at generating transferential involvement and affective insight in his audience, is, in his *Ecrits*, the "author" of institutional-professional knowledge. What theory's writing can never communicate, indeed what it must repress, is that language is also the lived extension of the body. Hence it lacks the affective charge inhabiting the literary work, and its attendant intersubjective effect. In other words, if we "translate" the struggle for articulation and emotional survival of the (post)colonial literary work into concepts and theory, we practice a transvaluation which circumscribes its emotional effect. We amputate its affectivity and the curative possibility of engagement with its emotional charge. I am not referring to the Aristotelian notion of catharsis which supposedly helps the spectator to resolve his or her own unconscious conflicts. I am referring to what Felman and Laub articulated as the text's power to evoke an attitude of sympathetic *witnessing* which makes it possible for the unconscious experience giving rise to the peculiar symptomaticity of the text, to find ear and expression in another subject. Sheer analysis, sheer objectification deprives the literary work of its effect of making the reader *witness* the atrocities of colonial rule, of transmitting the pain and uncertainty of subaltern subjectivity, of conveying its outrage at injustice. Indeed, the fact that the feeling of being postcolonial seems to be growing universal, may be owing to precisely the splitting reductiveness of contemporary culture which has commodified textuality.

If colonial practice arose out of the failure to imagine and experience the reality of the other as equal, theory, which splits fetishized intellectualization from emotional engagement, is complicit in that act of splitting repression. In contrast to theory, literature makes history available as cultural memory, as re-lived, more fully embodied experience. As psychoanalytic treatment demonstrates, change only takes place if insight is attended with affect. Without the imaginative capability for perceiving history through one's own emotional response which literature provides, the practise of theory might entail the repression of the effects of colonial history, rather than their working through. History will remain a repetition without progress, at best a forgetting, perhaps a repressive diminishment of the emotional range of consciousness. It is for this reason that I pointed to Derrida's and Lacan's practise of ignoring the fabula and story of literary works. While it is not so that the affective charge of the work of literature is located in its narrative embodiment of knowledge alone, it does seem true that if we only look at style to the exclusion of content (if we split the text), we disrupt the imaginative totality of the work, and fail to engage the full charge of its force. If the "true otherness" of the work of literature[68] is its function as conduit of conscious or unconscious affect, we "castrate" literature if we understand it as just a form of performative "writing." The trade-off

---

[68] Barbara Johnson's term in "The Frame of Reference: Poe, Lacan, Derrida," in Felman (ed.), *Literature and Psychoanalysis*, p. 505.

involved seems clear. Theory is "cleaner" than literature: Less feeling, less pain, less sweat, less tears. Moreover, in its abstractness, it seems "harder," more masculine, more difficult and prestigious, even when it stylizes itself as the feminine variant of the form. In short, the whole ideological structure of privilege is implied in our choice of a preferred approach towards rendering our understanding of history and culture. Here it will be understood that my method of pairing literature and theory, and reading them as mutually determined and determining discourses, was a political choice. It seemed a way of healing the breach which threatens to separate the reading of literature from theoretical reflection; it is also an attempt to relocate theory in the affective context from which it has struggled to escape on Daedalian wings.

Joyce's anamorphic mirror

What can't be coded can be decorded if an ear aye sieze what no
eye ere grieved for.

Finnegans Wake

Trauma is the curious condition of a split and yet redoubled state of
being: death-in-life. Death has been felt, but has not been accepted.
Although the conscious memory of the occasion is lacking, death has
inscribed itself on the psyche and/or in the body, and insists on manifesting itself as the compulsion to repeat. A force stronger than the will
programs the self, seemingly from outside; exiled from self-possession,
the self is at once self-consciously aware of that displacement. Joyce's
career was a struggle to constitute a discursive self in the language that
had marked his exclusion, as well as an attempt to appropriate the
language and dissolve his own foreignness within it. The only way he
could accomplish that task was by making a self-conscious attempt,
through his writing, to occupy the void and testify to the experience of
ultimate nothingness left by the appropriation of his culture by the
hegemony. Thus he could try to erode the seeming self-presence of the
hegemony from within, although he could never gain a sense of being
"at home" in language. As the author of *Ulysses* and *Finnegans Wake*, he
blurred the clarity and transparency of meaning with the darkness of ink
and Irish turf and mud. Thus he reflected the racial prejudice against
the Irish back upon the English canon.

It is in this attempt to stretch and decompose the hegemony that
Joyce invented and practiced the strategies of resisting textuality and
linguistic inventiveness which unsettle the mirroring function of western
representation. Dissemination, *différance*, supplementarity, invagination,
jouissance, the Real, "the Thing," are embodied features and principles
of Joyce's texts. They were Joyce's resources, sometimes, perhaps,
echoing lingering indigenous ways of relating to language in his successful battle with the hegemony of representation. In turning these rhetori-

cal effects into theoretical formulations in their fight against the logocentrism of western metaphysics or a reified Freudianism, Derrida and Lacan confirmed the importance of Joyce's writing to contem- porary western thought; but they also neutralized its political sting and muted its historical occasion. Moreover, they also circumscribe Joyce's affective force, and co-opt the instrument which might reflect and transmit the specificity and pain of the postcolonial struggle to a theory with a universalist bias. Thus his true disruptiveness and effect is domesticated.

That Joyce should have been such a rich resource for theory, is owing to the fact that his work stages the dilemma of our understanding of consciousness: is it one or two, single or divided? This is an ancient theological problem addressed in myths in many cultures,[1] which, as a debate about the nature of sexual difference, also engaged Derrida and Lacan. In Joyce, however, the question does not arise from intellectual bafflement. Irish experience brings the contradiction as a lived reality. The moment of Stephen's discursive trauma is predicated upon it. Eileen, the girl next door, whom Stephen intends to marry when grown-up, has a "different father and mother" (*P* 8). The historical division of religious difference inserts itself as a mysterious difference at the heart of familiarity. Joyce does not specify that Eileen is Protestant. He presents the incomprehensibility of division from the child's perspective. How can a "father and mother" be "different"? The religious difference is, of course, related to political division, and the present co-existence of the Irish Republic and Northern Ireland on the geographical territory of the one island. Difference, although radically divisive is not absolute, and perhaps so disruptive because of its ambiguity. Geography, a shared material location, holds together what ideology and history divide. Joyce's strategy of making the book the physical location where difference is played out enacts the real condition of Irish society; thus it would seem that Joyce's "embodied textuality" is the direct translation of the ambivalence of Irish existence. It is this translation which both baffled and inspired theory. My hope is that this recontextualization of the theoretical concepts of Derrida and Lacan will make them more natural tools in postcolonial studies.

However, there is a more pressing point. I also want to argue that Joyce's literary text holds an ethical appeal to the reader which theory as

[1] Mircea Eliade, *The Two and the One* (New York: Harper and Row, 1969).

such lacks.[2] His strategy of reflecting the condition of trauma back upon the reader demands a response to witness the blanks of history and so reinscribe the colonized subject into history – even if only as a virtual presence. If philosophy and psychoanalytic theory appropriate the strategies of articulation so hard-won by postcolonial writing, these discourses precisely frustrate such a pedagogy. The history of trauma is a history of forgetting. It is worrisome that theory should collude with our collective forgetting instead of helping to reclaim the experience which cannot be put into words (so that, belatedly, it may yet be worked through and mourned). As Adorno emphasized: "We will not have come to terms with the past until the causes of what happened then are no longer active. Only because these causes live on does the spell of the past remain to this very day unbroken."[3]

From *Dubliners* to *Finnegans Wake,* Joyce both demonstrates an intense compulsion to repeat, as well as a forward drive propelled by the author's self-conscious self-analysis which can never uncover the moment of trauma, but must keep endeavouring to do so – by digging ever deeper into the medium of representation, and unceasingly sending himself into circulation in ever-progressive splitting. As Joyce put it in *Finnegans Wake*: his writerly *persona* is "self exiled in upon his ego, a nightlong a shaking betwixtween white or reddr hawrors, noondayterrorised to skin and bone by an ineluctable phantom . . . writing the mystery of himself in furniture" ("furniture" is printing type; *FW* 184.5–10). He never succeeded in recovering a sense of familiar selfhood in the English language, and increasingly turned inward to the analysis of the rhetorical means of communication, the conventional structures of representation, and eventually the physical act of writing and material textuality: the book as object, the text as screen. His sense of self-identity eventually came to rest on the success of *Ulysses. Finnegans Wake*, in its rehearsal of Joyce's earlier work, as well as the record of contemporary events, provided a utopian *locus* of writerly subjectivity in process.

The similarity with Derrida's projection of subjectivity as dissemination will seem clear. For the Derrida of *The Postcard*, self-presence is no longer a home from which to depart, but the always elusive end to the

---

[2] As Samuel Weber demonstrates in an appendix to *Return to Freud: Jacques Lacan's Dislocation of Psychoanalysis*, Lacan's theory contains a clear ethical demand; and Derrida's political correctness cannot be doubted. I should not be construed as implying that theory is lacking in ethical awareness.

[3] Theodor W. Adorno, "What Does Coming to Terms With the Past Mean?" in *Bitburg in Moral and Political Perspective*, ed. Geoffrey Hartman (1959; Bloomington: Indiana University Press, 1986), p. 129.

quest for scriptural self-expression. It is also an aim which can never be guaranteed because the letter may go astray. This co-extensiveness between Derrida and Joyce is not only a tribute to both, it is also disturbing. Joyce's self-alienation stems from the specific historical condition of Irishness, whereas Derrida projects that state as a universal condition of subjectivity in an age of technological innovation. If we ignore the specificity of that difference, we also lose the hope of inactivating the causes of that history. Joyce's work, as I shall argue in this conclusion, keeps repeating its trauma with the demand that the reader witnesses and responds to its occasion, and by doing so finds the words to articulate the history of what can only manifest itself as an irreducible gap in Joyce's psyche and textuality. The burden is upon us as readers to reconstitute a narrative which will transform the symptomaticity of Joyce's textuality into knowledge. If we read Joyce as the literary analog to Derrida, we threaten to foreclose upon that ethical imperative contained in the embodied nature of his life's work. Moreover, Joyce calls upon us to address the crisis in western metaphysics not by means of rational understanding, theoretical sophistication, or even good will. His demand that the reader witnesses his discursive trauma, not inscribed into the text as story, but communicated nevertheless, re-opens the question of the relation of subjectivity to language in a new way. In responding to the affect of the embodied text, in engaging the work with patience and attentive empathy, listening as if we were the analyst trying to understand the patient, and in accepting its aggressive castrating effect, the reader undergoes the deconstitution which transforms subjectivity and which may undo the splitting effect of history. Indeed, the unique principle of Joyce's work is his insistence on the embodiment of textuality, his hope of encrypting its elusive meaning in the material presence of the work. For all its symptomaticity, Joyce's linguistic materialism contains the message to become aware of our splitting practices: voice and writing, affect and reason, body and language, enthusiasm and knowledge. How can we see subjectivity as a continuous holistic practice involving both a body and language simultaneously and at once?

Joyce's compulsion to repeat began as the drive to create the uncreated conscience of the race in writing a portrait of Dublin which held up to view its colonial paralysis. He would persist in the attempt to make the reader see the trauma of Irishness until the closing page of *Finnegans Wake*, long after his decision to go into exile on the European continent. This self-chosen exile, in addition to being an escape from

Irish constraint, seems the (repetitive) literalized acting out of the condition of a colonized subjectivity which has had self-difference (exile
from self-possession) inscribed at the moment of constitution. The
nomadic forward drive which led the Joyces to wander all over western
Europe and impelled Joyce to invent a new genre in each new work,
was fueled by a growing self-consciousness and the increasing insistence
of the compulsion to repeat as a form of forward flight to attempt and
uncover the source of the trauma. Looking self-reflexively in the mirror
of his own art, Joyce kept breaking new discursive territory in order to
attempt to articulate the story which, through the recovery of the
memory of trauma, might undo its consequences. Not only is each new
work an innovation of writerly style and technique. Joyce's progressive
self-consciousness, resembling that of the subject in psychoanalysis,
consistently moves its focus, shifting the *locus* of the dark irrecoverability
of the trauma of Irish subjectivity from outside the self to eventually
assume it himself as the blackness of Irishness in *Finnegans Wake*, which
also blackens the mirror of representation.

   Joyce began as the diagnostician wanting to hold up his "nicely
polished lookingglass" to the citizens of Dublin to "betray the soul of
paralysis," and write a chapter of the "moral history" which would
bring "spiritual liberation."[4] His fragmented portrait (fifteen short stories) reflects the self-censorship and repression necessary to function in
the social and emotional impoverishment of a society which is irre-
mediably split internally, owing to its colonial heritage. Each inhabitant
of Dublin suffers from scotoma, a restriction of vision and consciousness
necessary to survive, which is performatively mirrored in the gaps in the
text. Thus Joyce's short-story cycle, though it sets itself up as the
objective reflector, partakes discursively in this self-censorship. The
more closely we read *Dubliners*, the more lacunae we note in its seemingly smooth texture. The nicely polished looking-glass also forces us to
become conscious of the "castration" implicit in living in colonial
Dublin.

   At this point, Joyce still places the stain of darkness outside representation, in an "iris[h]maimed" (*FW* 489.31) Dublin society which supposedly refuses to see and acknowledge the truth of this vision. It is the
fragmentation of his text which betrays that the "castration" which its
author "sees" elsewhere also inhabits his authorial subjectivity. The nice
polish of the looking-glass is achieved by the splitting of the sub-

----

[4] I am quoting from Joyce's letters to Grant Richards, *LI*, pp. 63–64.

ject(matter) into fifteen separate stories with different protagonists of different sex and social backgrounds. However, in the subsequent self-mirroring self-dialectic of writing the autobiographical *A Portrait of the Artist*, this "nice polish" begins to crack apart into the repetitive structure of the "same anew." The text self-subversively embodies the performative self-difference within its own narration. As we noted, each chapter of the work re-enacts the same dilemma. The repetitive five chapters of the cracked looking-glass act out the self-difference which it tries to overcome within its own narration. The crack between the "familiar" and the "foreign," inscribed in a subaltern consciousness which must mirror itself in a language that it experiences as alien and which brings with it an ideological perspective which places the Irish as ignorant simian Micks, is now located *in* the text. This leads to an open-ended process of infinite self-projection and self-revision – a process of self-analysis interminable like psychoanalysis. The forward flight is only concluded rhetorically when the self-alienation and stagnation of Dublin culture are eluded in sending the artist into voluntary exile.

Ulysses, the next step, seems to enforce the conclusion that exile, rather than an escape from the condition of trauma, is its dramatized literalization. The unified subject of *A Portrait of the Artist* splits under this realization into two male figures. The text pairs the figure of Stephen Dedalus – whose "shape cannot be changed" according to his author – with the figure of the "exile within" society: the Wandering Jew Leopold Bloom. The son of a suicide and father of a dead son, Bloom, mourning a friend's death and attending a funeral, lives death-in-life. As we noted, his horrifyingly intense consciousness of death is only made bearable by the warmth of Molly's flesh. Instead of splitting the narrative into short stories or chapters which repeat the same story at a different level, *Ulysses* splits its portrait of Dublin into eighteen chapters, each with a wholly new style; and it splits its image of the maternal *imago* into castrating older women (the punitive mother and Aunt Dante) and vitally warm and still generative Molly Bloom. This epic is seemingly unified by its restriction of time and place and the "mythic method" of the parallel with Homer. Nevertheless, it splits between fabula-story on the one hand, and text on the other, projecting two perspectives on sexual difference. In doing so, *Ulysses* adds a whole new dimension to narrative representation in digging into the process of writing itself and fetishizing the procreative power of pen and print. The performativity of "the cracked lookingglass" of *A Portrait* makes place for a conscious counterfeit, an "epical forged check" (Joyce's words) or carnival mirror which is wondrously comic, but which definitively splits writing as performative process from writing as representation. Moreover, it dissolves authorial accountability. If *A Portrait* can still be read in the traditional manner in which we identify with a protagonist, *Ulysses* no longer leaves the reader a subject-position in the text with which to identify. We must abandon our habit of placing ourselves inside the world of the text by means of the projective identification with a character in the story. In fact, the text becomes an analytical-transferential mirror for the reader, in which one will always encounter one's own blind spots. Interpreting Joyce is risky, because our response tells at least as much about ourselves as about "what is truly there." Joyce's texts expropriate our self-presence. They visit the affliction of its lack upon the reader.

Finally, *Finnegans Wake* identifyingly stages itself in the dark crack of the irrecoverability of the memory of trauma, smearing the signifier with the darkness of non-remembrance, assuming the dissolution of subjectivity, and embodying what it means not to see or not to speak. Its setting, the wake of Tim Finnegan, dramatizes the liminality of a stage after the death of the body but before the departure of the soul; a condition of death experienced but not yet accepted: the condition of trauma. This self-conscious assumption of traumatic subjectivity is achieved at the expense of referentiality and narrative power. The text splits and repeats itself, replaying the reel of life and career as endless repetition and recirculation. Instead of achieving the memory of a moment before trauma, of recollecting the event which caused the fraying process of splitting, this flaunting demonstration of the presence of death *in* the self is based on and leads to increasing fragmentation, even of the signifier itself. The reader who engages this work stares in an anamorphic mirror which demonstratively inscribes the skull beneath the flesh and vitality of Irish history. Here Lacan's chapter on anamorphosis in his seminar on the gaze is pertinent. If the ordinary picture or the conventional story is a trap for the gaze facilitating the viewer's/reader's illusion of totality, anamorphosis (the incorparation of an image [here the skull] which can only be perceived as such from a different spatial position and perspective point) shows the "subject as annihilated" and as "the imaged embodiment of . . . castration."[5] *Finnegans Wake* includes the perspective point of the "death of the reader" in its hilarious carnavalization of western cultural history.

[5] *Four Fundamental Concepts of Psychoanalysis*, ed. Jacques Miller, trans. Alan Sheridan (New York: Norton, 1977), pp. 88–89.

Published on the eve of World War II, this dramatization of the gap of Irish subjectivity as the blackness of Irishness contains a clear appeal to come to terms with religious and racial difference,[6] to solve the problem of western metaphysics which cannot conceive of another as different yet equal without abjection or assigning hierarchical priority. It poses that question not through plot or discursive formulation, but dramatically, by imposing the condition of meaninglessness, of exclusion, and lack of speech upon the reader while itself becoming the secondary positivization of the nothing, the transcendental void, that ultimate kind of nothingness for which "Auschwitz" has become a historical signifier. *Finnegans Wake* is "a pure semblance devoid of any substantial support, and something 'more real than reality itself': in its very capacity of a pure semblance, it 'gives body' to a boundary which fixes the limits of (what we experience as) reality, i.e., it holds the place of, stands in for, what has to be excluded, foreclosed, if 'reality' is to retain its consistency."[7] The question *Finnegans Wake* asks in its voluntary sacrifice of all title to discursive self-presence, and its staging of the *sparagmos* of the body (also that of Christ or Freud's primal father) is when we shall ever learn. When shall we relinquish the dangerous illusions of self-presence, power, and objectivity based on the splitting of the world in a seeing subject and a perceived object, or a commanding reader and a patient text?

Joyce does not tell the story of the trauma, his life and work re-enact it. Nor does he ever recover the moment of its origin, he uncovers the death-in-life that is its effect. The increasingly conscious presence of death in Joyce's works is attended with, and won, owing to his constantly intensified assault on the English language, and eventually the medium of representation itself. Joyce tears through the screen of representation. But however assiduously Joyce may dig the field of language to search and find in its soil the hidden treasure of a tongue undefiled by "foreignness," or to uncover the memory of the moment when the "familiar" was split by the "foreign," what he best succeeds in is the dislocation once and for all of western representation, and the canonicity of the English novel, which will henceforth be "english."

Thus Joyce ends up assuming the fragmentation which the imposi-

---

[6] Whereas *Ulysses* chose a Jew as protagonist, *Finnegans Wake* is full of references to Shem's blackness and Anna Livia's Africanism. Note, however that Joyce nevertheless refuses to inscribe blackness as presence: "Anf pfor to pfinnish our pfun of a pfan coalding the keddle mickwhite . . ." (*FW* 596.31–32).

[7] Slavoj Žižek, *Tarrying with the Negative: Kant, Hegel, and the Critique of Ideology* (Durham: Duke University Press, 1993), p. 38.

tion of Irish subjectivity had inflicted upon him, and turns it into exemplary martyrdom (St. Stephen was the first martyr in the New Testament).[8] But there is also a contrary force at work in his texts: an attempt at psychic rememberment and the reincarnation of the dissevered subject. As in the myth of the reassembly of the dismembered god Osiris, Joyce tries to recreate the body *in* the text, to create a new corpus of sensibility, made of "synthetic ink" and "sensitive paper" :'for his own end out of his wit's waste" (*FW* 185.7–8). Writing with "double dye," Joyce the "alshemist" "brandishing his bellbearing stylo, the shining keyman of the worlds of change," "squirtscreens" the "squidself" "over every square inch of the only foolscap available, his own body, till by its corrosive sublimation one continuous present tense integument slowly unfold[s] all . . . cyclewheeling history" (*FW* 185.32–86.2).

If we accept the axiom of trauma and its psychological symmetry to colonization, this obsessive insistence on embodiment is not just a symptom of a particularly intense form of anxiety (the threat of severance of language from body), but an act of resistance against the violence with which Irish-Catholic colonial culture effectuates subjectivity. If subjectivity is constituted by a splitting of the self which facilitates self-reflection and self-correction by self-rejection, the refusal to detach and separate is both an act of loyalty to the moment of trauma to which it is a witness, as well as an attempt to suggest what is at stake in its occurrence by obsessively entwining what culture wishes to separate. This drive not only affects the separation of body and language, it also affects the crystallization of the amorphous sentience of the body into separate and rivaling organs. Joyce counters the centralizing phallic drive of his contemporaries Pound and Lawrence. To Wyndham Lewis's frustration he refused to relinquish his attachment to the ear. Joyce avoids the choice between eye and ear, since choice means loss. We cannot hear what is presented as writing, we cannot see what we are told. Although John Bishop claims that *Finnegans Wake* centers on "the closure of the eye and the eternal openness of the ear,"[9] I suggest otherwise. Joyce tries to bind the reader's eye and ear, the voice and the gaze, as it were to resist the crystallization around a single organ, frustrating the privileging of one organ, any single organ. Eye and ear are as a rule mentioned in paired conjunction throughout Joyce's works, becoming "ear aye" and "eye ere" (*FW* 482.34). It is as a pair that Joyce

---

[8] Also note Lacan's play on Joyce's sanctity in the formulation of the "sinthome."

[9] *Joyce's Book of the Dark: Finnegans Wake* (Madison: University of Wisconsin Press, 1986), p. 303.

mentions them even when arguing the legitimacy of his own paternity; and it will be remembered that the moment of trauma in *A Portrait* was a wounding of the ear by the threat to the eye. Indeed, the prime peculiarity of Joyce's later work is the defamiliarization of the reader's sight to make him or her dependent on simultaneous acoustic recognition for the decipherment of the sign. Joyce makes the eye (I) work in conjunction with the ear ("ear" pronounced "Eire" lends Joyce's refusal a political charge).

The point in talking about "bodily organs" such as penis/phallus, ear or eye, is that our culture uses body parts and sense organs as *loci* for truth or prestige ("seeing is believing"; the doubting Thomas needs touch; the Jewish tradition regards the eye as a distraction from the truth of the Word; and, as Martin Jay tells us in *Downcast Eyes*, twentieth-century French philosophy has tended to "denigrate" vision, inscribing a Hebraic alterity upon the self-evident clarity of Reason.[10]) In binding the voice to the eye, in yoking one to the other, Joyce should not be seen as providing a Hegelian *reconciliation* of Jewish and Hellenic metaphors of truth, as Lyotard also argued. Such a conclusion would fail to do justice to Joyce's recalcitrant elusiveness. The aim of his "verbicovisual presentment" (*FW* 341.19) is not a new truth, or another kind of truth, but a focus on the process which channels physical energy into the service of organ-rationalized ideology, colonizing the body and its sentience to make it chattel of the Idea. The difference lies, I would suggest, in a difference of intentionality and speech act. Instead of just constative or performative, Joyce's linguistic impetus which combines both modes, is that of *witnessing* as defined by Felman and Laub in *Testimony*: a demonstrative enactment of the affect which binds body to speech. Thus Joyce's "body-language" in turn pierces the ear or blinds the eye of rational signification, instituting the echoing, witnessing voice of rhythm and repetition.

In retrospect the traumatizing phrase "apologise, pull out his eyes" gains a curious additional meaning. In binding the eye to the ear, thus depriving the eye of its hegemony as a "transparent eyeball," while substituting darkness of echo, Joyce seems indeed to have accomplished the aim of "pulling out his eyes" (where "his" may be read as referring to western logocentrism). In Joyce's universe sentience and self-extension, body and language, intention and writing do not move in radically different universes as poststructuralist theory still assumes. Joyce's

---

[10] *Downcast Eyes: The Denigration of Vision in Twentieth-Century French Thought* (Berkeley: University of California Press, 1993.

aesthetic centers on embodiment without definitive crystallization. His body is not the gender-specific body, but a protean body, protecting itself from being harnessed to the aim of empire. But, we must ask, in being so protean did he not also sign the death warrant of his own textual body? Funerals, wakes, corpses, ghosts are as central to the Joycean text as sexuality and music – the body in *Finnegans Wake* is after all a decomposing corpse.

This refusal to pursue the light is also a dramatic reminder of what the body is, of what culture represses in its discursive colonization of the flesh. There is no more gruesomely emphatic body than a rotting cadaver. In insisting on the darkly physical nature of the body, Joyce reminds us that culture – man's self-extension of body into tool and language, as Elaine Scarry so brilliantly argues – is also an attempt to elevate himself above the suffering and toil of mute bodily existence.[11] Joyce also seems to have a more specifically political message: If, as *The Body in Pain* points out, creation is a double process in which the body is projected out into artifice, while the human body itself becomes an artifact, that doubling and splitting repeats itself in the social distribution of privilege. Under colonial rule one group or people is freed as much as possible from the limitations of bodily existence, or of the reminder of those limitations, while the others are reduced to body: slaves, servants, convicts, prostitutes. In insisting on the body in the text – a traumatized and decomposing body – Joyce bears witness to what colonial culture, perhaps especially contemporary western culture prefers to allow some to forget – that we share the burden of being flesh unequally. Some are able to live at a distance from the awareness of mutability of their bodies, engaged in its narcissistic cult, while the majority of human beings live in a painful awareness of being gut and bone. Need I remind my reader that the Great Famine made the impression of the precariousness of physical subsistence on Irish cultural memory indelible? From this perspective Joyce shares Albert Camus' notion of the specific task of literature as bearing witness to the body, to counter the official version of history, the ideological-hegemonic version in which death has become invisible as in the Gulf War. "In a civilization where murder and violence are already doctrines in the act of becoming institutions," it is the artist who, owing to his vocation, is "'Freedom's witness' as far as he 'testifies not to the Law, but to the body'"[12]

[11] *The Body in Pain: The Making and the Unmaking of the World* (Oxford University Press, 1985).
[12] Felman and Laub, *Testimony*, p. 108.

Joyce's "symptom" contains the real reminder that philosophy, art, technology are produced by the flesh. However, instead of labeling it "symptomatic," I wish to see it as an act of resistance against the hegemonic imposition of a structure of subjectivity which splits body from language. In fact, I propose that we understand Joyce's drive to bring the body into word as the product of a different way of conceiving the practice and substance of language, perhaps analogous to that of ancient Irish oral culture, preserving an incantatory mode. In ritual, words have the power to bring into being what they designate, they embody rather than represent. Just so, Joyce wants to create a utopia of unified sensibility within language itself.

Similarly, I argue that Joyce's splitting "ambivalence" or the "fetishism" of his linguistic materialism should not be understood from a Freudian perspective as a failure in mature adaptation. On the contrary, they testify to a resisting strategy of syncretism which makes it possible to express and hold contradictory truths at the same time.[13] Such resisting hybridity is not a lack of responsibility, but the concrete manifestation of the state of being of trauma, which is hybridity itself: death experienced but not accepted. As Bhabha points out: "It is from such an enunciatory space, where the work of signification *voids* the act of meaning in articulating a split-response – 'Ouboum,' 'true time in two longitudes,' that . . . texts of colonial nonsense and imperial aporia have to negotiate their discursive authority."[14]

Positioning itself in the twilight between sleep and awakening, *Finnegans Wake* is the embodiment of hybridity, as well as the erosion of the binary logic and stereotomy of western thought. In the semi-darkness of this theatre of limbo, where the spirit is leaving the decaying body, we do not know whether we are witnessing the approach of the end or a new beginning, the end of metaphysics or the awakening of a new conscience. In his essay "The Ends of Man," Derrida raises that uncertainty thus: "Must one read Nietzsche, with Heidegger, as the last of the great metaphysicians? Or, on the contrary, are we to take the question of the truth of Being as the last sleeping shudder of the superior man? Are we to understand the eve as the guard mounted around the house or as the awakening to the day that is coming, at whose eve we are? Is there any economy of the eve? Perhaps we are between these two eves, which are also two ends of man. But who, we?"[15]

The point of Joyce's ambivalence is precisely to place us in the middle

---

[13] See also *The Empire Writes Back*, p. 153.   [14] *Location of Culture*, p. 132.
[15] *Margins of Philosophy*, p. 136.

of that question without irritable reaching after a cognitive answer either way. Testifying to the historical occasion of the state of hybridity, he wants to re-open the question of the nature of the relationship of subjectivity to language which has brought us to an *impasse*, by making his readers *experience* the crisis. Instead of holding up a mirage of resolution, he wants his readers to witness and live the dark as a place of multiplicity of belief and productive differentiation, where different or independent perspectives (a Shem and a Shaun; or a Derrida and a Lacan, a Catholic and a Protestant) inhabit the same place. Because it is only through conscious (re-)experience (knowledge attended with affect as in the psychoanalytic cure) that genuine change takes place. Joyce can only initiate this process by speaking the split text with a forked tongue, and making the reader share its condition.

In fact, trauma, as a state of death-in-life, is a state of hybridity. *Finnegans Wake* contains both death and resurrection. The hybridity of this state asks us: is the trauma an encounter with death, or, on the contrary, "the ongoing experience of having survived it?"[16] This uncertainty may productively be related to Lacan's theory of "the two deaths": a death of the body, and a symbolic death which confirms and effectuates the first when the ritual of burial finalizes the passing away of the spirit in interring the lifeless body. This distinction is pertinent in our contemporary culture which characterizes itself by its denial of death. On television and movie screen we see examples of the first death without the confirmation and seal of the second. Thus characters like Tom and Jerry suffer death and damage in one installment to jump up and begin new adventures without a sign of wear or tear. Death occurs, but is not terminal. It is as if over and above their natural, material bodies (belonging to the cycle of generation and corruption) such characters possess "another body, a [charmed] body composed of some other substance, one excepted from the vital cycle – a sublime body."[17] Their true end comes at the end of the performance, when the movie or story ends, or when they accept death as their necessary destiny – as when death is accepted and symbolized in the Catholic ritual of death-bed confession. In our technological culture this playground of invulnerability, product of an age which has given us the tools to repress our mutability, extends beyond fiction or the moviescreen to our own perception of reality. Our cultural habitat would seem the forgetting of history, and a denial of death.

[16] Caruth, *Unclaimed Experience*, p. 7.
[17] I am using Slavoj Žižek's paraphrase in *The Sublime Object of Ideology*, p. 134.

On the stage "between the two deaths," Lacan, in Žižek's para-phrase, places two figures, two alternative ways of being "in between," offering a choice between "sublime beauty or [a] fearsome monster." The figure of sublime beauty is Antigone, whose "symbolic death, her exclusion from the symbolic community of the city, precedes her actual death and imbues her character with sublime beauty." The other figure is the ghost of Hamlet's father who "represents the opposite case – actual death unaccompanied by symbolic death, without a settling of accounts – which is why he returns as a frightful apparition until his debt has been paid."[18] We might see these two figures as the allegorical representatives of, respectively, Freud's mourning and melancholia.

In its hybridity, embodied textuality, and repetition compulsion, Joyce's *œuvre*, his *corpus*, might be understood as the symptomatic refusal to mourn the loss of the sentient material body, and its attempted remedy: a utopian substitution of art for life. If we see Joyce that way we make him into a representative modernist author like Ezra Pound, and place him as a version of Lacan's ghost of Hamlet's father. My sugges-tion in these pages has been to read Joyce's textuality as the *witnessing* of a history that cannot be told or be made present to itself, but which the text acts out, speaking beyond its knowledge. This would seem to shift Joyce towards Lacan's Antigone. Lacan's dualism would seem to force us into making a choice.

However, we are placed in a different position than Lacan. He speaks about literary figures whose meaning seems relatively fixed, whereas we are readers of a *corpus*, a body of text which was designed not to congeal into a definitive meaning precisely because its author needed us to witness it. Owing to its overdetermination, we, Joyce's readers, will always be given the final say about the meaning of his work, the "cropse of our seedfather" as well as the "bunk of our breadwinning" (*FW* 55.8). We hold the power to close the book and bury Joyce by imposing a definitive meaning on his work. Appropriation of the specificity of his textuality to purely theoretical ends is one way of trying to do so; re-absorbing him into the hegemony under the rubric of modernism or postmodernism is another. In addition, there is a way of keeping the book open while not "reading" it. Searching for puzzles and allusions, trying to solve the riddle of *Finnegans Wake*, we skirt the reality of Joyce's experience while seemingly engaging with its record. C. G. Jung already named *Ulysses* "a devotional book for the object-besotted, object-ridden

[18] *Ibid.*, p. 135.

white man."[19] Some Joyce criticism seems to provide proof for Jung's claim. In my opinion, answering the appeal of Joyce means not to try and "bury" him by means of a definitive reading. Nor does it mean using his writings as an escapist playing field in which we can elude the actuality of history's effect. It means acknowledging the specificity of his text as the re-enacting resistance against the imposition of a colonial subjectivity which splits body and language, self and social inscription. Only then will Joyce's ghost stop walking. This offers a third possibility of seeing Joyce not as a version of Hamlet's father, nor as a modern Antigone, but as a unique, exceptional irruption into the reality of history of a strategy of resistance against dying the second death even though the first is inevitable, in the hope that the history which cannot be grasped may eventually come to consciousness in the reader.

If the "terrible beauty" of Antigone's symbolic death comes from her courage to persist in faith at the price of exclusion from the community of the city, she derives her courage from a belief in a transcendent truth. The sublime and terrible beauty of Joyce comes from his self-chosen wounded exile from the symbolic of his age, while fiercely and blindly holding on to the act of utterance, to speech without vision of a final truth. He does so because speech provides the only resistance against being molded into an organ of hegemonic truth; but also because continued speech is the only way of not being annihilated by pain. Joyce's trauma bespeaks survival.

"Literature bears testimony not just to duplicate or to record events but to make history available to the imaginative act whose historical unavailability has prompted, and made possible, a holocaust," Felman and Laub point out. Their claim, which holds not only for World War II, inspired me to write this book and argue that Joyce's colonial experience concerns us all. Until buried properly, the dead return. Unless we learn to read him properly, Joyce will keep haunting us. As I said, one of the questions with which Lacan teased his audience was: "Why did Joyce publish *Finnegans Wake*?" How do we know that the unreadable nonsense of *Finnegans Wake* is meaningful? In his Seminar I, Lacan himself addresses a similar question in the context of the relationship between analyst and patient. His example is from the *Odyssey*: Circe's swine grunting at Ulysses. The question rises "What do they want to say?" More specifically, how does one know that this grunting constitutes speech? What is speech? Is this speech because the swine

<hr>

[19] "*Ulysses*: A Monologue", p. 216.

express their emotional ambivalence about Ulysses whom they miss? According to Lacan, the grunting of the swine only becomes speech when someone poses himself the question what it wants to say. Ultimately and primarily, speech is the means of finding recognition. But the burden of granting recognition and creating understanding rests with the listener – in our case, the reader. Speech as such is ambivalent and absolutely unfathomable. We shall never know whether what the patient says is true or not. Foundational truth in speech is a *mirage*; and it is this primary mirage which assures us of being in the realm of speech.[20] We may transpose the question of the intelligibility of speech to *Finnegans Wake* which is both ambivalent and places the reader in acute uncertainty about having one's leg pulled. Just as Circe's swine still want to be recognized as the companions of Ulysses, Joyce, by reducing speech to the primal feature of the claim for human recognition – while suspending the question of referential truth – still makes an appeal for our recognition. *Finnegans Wake* simplifies language and representation to the "speech act" of the appeal.

Responding to that appeal means that we suffer the performative displacement of the inarticulateness of the text.[21] We must share the deconstitution or fading of the subject, the darkness of meaninglessness, the loss of voice and subjectivity of the colonized subject. We, the reader, placed in the shoes of Ulysses, must receive the very gap between our own apparently stable structure of subjectivity in language and that of the inarticulate text. Unless we witness it with empathy, we reduce the text to alienated otherness and repeat the colonizing gesture. Moreover, the implicit pedagogy of *Finnegans Wake* asks the reader to formulate the narrative, the coherent tale and the cogent claim, in short to write the history of the trauma to which the text has had no access.

Joyce's genius as a writer is that he should – again syncretically – have packaged this appeal in the rhetorical structure of a cosmic joke. As Freud argued, a joke is only a joke if it produces laughter. Like trauma, the joke constitutes its own identity through its after-effect. Its rhetoric demands a witnessing "reader." Without response there is no joke, nor is the teller witty. Thus the effect of the joke retrospectively constitutes

[20] I have given a paraphrase of *Les Ecrits techniques de Freud: 1953–54*, texte établi par Jacques-Alain Miller (Paris: Seuil, 1975), p. 264.
[21] For a more detailed analysis of the reading process of *Finnegans Wake* from a reader-response point of view, which arrives at similar conclusions from a different perspective (reader-response criticism), I refer to Gabriele Schwab's "'I, a Self the Sign': Language and Subjectivity in *Finnegans Wake*," in *Subjects without Selves: Transitional Texts in Modern Fiction* (Cambridge: Harvard University Press, 1994), pp. 95–131.

its identity and confirms the projected self-identity of its teller. The addressee, the second person, affirms the speaker as a first person. From the beginning of *A Portrait*, Joyce inscribes the consciousness of his protagonist in the self-alienated third person "he." "He was baby tuckoo" (*P* 7). When we respond to Joyce's text, we transform the alienated third person "he" into the direct and personal "you," facilitating the subject's accession to the first-person "I."

As we know, a listener cannot consciously intend to laugh. Laughter involves the activity of the unconscious. Laughter is an involuntary response of the whole person, including the body's reaction. "The convulsive, spasmodic movements by which the body expels, as it were, its inner energies, suggest allegorically the kind of dislocation triggered by the joke, in which the self-contained subject becomes both the agent and the theater of an alterity whose transgression confirms and reproduces *Hemmungen* it momentarily transcends," as Samuel Weber writes. What the rhetorical structure of the joke effectuates is "precisely not a return of the same, but a movement of violent effraction. Its singularity consists in this return of alterity, of the excluded, of the repressed."[22] I need not testify here to the hilariously comic effect of *Finnegans Wake*. Others have done so, among whom Jean-Michel Rabaté.[23] In packaging the mute appeal for recognition and subjectivity as a joke, Joyce enlists our involuntary, physical response to his writing – the pleasure it gives serving as lure to attachment. However, beyond our laughter, *Finnegans Wake* – also Joyce's road to Calvary – demands and needs the imaginative act of our witnessing empathy. Failing that, history will keep repeating itself. One of the last words of *Finnegans Wake*, before a new cycle of history begins, is the dying "mememormee!", asking at once for symbolizing remembrance after death ["remember me"] as well as containing a desperate plea for the witnessing recognition by the reader ["me, more me"]. Perhaps we need to learn to read in a wholly new way.

---

[22] "The Blindness of the Seeing Eye: Psychoanalysis, Hermeneutics, *Entstellung*," in *Institution and Interpretation* (Minneapolis: University of Minnesota Press, 1987), p. 83.
[23] See "Lapsus ex Machina" in *Post-Structuralist Joyce*.

Bibliography

Abraham, Nicolas and Maria Torok, *L'Ecorce et le noyau*, 2nd edn., Paris: Aubier-Montaigne, 1987.

Adorno, Theodor W., "The Position of the Narrator in the Contemporary Novel," in Rolf Tiedemann (ed.), *Notes to Literature 1*, trans. Shierry Weber Nicholsen, New York: Columbia University Press, 1991.

"What does Coming to Terms with the Past Mean?" in Geoffrey Hartman (ed.), *Bitburg in Moral and Political Perspective*, Bloomington: Indiana University Press, 1986, pp. 114–29.

Anderson, Benedict, *Imagined Communities: Reflections on the Origin and Spread of Nationalism*, Rev. edn., London: Verso, 1991.

Apter, Emily, *Feminizing the Fetish: Psychoanalysis and Narrative Obsession in Turn-of-the-Century France*, Ithaca: Cornell University Press, 1991.

Arp, Jean, *On my Way: Poetry and Essays 1912–1947*, New York: Wittenborn, 1948.

Ashcroft, Bill, Gareth Griffiths, and Helen Tiffin, *The Empire Writes Back: Theory and Practice in Post-Colonial Literatures*, London: Routledge, 1989.

Attridge, Derek, *Peculiar Language: Literature as Difference from the Renaissance to James Joyce*, Ithaca: Cornell University Press, 1988.

(ed.), *Acts of Literature: Jacques Derrida*, London: Routledge, 1992.

and Daniel Ferrer (eds.), *Post-Structuralist Joyce: Essays from the French*, Cambridge: University of Cambridge Press, 1984.

Aubert, Jacques (ed.), *Joyce avec Lacan*, Paris: Navarin, 1987.

Bal, Mieke, *An Introduction to the Theory of Narrative*, trans. Christine van Boheemen, University of Toronto Press, 1985.

"The Narrating and the Focalizing: A Theory of the Agents in Narrative," *Style* 17 (1983), 234–70.

Banville, John, "Survivors of Joyce," in Augustine Martin (ed.), *The Artist and the Labyrinth*, London: Ryan, 1990, pp. 73–81.

Barth, John, *Lost in the Funhouse*, 1968; repr. New York: Bantam Books, 1969.

Barthelme, Donald, *Snow White*, 1967; repr. New York: Atheneum, 1984.

Barthes, Roland, *Image/Music/Text*, trans. Stephen Heath, New York: Hill & Wang, 1977.

The Pleasure of the Text, trans. Richard Miller, New York: Hill & Wang, 1975.

211

Baudrillard, Jean, *America*, trans. Chris Turner, London: Verso, 1988.
For a Critique of the Political Economy of the Sign, trans. Charles Levin, St. Louis: Telos Press, 1981.
Symbolic Exchange and Death, trans. Mike Gane, London: SAGE, 1993.
Bazin, André, "The Ontology of the Photographic Image," in *What is Cinema?* 2 vols., trans. Hugh Gray, Berkeley: University of California Press, 1971.
Beckett, Samuel, "Dante . . . Bruno. Vico . . . Joyce," *James Joyce/Finnegans Wake: A Symposium*, 1929; repr. New York: New Directions, 1972.
Benjamin, Walter, *The Origin of German Tragic Drama*, trans. John Osborne, London: Verso, 1977.
Bennington, Geoff, "The Field and the Fence," *Oxford Literary Review* 4 (1980), 82–88.
and Jacques Derrida, *Jacques Derrida*, University of Chicago Press, 1993.
Benstock, Bernard (ed.), *James Joyce: The Augmented Ninth*, New York: Syracuse University Press, 1988.
Bhabha, Homi K., "DissemiNation: Time, Narrative, and the Margins of the Modern Nation," in Homi K. Bhabha (ed.), *Nation and Narration*, London: Routledge, 1990, pp. 291–323.
The Location of Culture, London: Routledge, 1994.
"Representation and the Colonial Text: Some Forms of Mimeticism," Frank Gloversmith (ed.), *The Theory of Reading*, Brighton: Harvester, 1984, pp. 93–122.
Bishop, John, *Joyce's Book of the Dark: Finnegans Wake*, Madison: University of Wisconsin Press, 1986.
Boehm, Beth A., "Educating Readers," in James Phelan (ed.), *Reading Narrative*, Columbus: Ohio State University Press, 1989, pp. 102–20.
Borch-Jacobsen, Mikkel, *The Emotional Tie: Psychoanalysis, Mimesis, and Affect*, trans. Douglas Brick et al., Stanford University Press, 1992.
Bosinelli, R. M. et al. (eds). *Myriadminded Man: Jottings on Joyce*, Bologna: CLUEB, 1986
Bosinelli, R. M., Carla Marengo, and Christine van Boheemen (eds.), *The Languages of Joyce*, Philadelphia: John Benjamins, 1992.
Briggs, Austin, "The Full Stop at the End of 'Ithaca': Thirteen Ways – and Then Some – of Looking at a Black Dot," *Joyce Studies Annual*, Austin: University of Texas Press, 1996, pp. 125–45.
Brivic, Sheldon, "Joyce in Progress: A Freudian View," *James Joyce Quarterly* 13 (1976), 306–27.
Joyce's Waking Women: An Introduction to "Finnegans Wake," Madison: University of Wisconsin Press, 1995.
Brooks, Peter, *Body Work: Objects of Desire in Modern Narrative*, Cambridge: Harvard University Press, 1993.
Reading for the Plot: Design and Intention in Narrative, Oxford: Clarendon Press, 1984.
Brown, Richard, *James Joyce and Sexuality*, Cambridge University Press, 1985.

Budgen, Frank, *James Joyce and the Making of "Ulysses,"* 1934; repr. Bloomington: Indiana University Press, 1960.

Butler, Judith, *The Psychic Life of Power: Theories in Subjection,* University of Stanford Press, 1997.

Cain, William E. (ed.), *Philosophical Approaches to Literature: New Essays on Nineteenth- and Twentieth-Century Texts,* Lewisburg: Bucknell University Press, 1984.

Carrol, David, *The Subject in Question,* University of Chicago Press, 1982.

Caruth, Cathy (ed.), *Trauma: Explorations in Memory,* Baltimore: Johns Hopkins University Press, 1995.

  Unclaimed Experience: Trauma, Narrative, and History, Baltimore: Johns Hopkins University Press, 1996.

Chaitin, Gilbert D., *Rhetoric and Culture in Lacan,* Cambridge University Press, 1996.

Chen, Xiaomei, *Occidentalism,* Oxford University Press, 1995.

Cheng, Vincent J., " 'Goddinpotty': James Joyce and the Language of Excrement," in R. M. Bosinelli et al. (eds), *The Languages of Joyce,* pp. 85–103.

  Joyce, Race, and Empire, Cambridge University Press, 1995.

Cheyette, Bryan, " 'Jewgreeek is Greekjew': The Disturbing Ambivalence of Joyce's Semitic Discourse in *Ulysses,*" *Joyce Studies Annual,* Austin: University of Texas Press, 1992, pp. 32–56.

Cixous, Hélène, "Devant le Pome," *James Joyce: Cahiers de l'Herne,* Paris: L'Herne, 1985, pp. 193–203.

  "The Laugh of the Medusa," *Signs* 1 (1976), 875–93.

  " 'Mamâe, disse ele,' or, Joyce's Second Hand," *Poetics Today* 17 (1996), 339–67.

Couturier, Maurice and Régis Durand, *Donald Barthelme,* London: Methuen, 1982.

Crowther, Paul, *Critical Aesthetics and Postmodernism,* Oxford University Press, 1993.

Cunningham, Valentine, "Renoving that Bible: The Absolute Text of (Post)Modernism," in Frank Gloversmith (ed.), *The Theory of Reading,* Brighton: Harvester, 1984. pp. 1–51.

Davison, Neil R., *James Joyce's "Ulysses" and the Construction of Jewish Identity,* Cambridge University Press, 1995.

Deane, Seamus, "Joyce and Nationalism," in Colin MacCabe (ed.), *James Joyce: New Perspectives,* pp. 168–84.

  (ed.), *The Field Day Anthology of Irish Writing,* 3 vols., Derry: Field Day Publications, 1991.

Deming, Robert H. (ed.), *James Joyce: The Critical Heritage I 1907–1927,* London: Routledge & Kegan Paul, 1977.

Derrida, J., *La Dissémination,* Paris: Seuil, 1972.

  "Geslecht: différance sexuelle, différance ontologique," Martin Haar (ed.), *Martin Heidegger,* Paris: L'Herne, 1983, pp. 419–30.

Glas, trans. John P. Leavy, Jr. and Richard Rand, Lincoln: University of Nebraska Press, 1986.

"The Law of Genre," trans. Avital Ronell, *Critical Inquiry* 7 (1980), 55–81.

"Living On. Borderlines," in Harold Bloom et al., *Deconstruction and Criticism*, trans. James Hulbert, New York: Continuum, 1979, pp. 75–177.

Margins of Philosophy, trans. Alan Bass, University of Chicago Press, 1972.

Mémoires d'aveugle: l'autoportrait et autres ruines, Paris: Réunion des musées nationaux, 1990.

Of Grammatology, trans. Gayatri Chakravorty Spivak, Baltimore: Johns Hopkins University Press, 1976.

The Postcard: From Socrates to Freud and Beyond, trans. Alan Bass, University of Chicago Press, 1987.

"Pour l'amour de Lacan," in N. Avtonomova et al. (eds), *Lacan avec les philosophes*, Paris: Albin Michel, 1991.

Psyché: Inventions de l'autre, Paris: Galilée, 1987.

Résistances: de la psychanalyse, Paris: Galilée, 1996.

"Speculations – On Freud," *Oxford Literary Review* 3 (1978), 78–97.

The Truth in Painting, University of Chicago Press, 1987.

"Two Words for Joyce," in Attridge and Ferrer (eds.), *Post-Structuralist Joyce*, pp. 145–60.

"Ulysses Gramophone: Hear Say Yes in Joyce," in Benstock (ed.), *James Joyce: The Augmented Ninth*, pp. 27–77.

Writing and Difference, trans Alan Bass, University of Chicago Press, 1978.

Devlin, Kimberly, "Pretending in 'Penelope': Masquerade, Mimicry, and Molly Bloom," *Novel* 25 (1991), 71–89.

Wandering and Return in "Finnegans Wake": An Integrative Approach to Joyce's Fiction, Princeton University Press, 1991.

Dijkstra, Bram, *Idols of Perversity: Fantasies of Feminine Evil in Fin-de-Siècle Culture*, Oxford University Press, 1986.

Doane, Mary Ann, *Femmes Fatales: Feminism, Film Theory, Psychoanalysis*, New York: Routledge, 1991.

Doležel, Lubomír, *Narrative Modes in Czech Literature*, University of Toronto Press, 1973.

Domenichelli, Mario, "Implosion, Hyperreality and Language in *Finnegans Wake*," in R. M. Bosinelli et al. (eds.), *Myriadminded Man: Jottings on Joyce*, pp. 277–93.

Duffy, Enda, *The Subaltern "Ulysses,"* Minneapolis: University of Minnesota Press, 1994.

Dutton, Dennis, "Why Intentionalism Won't Go Away," in Anthony J. Cascardi (ed.), *Literature and the Question of Philosophy*. Baltimore: Johns Hopkins University Press, 1987, pp. 192–210.

Eagleton, Terry, *Ideology: An Introduction*, London: Verso, 1991.

Eco, Umberto, *L'Œuvre ouverte*, Paris: Seuil, 1965.

A Theory of Semiotics, Bloomington: Indiana University Press, 1976.

"Ur-Fascism," *New York Review of Books*, July 22, 1995.

Eliade, Mircea, *The Two and the One*, trans. J. M. Cohen, New York: Harper & Row, 1969.

Eliot, T. S. "*Ulysses*, Order and Myth," *Dial* 75 (1923), 480–83; repr. in Deming (ed.), *The Critical Heritage*, pp. 268–72.

Ellmann, Maud, "The Ghosts of 'Ulysses'," in Bosinelli et al. (eds.), *The Languages of Joyce*, pp. 103–21.

Ellmann, Richard, *James Joyce*, new and rev. edn., Oxford University Press, 1982.

(ed.), *Selected Letters of James Joyce*, New York: Viking Press, 1975.

Epstein, E. L., "James Joyce and the Body," in E. L. Epstein (ed.), *A Starchamber Quiry: A James Joyce Centennial Volume 1882–1982*, London: Methuen, 1982, pp. 71–107.

Faulkner, William, *Absalom, Absalom!* 1936; repr. New York Vintage Books, 1972.

Felman, Shoshana, "To Open the Question," in Felman (ed.), *Literature and Psychoanalysis*, pp. 5–10.

"Turning the Screw of Interpretation," in Felman (ed.), *Literature and Psychoanalysis*, pp. 94–207.

(ed.), *Literature and Psychoanalysis: The Question of Reading: Otherwise*, Baltimore: Johns Hopkins University Press, 1982.

and Dori Laub, *Testimony: Crises of Witnessing in Literature, Psychoanalysis, and History*, London: Routledge, 1992.

Felstiner, John, *Paul Celan: Poet, Survivor, Jew*, New Haven: Yale University Press, 1995.

Flood, Jeanne A., "Joyce and the Maamtrasna Murders," *James Joyce Quarterly* 28 (1991), 879–89.

Fokkema, Douwe and Elrud Ibsch, *Modernist Conjectures: A Mainstream in European Literature 1910–1940*, London: Hurst, 1987.

Foster, Hal, " 'Primitive Scenes,' " *Critical Inquiry* 21 (1993), 69–103.

Foucault, Michel, *Ethics: Subjectivity and Truth*, ed. Paul Rabinow, trans. Robert Hurley et al., *The Essential Works of Michel Foucault*, vol 1., Harmondsworth: Allen Lane/Penguin, 1997.

The History of Sexuality vol. 1: An Introduction, trans. Robert Hurley, New York: Pantheon Books, 1978.

"What is an Author?" in Josué V. Harari (ed.), *Textual Strategies: Perspectives in Post-Structuralist Criticism*, Ithaca: Cornell University Press, 1979.

Freud, Sigmund, *The Standard Edition of the Complete Psychological Works of Sigmund Freud*, ed. James Strachey, London: Hogarth, 1964–74.

Friedman, Susan Stanford, "(Self)Censorship and the Making of Joyce's Modernism," in Friedman (ed.), *Joyce: The Return of the Repressed*, pp. 21–58.

Friedman, Susan Stanford (ed.). *The Return of the Repressed*. Ithaca: Cornell University Press, 1993.

Froula, Christine, *Modernism's Body: Sex, Culture, and Joyce*, New York: Columbia University Press, 1996.

Gadet, Françoise, *Saussure and Contemporary Culture*, trans. Gregory Elliott, London: Century Hutchinson, 1989.

Gaiser, Gottlieb (ed.), *International Perspectives on James Joyce*, New York: Whiston, 1986.

Gallop, Jane, "Lacan and Literature: A Case for Transference," *Poetics* 13 (1989), 301–08.

Gates, Henry Louis, *The Signifying Monkey*, Oxford University Press, 1989.

(ed.), *Race, Writing, Difference*, University of Chicago Press, 1986.

Genette, Gérard, *Introduction à l'architexte*, Paris: Seuil, 1979.

Gifford, Don, *Notes for Joyce: "Dubliners" and "A Portrait of the Artist as a Young Man,"* New York: Dutton, 1967.

and Robert J. Seidman., *Notes for Joyce: An Annotation of James Joyce's "Ulysses,"* New York: Dutton, 1974.

Gilbert, Sandra M., "Woman's Sentence, Man's Sentencing: Linguistic Fantasies in Woolf and Joyce," in Jane Marcus (ed.), *Virginia Woolf and Bloomsbury: A Centennial Celebration*, London: Macmillan, 1987.

and Susan Gubar, *No Man's Land: The Place of the Woman Writer in the Twentieth Century, vol. 1: The War of Words*, New Haven: Yale University Press, 1989.

Gilbert, Stuart (ed.), *Letters of James Joyce. vol. 1*, London: Faber & Faber, 1957.

Gilman, Sander L., *Freud, Race, and Gender*, University of Princeton Press, 1993.

Golding, John, "Cubism," in Tony Richardson and Nikos Stangos (eds.), *Concepts of Modern Art*, New York: Harper & Row, 1974, pp. 53–82.

Grosz, Elisabeth, "Lesbian Fetishism," in Emily Apter and William Pietz (eds.), *Fetishism as Cultural Discourse*, Ithaca: Cornell University Press, 1993, pp. 101–18.

Haar, Martin (ed.), *Martin Heidegger*, Paris, L'Herne, 1983.

Hart, Clive, *Structure and Motif in "Finnegans Wake,"* London: Faber & Faber, 1962.

Hart, Clive and David Hayman (eds.), *James Joyce's "Ulysses": Critical Essays*, Berkeley: University of California Press, 1974.

Hassan, Ihab, *Paracriticisms: Seven Speculations of the Times*, Urbana: University of Illinois Press, 1975.

Hayman, David, "Cyclops," in Hart and Hayman (eds.), *James Joyce's "Ulysses,"* pp. 243–77.

"The Fractured Portrait," in Bosinelli (ed.), *Myriadminded Man*, pp. 79–89.

"I Think her Pretty: Reflections of the Familiar in Joyce's Notebook VI.B.5," *Joyce Studies Annual*, Austin: University of Texas Press, 1990, pp. 43–60.

"Ulysses": The Mechanics of Meaning, Englewood Cliffs, NJ: Prentice Hall, 1970.

Heath, Stephen, "Men in Feminism: Men and Feminist Theory," in Alice Jardine and Paul Smith (eds.), *Men in Feminism*, London: Methuen, 1987, pp. 41–46.

Herring, Phillip F. (ed.), *Joyce's Notesheets and Early Drafts for Ulysses: Selections from*

the Buffalo Collection, Charlottesville: University of Virginia Press, 1971.
Joyce's "Ulysses" Notesheets in the British Museum, Charlottesville: University of Virginia Press, 1972.
Joyce's Uncertainty Principle, Princeton University Press, 1987.
Horkheimer, Max and Theodor W. Adorno, *Dialectic of Enlightenment*, trans. John Cumming, 1947; New York: Seabury Press, 1972.
Hutcheon, Linda, *A Poetics of Postmodernism: History, Theory, Fiction*, New York: Routledge, 1988.
Ian, Marcia, *Remembering the Phallic Mother: Psychoanalysis, Modernism, and the Fetish*, Ithaca: Cornell University Press, 1993.
Innes, C. L., *Woman and Nation in Irish Literature and Society 1880–1935*, Hemel Hempstead: Harvester-Wheatsheaf, 1993.
Irigaray, Luce, *Je, tu, nous: Toward a Culture of Difference*, trans. Alison Martin, London: Routledge, 1993.
    This Sex Which Is Not One, trans. Catherine Porter, Ithaca: Cornell University Press, 1985.
Jackson, John Wyse and Bernard McGinley (eds.), *James Joyce's "Dubliners": An Annotated Edition*, London: Sinclair-Stevenson, 1993.
Jameson, Fredric, "Imaginary and Symbolic in Lacan: Marxism, Psychoanalytic Criticism and the Problem of the Subject," in Felman (ed.), *Literature and Psychoanalysis*, pp. 338–96.
    "Ulysses in History," in W. J. McCormack and Alistair Stead (eds.), *James Joyce and Modern Literature*, London: Routledge & Kegan Paul, 1982, pp. 126–41.
Jardine, Alice A., *Gynesis: Configurations of Woman and Modernity*, Ithaca: Cornell University Press, 1985.
Jay, Martin, *Downcast Eyes: The Denigration of Vision in Twentieth-Century French Thought*, Berkeley: University of California Press, 1993.
    Forcefields: Between Intellectual History and Cultural Critique, London: Routledge, 1993.
Johnson, Barbara, "The Frame of Reference: Poe, Lacan, Derrida," in Felman (ed.), *Literature and the Question of Psychoanalysis*, pp. 457–505.
    "Translator's Introduction," in Jacques Derrida, *Dissemination*, University of Chicago Press, 1981, pp. vii–xxxiii.
Johnson, Jeri, " 'Beyond the Veil': *Ulysses*, Feminism, and the Figure of Woman," in Christine van Boheemen (ed.), *Joyce, Modernity and its Mediation*, Amsterdam: Rodopi, 1990, pp. 201–28.
Jolas, Eugene, "The Revolution of Language and James Joyce," in Samuel Beckett et al., *James Joyce / Finnegans Wake: A Symposium*, pp. 79–92.
Jousse, Marcel, *L'Anthropologie du geste*, Paris: Resma, 1969.
    La Manducation de la parole, Paris. Gallimard, 1975.
Joyce, James, *The Critical Writings of James Joyce*, Ellsworth Mason and Richard Ellmann (eds.), New York: Viking, 1959.
    Finnegans Wake, New York: Viking, 1939.

Giacomo Joyce, London: Faber & Faber, 1968.

Poems and Shorter Writings, eds. Richard Ellmann, A. Walton Litz and John Whittier-Ferguson, London: Faber & Faber, 1991.

A Portrait of the Artist as a Young Man: Text, Criticism, and Notes, Chester G. Anderson (ed.), New York: Viking Press, 1968.

Selected Letters of James Joyce, ed. Richard Ellmann, New York: Viking Press, 1975.

Stephen Hero, eds. John J. Slocum and Herbert Cahoon, New York: New Directions, 1959.

Ulysses: The Corrected Text, Hans Walter Gabler, Wolfgang Steppe and Claus Melchior (eds.), New York: Random House, 1986.

Jung, Carl Gustav, "Ulysses: A Monologue," *Europäische Revue* 8 (1932); repr. in Leonard Manheim and Eleanor Manheim (eds.), *Hidden Patterns: Studies in Psychoanalytic Literary Criticism*, New York: Macmillan, 1966, pp. 192–219.

Kaufmann, Michael, *Modernism, Postmodernism, and Print*, Lewisburg: Bucknell University Press, 1994.

Kearney, Richard, "Myth and Motherland," in Seamus Deane (ed.), *Ireland's Field Day*, University of Notre Dame Press, 1986, pp. 74–78.

Kendrick, Walter, *The Secret Museum: Pornography in Modern Culture*, New York: Viking Press, 1987.

Kenner, Hugh, *Joyce's Voices*, London: Faber & Faber, 1978.

"The Portrait in Perspective," in William M. Chase (ed.), *Joyce: A Collection of Critical Essays*, Englewood Cliffs: Prentice Hall, 1974, pp. 33–50.

Kinsella, Thomas, "The Irish Writer," in Seamus Deane (ed.), *The Field Day Anthology of Irish Writing*, vol. 3, pp. 625–30.

Kofman, Sarah, *The Enigma of Woman: Woman in Freud's Writing*, trans. Catherine Porter. Ithaca: Cornell University Press, 1985.

Kristeva, Julia, "Joyce 'The Gracehoper,' Or: The Return of Orpheus," in Benstock (ed.), *James Joyce: The Augmented Ninth*, pp. 167–81.

Revolution in Poetic Language, trans. Margaret Waller, New York: Columbia University Press, 1984.

Semeiotikè: Recherches pour une semanalyse, Paris: Seuil, 1969.

Soleil noir: dépression et mélancholié, Paris: Gallimard, 1987.

Kuberski, Philip, "The Joycean Gaze: Lucia in the I of the Father," *Substance* 46 (1985), pp. 49–67.

Kumar, Udaya, *The Joycean Labyrinth: Repetition, Time, and Tradition in "Ulysses,"* Oxford: Clarendon Press, 1991.

Lacan, Jacques, *Ecrits: A Selection*, trans. Alan Sheridan, New York: Norton, 1977.

Encore, ed. Jacques-Alain Miller, Paris: Seuil, 1975.

Four Fundamental Concepts of Psychoanalysis, ed. Jacques-Alain Miller, trans. Alan Sheridan, Harmondsworth: Penguin Books, 1986.

"Joyce le symptôme 1"; "Joyce le symptôme 2"; "Le sinthome; séminaire du 18 novembre 1975"; "Le sinthome; séminaire du 20 janvier 1976," in

Jacques Aubert (ed.), *Joyce avec Lacan*, Paris: Navarin, 1987, pp. 21–67.

Les écrits techniques de Freud 1953–54, ed. Jacques-Alain Miller, Paris: Seuil, 1975.

"Lituraterre," *Littérature* 1,3 (1971): 3–10.

Le Transfert 1960–61, ed. Jacques-Alain Miller, Paris, Seuil, 1991.

Television: A Challenge to the Psychoanalytic Establishment, trans. Denis Holier, Rosalind Kraus, Annette Michelson, and Jeffrey Mehlman, New York: Norton, 1990.

Lakoff, George and Mark Johnson, *Metaphors we Live By*, University of Chicago Press, 1980.

Laplanche, Jean, *Problématiques 2: Castration, Symbolisations*, Paris, PUF, 1980. and J.-B. Pontalis, *The Language of Psychoanalysis*, trans. Donald Nicholson-Smith, London: Hogarth, 1983.

Lasch, Christopher, *The Culture of Narcissism: American Life in an Age of Diminishing Expectations*, New York: Warner Books, 1979.

Laub, Dori and Daniel Podell, "Art and Trauma," *The International Journal of Psychoanalysis* 76 (1995), 991–1005.

Lawrence, K., *The Odyssey of Style in "Ulysses,"* Princeton University Press, 1981.

Leerssen, Joep, *Remembrance and Imagination: Patterns in the Historical and Literary Representation of Ireland in the Ninteenth Century*, Cork University Press, 1996.

Lernout, Geert, *The French Joyce*, University of Michigan Press, 1990.

Levitt, Morton P., *Modernist Survivors: The Contemporary Novel in England, the United States, France, and Latin America*, Columbus: Ohio State University Press, 1987.

Leys, Ruth, "Traumatic Cures: Shell Shock, Janet, and the Question of Memory," *Critical Inquiry* 20 (1994), 623–63.

Lifton, Robert Jay, *The Broken Connection: On Death and the Continuity of Life*, New York: Simon and Schuster, 1979.

Litz, A. Walton, "Ithaca," in Clive Hart et al. (eds.), *James Joyce's "Ulysses": Critical Essays*, pp. 385–406.

Lloyd, David, *Anomalous States: Irish Writing and the Postcolonial Moment*, Durham: Duke University Press, 1993.

Lyotard, Jean-Francois, *La Condition postmoderne: rapport sur le savoir*, Paris: Minuit, 1979.

The Differend: Phrases in Dispute, Minneapolis: University of Minnesota Press, 1988.

"Going Back to the Return," in Bosinelli et al. (eds.), *The Languages of Joyce*, pp. 193–222.

The Postmodern Condition: A Report on Knowledge, trans. Geoff Bennington and Brian Massumi, Minneapolis: University of Minnesota Press, 1984.

MacCabe, Colin, *James Joyce and the Revolution of the Word*, London: Macmillan, 1978.

(ed.), *James Joyce: New Perspectives*, Sussex: Harvester, 1982.

McGee, Patrick, *Paperspace: Style as Ideology in Joyce's "Ulysses,"* Lincoln: University of Nebraska Press, 1988.

McHale, Brian, *Postmodernist Fiction*, New York: Methuen, 1987.

McHugh, Roland, *Annotations to "Finnegans Wake,"* Baltimore: Johns Hopkins University Press, 1980.

The Finnegans Wake Experience, Dublin: Irish Academic Press, 1981.

Mailer, Norman, *Why Are We in Vietnam?* New York: Berkeley Medallion Books, 1968.

Meltzer, Françoise, " 'Eat your *Dasein*': Lacan's Self-consuming Puns," in Jonathan Culler (ed.), *On Puns: The Foundation of Letters*, Oxford: Blackwell's, 1998, pp. 156–64.

Melville, Stephen, "Psychoanalysis and the Place of *Jouissance*," *Critical Inquiry* 13 (1987), 348–71.

Milesi, Laurent "The *Poe*tics of 'The Purloined Letter' in *Finnegans Wake* (narrative foresight and critical afterthought)," in *A Collideorscape of Joyce*, ed. Ruth Frehner and Ursula Zeller, Dublin: Lilliput Press, 1998, pp. 306–23.

Miller, J. Hillis, "From Narrative Theory to Joyce: From Joyce to Narrative Theory," in Benstock (ed.), *The Seventh of Joyce*, Bloomington: Indiana University Press, 1982, pp. 3–5.

Mitchell, Juliet and Jacqueline Rose (eds.), *Feminine Sexuality: Jacques Lacan and the Ecole Freudienne*, London: Macmillan, 1982.

Morace, Robert A., "Donald Barthelme's *Snow White*: The Novel, the Critics, and the Culture," *Critique: Studies in Modern Fiction* 26 (1984), 1–10.

Moreiras, Alberto, "Pharmaconomy: Stephen and the Daedalids," in Friedman (ed.), *The Return of the Repressed*, pp. 58–89.

Morrison, Tony, *Playing in the Dark: Whiteness and the Literary Imagination*, Cambridge: Harvard University Press, 1992.

Muller, John P. and William J. Richardson (eds.), *The Purloined Poe: Lacan, Derrida, and Psychoanalytic Reading*, Baltimore: Johns Hopkins University Press, 1988.

Nadel, Ira B., *Joyce and the Jews*, London: Macmillan, 1989.

Nancy, Jean-Luc and Philippe Lacoue-Labarthe, *Le Titre de la Lettre: Une Lecture de Lacan*, Paris: Galilée, 1973.

Nietzsche, Friedrich, *On the Genealogy of Morals and Ecce Homo*, ed. and trans. Walter Kaufman, New York: Vintage Books, 1969.

Nolan, Emer, *James Joyce and Nationalism*, London: Routledge, 1995.

Norris, Margot, "Joyce's Heliotrope," in Morris Beja and Shari Benstock (eds.), *Coping with Joyce*, Columbus: Ohio State University Press, 1989, pp. 3–24.

Joyce's Web: The Social Unravelling of Modernism, Austin: University of Austin Press, 1992.

Parrinder, Patrick, "The Strange Necessity: James Joyce's Rejection in England (1914–30)," in MacCabe (ed.), *James Joyce: New Perspectives*, pp. 151–67.

Pearce, Richard, "What Joyce after Pynchon?" in Morris Beja, Phillip Herring, Maurice Harmon, and David Norris (eds.), *James Joyce: The Centennial Symposium*, Urbana: University of Illinois, pp. 43–47.

Power, Arthur, *Conversations with James Joyce*, London: Millington, 1974.

Praz, Mario, *The Romantic Agony*, trans. Angus Davidson, Oxford University Press, 1979.

Quinones, Ricardo J., *The Changes of Cain: Violence and the Lost Brother*, University of Princeton Press, 1991.

Rabaté, Jean-Michel, "Discussion," in Benstock (ed.), *James Joyce: The Augmented Ninth*, pp. 204–07.

James Joyce: Authorized Reader, Baltimore: Johns Hopkins University Press, 1991.

Joyce upon the Void: The Genesis of Doubt, London: Macmillan, 1991.

"Lapsus ex Machina," in Attridge and Ferrer (eds.), *Post-Structuralist Joyce*, pp. 79–103.

Ray, Sangeeta, "Gender and the Discourse of Nationalism in Anita Desai's *Clear Light of Day*," *Genders* 20 (1994), 96–119.

Restuccia, Frances L., *Joyce and the Law of the Father*, New Haven: Yale University Press, 1989.

Richardson, John, *A Life of Picasso, vol. 2: The Painter of Modern Life*, London: Cape, 1996.

Riquelme, John Paul, *Teller and Tale in Joyce's Fiction: Oscillating Perspectives*, Baltimore: Johns Hopkins University Press, 1983.

Roudinesco, Elizabeth, *Jacques Lacan & Co.: A History of Psychoanalysis in France 1925–85*, trans. Jeffrey Mehlman, University of Chicago Press, 1990.

Rubin, William, "From Narrative to 'Iconic' in Picasso: The Buried Allegory in *Bread and Fruitdish on a Table* and the Role of *Les Demoiselles d'Avignon*," *Art Bulletin* 65 (1983), 615–49.

Scarry, Elaine, *The Body in Pain: The Making and the Unmaking of the World*, New York: Oxford University Press, 1985.

Schwab, Gabriele, *Subjects Without Selves: Transitional Texts in Modern Fiction*, Cambridge: Harvard University Press, 1994.

Sebeok, T. A., *Style in Language*, Cambridge: MIT Press, 1961.

Senn, Fritz, *Inductive Scrutinies: Focus on Joyce*, Dublin: Lilliput Press, 1995.

Silverman, Kaja, *The Threshold of the Visible World*, New York: Routledge, 1997.

Spivak, Gayatri, "Can the Subaltern Speak?: Speculations on Widow Sacrifice," *Wedge* 7 (1985), 120–30, repr. (abbreviated) in Bill Ashcroft, Gareth Griffiths and Helen Tiffin (eds.), *The Postcolonial Studies Reader*, London: Routledge, 1995.

"Love Me, Love My Ombre, Elle," *Diacritics* 14.4 (1984), 19–36.

Shechner, Mark, *Joyce in Nighttown: A Psychoanalytic Inquiry into "Ulysses"*, Berkeley: University of California Press, 1974.

Staten, Henry, "The Decomposing Form of Joyce's *Ulysses*," *PMLA* 112 (1997), 380–92.

Eros in Mourning: Homer to Lacan, Baltimore: Johns Hopkins University Press, 1995.

Stevens, Wallace, *The Palm at the End of the Mind: Selected Poems and a Play*, ed. Holly Stevens, New York: Vintage, 1972.

Suleiman, Susan Rubin, *Subversive Intent: Gender, Politics and the Avant-Garde*, Cambridge: Harvard University Press, 1991.

Tardits, Annie, "Joyce in Babylonia," in *The Languages of Joyce*, ed. R. M. Bosinelli et al., pp. 229–48.

Thiher, Allen, *Words in Reflection: Modern Language Theory and Postmodern Fiction*, University of Chicago Press, 1984.

Tifft, Stephen, "The Parricidal Phantasm: Irish Nationalism and the *Playboy* Riots," in Andrew Parker, Mary Russo, Doris Sommer, and Patricia Yaeger (eds.), *Nationalisms and Sexualities*, London: Routledge, 1992, pp. 313–43.

Toolis, Kevin, *Rebel Hearts: Journeys with the IRA's Soul*, London: Picador, 1996.

Topia, André, "The Matrix and the Echo: Intertextuality in *Ulysses*," in Attridge (ed.), *Poststructuralist Joyce*, pp. 103–27.

Transition: A Paris Anthology, intr. Noel Riley Fitch, New York: Anchor Books, 1990.

Tymoczko, Maria, *The Irish "Ulysses"*, Berkeley: University of California Press, 1994.

Valente, Joseph, *James Joyce and the Problem of Justice: Negotiating Sexual and Colonial Difference*, Cambridge University Press, 1995.

Van Boheemen-Saaf, Christine, "Deconstruction After Joyce," in Bonnie Kime Scott (ed.), *New Alliances in Joyce Studies*, Newark: University of Delaware Press, 1988, pp. 29–37.

The Novel as Family Romance: Language, Gender, and Authority from Fielding to Joyce, Ithaca: Cornell University Press, 1987.

"Purloined Joyce," in John Brannigan, Geoff Ward, and Julian Wolfreys (eds.), *Re:Joyce: Text, Culture, Politics*, London: Macmillan, 1998, pp. 246–58.

Weber, Samuel, *Institution and Interpretation*, Minneapolis: University of Minnesota Press, 1987.

Return to Freud: Jacques Lacan's Dislocation of Psychoanalysis, Cambridge University Press, 1991.

Weir, Lorraine, *Writing Joyce: A Semiotics of the Joyce System*, Bloomington: Indiana University Press, 1989.

Welch, Robert, *Changing States: Transformations in Modern Irish Writing*, London: Routledge, 1993.

Werner, Craig Hansen, *Paradoxical Resolutions: American Fiction since Joyce*, Urbana: University of Illinois Press, 1982.

Williams, Linda, *Hard Core: Power, Pleasure, and the Frenzy of the Visible*, Berkeley: University of California Press, 1989.

Wimsatt, William K. and Monroe C. Beardsley, "The Intentional Fallacy," *Sewanee Review* 54 (1946), 568–88.

Wiseman, Mary Bittner, "Rewriting the Self: Barthes and the Utopias of Language," in Anthony J. Cascardi (ed.), *Literature and the Question of Philosophy*, Baltimore: Johns Hopkins University Press, 1987.

Young, Robert, *White Mythology: Writing History and the West*, London: Routledge, 1990.

Žižek, Slavoj, *Enjoy Your Symptom: Jacques Lacan in Hollywood and Out*, London: Routledge, 1992.

Everything you Always wanted to Know about Lacan (But Were Afraid to Ask Hitchcock), London: Verso, 1992.

The Sublime Object of Ideology, London: Verso, 1992.

Tarrying with the Negative: Kant, Hegel, and the Critique of Ideology, Durham: Duke University Press, 1993.

"Why Lacan is not a 'Post-Structuralist'," *Newsletter of the Freudian Field* 1 (1987), 31–40.

Index

224

Printed in the United Kingdom
by Lightning Source UK Ltd.
118824UK00001B/251

9 780521 035316